HUMAN DESIGN
THE REVELATiON

A guide to basic Concepts, Centres Types and Definition

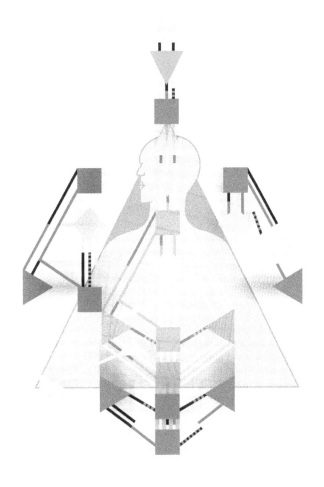

Richard Rudd

GENE KEYS

Second edition published in Great Britain and USA 2021
by Gene Keys Publishing Ltd
Lytchett House, 13 Freeland Park
Wareham Road, Poole BH16 6FA

Richard Rudd

HUMAN DESIGN

THE REVELATION
A guide to the Basic Concepts, Centres, Types and Definition
with introduction by Ra Uru Hu

Hardback Edition ISBN: 978-1-9996710-7-5
Kindle Edition ISBN: 978-1-8380487-7-8

genekeys.com

When we first come into contact with our Human Design chart, it is as though an implosion takes place inside us. For many people, this event initiates a deep shattering of their conditioning that they will have to grapple with over the following months and years. This book is designed to help anyone understand the basics of Human Design, and to learn to read your own chart. It offers each person support and understanding in the personal process that they are moving through as they come to understand about themselves. This is not a training manual, although it happens to offer a good grounding for anyone interested in going down that road. The real purpose of this book is to help you to become yourself.

Richard Rudd

CONTENTS

INTRODUCTION

Welcome to the world of Human Design. You are standing at the threshold of a great journey of discovery. Through this book, you have the opportunity to take an odyssey as ancient as time itself. The words and techniques may have changed to suit the modern psyche, but the goal remains the same. The goal is YOU. This is the journey that all people must some day take; it is the journey home, to the very heart of who you are. If you are reading this, then perhaps you are ready to take this journey. By now you may have already obtained your Human Design Chart. You will probably know which of the four Types you are and where your decision-making Authority comes from.

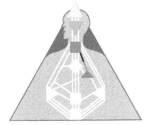

If you are a Manifestor, you may be beginning to remember the fire that burns deep within you – the fire that you have probably allowed so many people to dampen.

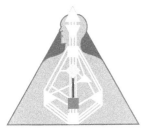

If you are a Generator or a Manifesting Generator, you may feel completely liberated to learn what you have always suspected about yourself – that you are not designed to be a 'go-getter', and as you relax, things happen more smoothly.

If you are a Projector, you may feel a sense of relief that you do not have to 'do' anything in order to get the recognition that you know you deserve – that you have only to wait and your invitation will come.

If you are a Reflector, you may have finally understood why you feel so different from everyone around you – you may well be excited to learn more about your extraordinary Design.

WHAT IS THE PURPOSE OF THIS BOOK?

1. SUPPORT

This book is designed in a very specific way. It has two main aims, the first of which is Support. From the moment we learn about our Design, a new potential begins to stir within us. These first months and years are in many ways the most delicate part of our journey. In the same way that a young seed is vulnerable when first planted in new soil, our psyche has to undergo a deep restructuring as we come to terms with new concepts of who and what we really are.

This book is only the beginning. It guides each of us through the door of self-discovery and nurtures us as we move through our process. As you learn about yourself through your Human Design, you may begin to feel different about yourself. It will bring many gifts into your life. So above all, we must be patient and allow the process time to unfold. For each of us, self-realisation comes in its own mysterious way and follows its own hidden timing. There is nothing we can do to speed it up or slow it down. There may be doubts and dark times. That is common with any new paradigm shift. Human Design is many things, and most often in the beginning it can seem confusing. Time is the great key. Only by waiting will our rewards emerge.

2. EDUCATION

The second purpose of this book is education. You will learn all the basic keys of Human Design: the calculation, the centres and most importantly, Type, Strategy and Authority. After reading this manual you will have all the necessary background to experiment. This is an absolute prerequisite before you go any deeper into the knowledge. This is a deeply practical training that will be focused on you. It gives you many insights about your own Design, but it will not teach you how to do a professional analysis of a chart. Having said that, we have also included a fair amount of theory in this manual. We will look at both the scientific background to Human Design as well as explore the mystical cosmology given in the revelation of this knowledge. We hope you enjoy reading this material and find the journey inspiring.

WHAT IS THE HUMAN DESIGN SYSTEM?

The Human Design System is a Synthesis. Synthesis is an easily used word these days, but it is not so easily understood. For something to be a true Synthesis, it must include everything. If anything is left out, then it cannot be called a true Synthesis. Human Design contains all systems from all walks of life because it is founded upon fundamental genetic principles that are the foundation of all life. It is neither a teaching, nor is it a technique. It does not require a master; neither does it require intelligence, study or effort.

One of the best ways to describe Human Design is as a mutation. It is a mutation of consciousness itself, and as such it spreads quickly. It spreads through the living cells of our bodies, even while it enters through our minds. Once we have heard our true genetic strategies, whenever we forget to follow them, this remembrance inside us flares up again, and again, until we get it.

Suffering is an important aspect of Human Design because every time we resist our suffering, we realise that we must be resisting our true nature. Thus the more we accept our own suffering, the less hold it has upon us, and the deeper the transformation goes inside us. Those who stay with the process will discover that the transformation that overtakes them leads to only one place – a place of Surrender.

HOW TO USE THIS BOOK

Like the DNA helix itself, two different paths are intertwined within this book:

The first path is the mental path, as we study the Human Design System itself, at the conscious level. It is represented in this training manual by the writing in black. This is when we exercise the logical side of the brain.

The second path is the physical path, and this is the path that can only be seen over time. It is represented in this training manual by the writing in red. It operates unconsciously within us at a level below our conscious access. This is where the mutation operates, deep within the cells of our body, as the old ingrained behaviour patterns of our conditioning slowly begin to unwind. This is when we exercise the abstract side of the brain.

For each of us, revelations await. There are always those moments when the hidden side comes to the surface and we glimpse the magic of the forces of nature at work within us. This is the magic of Synthesis. It is something totally new to the world, and something we are barely ready for as a species. Old knowledge is always safe, but new knowledge is heresy. This is a journey we will have to feel our way into as pioneers. We are a generation born on the cusp of a great turning point in consciousness, and our only responsibility is to thoroughly enjoy that privilege.

PART 1: A GUIDE TO BASIC CONCEPTS

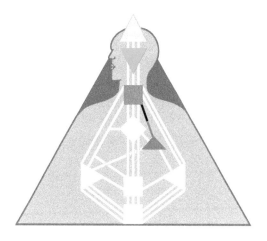

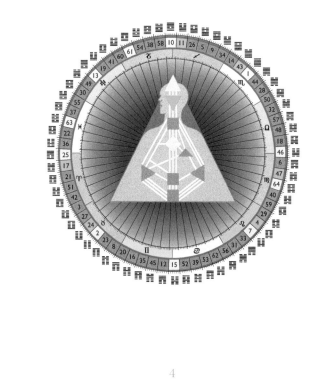

1. INTRODUCTION TO THE SPIRIT OF HUMAN DESIGN

-by Ra Uru Hu

The Human Design System is not a belief system. It doesn't require that you believe in anything. It doesn't require that you believe in me. It is not stories. It is not philosophy. It is a concrete map to the nature of being. It is a logical way in which we can see ourselves.

With Human Design, just knowing the simple mechanics of your design is enough to make a vast difference in your life. The irony of what it is to be a human being is that we are caught at the surface of understanding and accepting our nature and the cosmos around us. We are just at the surface. It doesn't matter how intelligent we are. It doesn't matter the labels that we attach to that intelligence - whether we call it enlightened or whether we call it genius. There is a vast underlying ignorance of how our bodies operate.

The Human Design System is a reading of your genetic code. This ability to be able to detail the mechanics of our nature in such depth is obviously profound because it reveals our complete nature in all its subtleties. However, it is not necessary for you to know Human Design in great depth. That is the job of the professional analyst. What this work aspires to communicate is simply the surface mechanics of your nature. That will give you grounding in your life that is immediately going to bring a difference to your life process.

These essential truths are simple because they are mechanical. The way in which our genes operate is purely mechanical, and the moment we try to interfere with their operation we descend into a life of confusion, chaos, and pain. In the end, our genes will have their way.

We are passengers in these bodies. We are passenger consciousness experiencing life going by. Buddha taught that the body is not yours. It is not. Yet at the same time, we are totally dependent on it. This is the tragedy of a sick body. We are totally dependent on our vehicles. To learn how to operate them properly immediately brings benefits. This is not complex and it will not be in complex language. It is very straightforward and very logical. It is accessible to anyone of any age. It is knowledge for the world.

In my teaching of Human Design and the training of Human Design analysts, students of mine have ranged from fourteen years old to being well into their eighties. There is no limitation and there is no barrier denying anyone from grasping these essential truths about themselves. This is not simply about saying, 'Aha, I'm this or I'm that'. This is not just another profiling system. It is about having the opportunity to do something with the knowledge. It is about being able to be able to act on it and experiment with its logic. This brings the remarkable experience of finding and ultimately living one's true life.

All learning, that is real learning, takes seven years. It takes approximately seven years to change almost all of the cells in the body ('almost' because most of the cells change, but the nerve cells and the bones stay the same). We live in a seven-year cycle. The moment that you begin to come to your own nature, the moment that you allow your body to live its life without resistance, you begin a deep process of de-conditioning. Seven years later, you emerge, quite literally, as a new being: yourself.

It's one of the great jokes that human beings don't get to live out their own lives. It is because they don't get to live out their own lives, that life seems to be such a difficult experience for them. We know that there is a lot of cant around about being yourself. It is all fine and good for somebody to stand up and tell you to be yourself, but first you have to know who that self is.

In my professional work, I have now given between five and six thousand individual readings. Wherever that has been, and regardless of culture or country, I have found there to be one prevailing disease. That disease is self-hatred, and it thrives wherever you find something about yourself that you would like to change. Self-hatred varies in intensity from being just beneath the surface of the consciousness to being full-blown. It is the most human of ironies that self-hatred is truly misplaced because most people do not know themselves. They actually hate the wrong person. They are actually dissatisfied with the wrong person.

Most human beings don't like themselves, and they don't like themselves because they truly do not know who they are. Most human beings have never lived the experience of being themselves, nor seen the beauty of what their true life holds. It is time to see that this is not, as the ancients claim, the planet of suffering, but in fact, an opportunity for a glorious awareness.

Human Design is not about guarantees or promises. This is not saying that if you live out your own nature, you're going to be the wealthiest or the most beautiful. It is not about being better or best. It is about being yourself.

Life is a duality, and this is revealed through our moralities. There is always going to be this and that. There is always going to be the good and the bad.

There is always going to be success and there is always going to be failure. That is the nature of what it is to be human and to live out the spectrum of human experience.

The moment that you live out your own nature and you enter into life correctly, this is the moment that you get what is correct for you. You get the correct career and you get the correct relationships. So, you see, it does not matter whether you are a success or not, because there will be no suffering, despite your state. You will be living out your nature and it will be clear to you that what is there for you is right for you. Whatever that might be. Only then, finally, will there be no part of you that can say: 'I wish I could be something or somewhere else'.

We are overwhelmed in our western culture with improvement propaganda. The hucksters cry 'be thinner, wiser, faster, richer'. There are all kinds of purveyors of teachings who beckon us to follow 'their' way. All human beings suffer from the propaganda of generalisations. Without knowing oneself, one can so easily be lost in this propaganda. You do not have to change anything. It is simply a matter of becoming yourself and becoming aware of yourself.

The Human Design System opens the door to the potential of self-love. Finding self-love is also about finding a greater love, a love for life and a love for others through understanding. Throughout this book, in seeing yourself and in coming to understand how you can live out your own nature, please pay attention to the importance of that in your relationships with others. So many of our difficulties in this life are because we have great difficulties in our relationships, whether they are our career relationships or whether they are our personal relationships. What is true for the individual, a lack of understanding about one's own nature, is also true for relationships. Relationships operate out of genetic imperatives based on mechanical laws.

To be yourself is to bring into your life those beings that are truly for you. This knowledge is about how you do that simply, so that you too can benefit from the best possible associations. Correct associations allow you not only to be seen and understood by others, but also allow you to understand them. As a parent, this has been an essential ingredient in the well being of my children.

Human Design is logical, mechanical knowledge. It is not theorising nor philosophy. It is about being able to do practical things with knowledge that brings practical benefits. I hope you enjoy this book. Enjoy the fact that there really is knowledge in the world that is truly valuable. Enjoy the fact that you too can participate in becoming a healthy self-loving human being.

RA URU HU

2. JUXTAPOSITION THEORY
THE FOUNDATION OF HUMAN DESIGN

This symbol appears many times within the field of Human Design. Revealed along with the system, it is know as the 'Juxtapose' and represents the fundamental duality of all life.

At the heart of the Human Design System lies a single, vital beating heart. It is called Juxtaposition Unified Theory (JUT). It is in fact, a very advanced and complex scientific theory of our universe based on 9 dimensions. The details of JUT are not for the faint-hearted, and one needs more than a rudimentary understanding of theoretical physics to begin to penetrate the logical core of this knowledge. Therefore, in this first training, we will keep everything as simple and clear as possible.

In simple language, Juxtaposition Theory is about chickens and eggs. Which came first? The answer according to Human Design is neither. They began together, inseparable but opposite, not integrated but juxtaposed. The word Juxtaposition points towards the existence of two forces that stand next to each other. They do not become one. In fact the juxtaposition of two forces creates a third force. This is a basic pattern that also lies at the heart of the Human Design revelation; that all life is a duality and has always been so, even from the beginning. With duality, you have friction, and out of friction comes life itself.

The basis of Juxtaposition Theory is that the universe is not one single entity, as the name 'UNI verse' suggests. In fact, we live in a 'Bi verse', because it is made up of two very different sets of forces. The universe that we see and that our scientists study is actually only an aspect of the greater duality. To put it simply, we can only see half the story.

When physicists first began studying the elements of the atomic world, they found something rather extraordinary that was very puzzling to them. They discovered that particles and waves, the building blocks of life, seemed to regularly transform into one another. Obviously, they knew that this was impossible, so they begun to speculate that they themselves were actually affecting the experiment. This gave rise to a whole new exciting set of theories involving further dimensions. Superstring Theory is the name of the most popular current model for explaining our universe, and it is based on the existence of other dimensions beyond our 3 dimensional perceived world.

According to Juxtaposition Theory, the physicists are getting closer to the truth. We live in a four dimensional world (the 4th dimension being time/space) and anything we measure, scientifically or otherwise, is limited by these four dimensions. Metaphysically speaking, we inhabit the Yang world of Light. But there exists alongside our perceived world another world. Alongside our world, juxtaposed, is the Yin world of Darkness.

The Yin world is a five dimensional world and cannot be seen by us, even though its laws govern all existence.

If you are now feeling lost, let me give you an image. Our perceived universe is a foetus growing in the womb of another unseen universe. In other words, we think we are alone, but something else knows that we are not! This is exactly the image that was given when the Human Design System was revealed. We are an unborn entity, and until we are born, we will not be able to see the bigger picture. Interestingly enough, the very latest scientific theories are based on a model known as the 'Braneworld', which postulates that our universe is surrounded by a membrane that obscures us from the higher dimensions.

The whole point of all this is to understand that Human Design is founded upon something that we cannot see, and thus it has to be tested rather than believed. One of the greatest challenges to a sceptical mind is the correlation between who we are and the time of our birth. Human Design is not about proving anything on the mental level. It is the experience of actually living our design that will finally prove the value of this knowledge to each one of us. The proof of the pudding, as always, lies in the eating.

Between the Conscious and the Unconscious
The Mind has put up a swing:
All earth's creatures, even the supernovas,
Sway between these two trees,
And it never winds down.
Angels, animals, humans, insects by the million,
Also the wheeling sun and moon;
Ages go by, and it goes on.
Everything is swinging: heaven and earth, water and fire
And the secret one slowly growing a body.

Kabir saw that for fifteen seconds,
And it made him a servant for life.

KABIR

3. HUMAN DESIGN - WHERE SCIENCE MEETS MAGIC
THE SCIENCE

Some time around 15 billion years ago, according to the physicists, an event took place that they call the big bang. This was the beginning of what we call the universe. The most extraordinary thing about that moment is that everything that has mass existed in an object that was smaller than a single atom. That is very difficult to imagine. Something ignited that and so the universe began to expand. As it expanded, it divided up into a basic duality.

In the above illustration, we can see the beginning of the dualistic universe in which we live. The first thing that happened after the Big Bang is that everything divided into two families. Here, we are using the eastern terms YIN and YANG to represent MATTER and ENERGY.

The Yin family is fundamentally material. The Yin family is made up of 6 Quarks. Scientists gave these things nice names. These quarks are called Up, Down, Strange, Charm, Beauty and Truth (sometimes also called Bottom and Top). Two of these 6 quarks, namely Up and Down, come together in two groups and they form what we call the Proton and the Neutron. These strange sounding objects make up the material building blocks of the universe.

The Yang family is fundamentally energy, or at least it was always considered to be until fairly recently. This family is made up of Leptons, and you may notice that there are six of them as well - 3 different types of electrons and 3 types of something called Neutrinos.

These 2 families then join together; that is the electron from one side comes together with the proton and neutron from the other side, and as we learned in school, they form the atom. The stars, the trees, the birds, you and me, we are all atomic in nature. The joke in this is that if you count up everything we know as atomic in the universe - all the stars, the galaxies and super clusters and planets, in other words everything that we know and can see - you are going to discover that it only represents 10% of the mass of the whole universe. It is only 1/10 of the physical material of the universe. The rest of the universe is known rather obscurely as 'dark matter', and that is what the scientists have been looking for.

And then the Neutrino entered onto the scene. For a very long time, the scientists thought that the Neutrino was just pure energy. However, in 1995 they discovered and proved that the Neutrino bears an infinitesimal mass. What we now know is that the largest of the Neutrinos is about one-millionth of the weight of a proton. That is extremely light, but nonetheless it is material. The other fact that is known about the Neutrino is that it travels slower than light, which means that it cannot be pure energy.

Neutrinos are only made in stars. They are the breath of stars. Our sun is such a star, and out of that star comes an endless stream of neutrino information which is material information passing through us. There are more Neutrinos than anything else in the universe. For every square inch of space on our earth, 3 trillion Neutrinos pass through that place, every second all the time. These tiny bits of information are penetrating us every second all the time, which means that we live in a vast information-field. This is what the ancients referred to as the 'Prana' or 'Chi'.

A TALE OF ENCOUNTER
By Ra Uru Hu

I had a house in Ibiza. It was called C´as Coxtu. When I stepped out and left everything behind, I left that house. In the back of the house was an ancient ruina, where the original house had once been. It died about 300 years ago. All that was left was one room. The rest were all broken down walls, but that one room had been fixed up by the previous owner of the house so it could be used as a kind of study or extra bedroom. It was not very pretty but it was functional. I had a friend of mine who was an English poet, and he had no place to live and I told him that he could come and live in this ruina. Some time later, he would return the service, because one day he came to me and said: 'I have a place for you to live. You should really get off the ground. You've been on the ground too long. Why don't you come and live in this ruina that you gave to me. I have to go to England anyway.'

C´as Coxtu

So I moved into this ruina, into this one room. It had a platform inside, with a desk and a bookshelf, which was full of books and herbs. My friend was a herb collector. There was also this one door, which had an ancient old key - one of these huge iron keys. Around the time that my daughter was born, I used to draw in diaries. They were symbol diaries of my life and contained no words. They only contained my drawings. On every single page there was a drawing of this key. That was many years before all this. Anyway, there was this wonderful key that opened up this door. There was also a Dutch couple. They were fascinated by my life process. I was quite notorious by that stage and considered by most people to be dangerous. They were fascinated with me and they would come once a week and collect me. They would bring me to their house and they would turn on their tape recorder and they would just let me talk. I talked about what I was going through in my process. They would give me a nice lunch, they would give me some pesetas and then they would send me home. It kept me alive.

On January 3rd, 1987, a day like any other day, I visited them as usual. They had picked me up in the morning. I was disturbed that day because I had an enormous pain in my mouth, a toothache. When the day was done, my host said to me: 'Do you need anything?' I said: 'Do you have anything for a toothache?' and he offered me something homeopathic which had no effect on me. Then they drove me back to the highway near my ruina.

I give names to everything. I even give names to the things I cook. I lived with a dog at that time. He was the only animal in my life that was never a pet. He never was anything close to being a pet. His name was Barley Baker. All my animals have last names. Barley was savage. He was a natural born killer. He had a master that never fed him because I never had anything. So he had to feed himself, and so he would hunt sheep. He would do all the things that carnivores do. The only thing was that he knew me from the moment that he was two days old, when he was given to me by the daughter of a friend of mine. So he knew my scent and he was all right with me. But he did not like people. I watched him one day kill a dog in a dog fight. He was savage.

So I arrive. It is dark. It is wintertime and it is dark early. I arrive at the bottom of the hill, at the highway, and the moment I step onto the path I can feel him. If you live that kind of a life you have a deep connection to animals. He just immediately picks up my smell and he knows that I am there and comes and he says hello. We climb up the hill and when we get to the top of the hill, there is a terrace. We go along the terrace and as we are walking along the way, what is in front of me is the original front door of the house. But the only thing that was there is the archway. The walls and the ceiling were gone. You can look through the archway and you can see the room that the ruina was. The room they had built for their first child because it was the smallest room in the house. The room sat over a cistern, an empty well. The well dried about two hundred years ago. It is why the house was given up. So this room was sitting over a cavern. Inside of the room there was a butane bottle that ran a little gas stove and above the platform where I slept hanging from a beam there was a kerosene lantern. This lantern had never been on, because it was out of kerosene and I could not afford either to get it nor where to get it.

So I am walking along with Barley along this terrace and when I get outside of the main entrance to the house, outside of the archway, I already begin to feel uncomfortable. I don't know why, but anyway in that moment I feel a tightening in my stomach muscles. I step through the old archway and I realise, because it is a shock to me, that there is light underneath my door. This is an ancient Ibiza door. It has this one big iron key. There is only one key. You can't break that lock. It is not the kind of door where you can get in. But it was more that light that disturbed me. Occasionally, I would have a candle but rarely did I have light. I am an Aries. It is easy for me to go to sleep at five o'clock in the afternoon and get up at four o'clock in the morning. I lived in my own world. It did not make any difference to me. So I was standing there and there was light under the door and Barley who normally goes ahead of me is behind me. I am very aware of the fact that he is behind me and that he is not interested in all of that. He is not moving. It was the first joke for me because the door was very close to me and I shouted at it. I shouted: Who is there? This is my joke. The ruina sits on a hill that goes down into a valley. On the other side, there is a whole ring of hills. So in this night, in the dark with this strip of light under the door I hear my own voice echoing through the valley. Who is there?

I got closer to the door I thought that maybe the English poet who told me that I could live in this ruina, maybe he had made another key and maybe he was there. So I got closer to the door and I shouted louder into the door only to hear my echo. So I took this magical key of out my pocket. I can remember putting the key in the keyhole and turning it and I push the door. When I push the door there was a lot of things going on at the same time. When I push the door I was stepping into the doorway. Barley was coming quickly now towards the house and as I push the door open and as I stepped on the threshold a lot of things happened. It is hard to tell these things sequentially. They all just happened together. I saw the lantern above my bed. It was lit. There was a flame in the lantern and the lantern was turning clockwise over my bed. At the same moment that I was aware that the lantern was turning, Barley had just come in the door and fell down like somebody had shot him. His whole body collapsed. I entered into something which I don't know how to describe.

The Revelation

My whole body seemed to explode. There was a kind of pressure in my head. In the moment of this pressure I hear this…

The way in which we experience things is conditioned through our history and our culture, our background. I spent most of my life being a very arrogant man and somebody who demeaned the intelligence of others. I respected no authority. There was no one who was going to impose his nature, his will or his thoughts on me. I had never been humiliated in my life. But, all of a sudden, there was this dark hard, cold, male voice, frightening, with a flavour of intelligence that I did not know and it said to me: Are you ready to work? My body exploded. I mean the water in my body exploded. I had rivulets of water coming off the top of my skull. I had a whole pool of my own water that I was standing in. I was like one of these people that runs a marathon for 25 kms and they get totally dehydrated and there is no water in the body. The moment that all the water was out of my body, every single muscle of my body began to cramp. It is hard to describe the intensity of the pain. Pain is a very subjective thing. I have an enormous tolerance for pain. In that experience, I have never known anything so painful in my whole life. That is why I call what was happening to me a rape. My body was violated. I was in agony. All of that happened very quickly. All of that perception: the dog, the light, the voice, the water. There was a moment where I assumed that I was about to die. It seemed very clear to me. Somewhere inside of me I knew that something was ripping me apart. Then something very strange happened. There was this sensation. It started in my right hip. I know the place. As a matter of fact, I never have been massaged except for once. The person who did the massage, when they got to that point they said: Oh, you can't touch this point. It was very strange. This place is where the energy body, the energy suit - that is how I call it - started. It feels like when your foot or your hand goes to sleep. There is this deafness, the dumbness but it is also a kind of tingling. It is sort of like that. It started in my hip and it moved both, down and up at the same time. It did not eliminate my pain but it did something to it. It don't know what.

For eight days I lived with this energy sheath around my body which made it very difficult for me to follow the instructions of the voice. It is was very difficult for me to grip a pen. It was almost impossible. The first day I did not really think that I could do that because I could not feel it in my hand. Aside from the fact that is was painful. The only time that the pain would go away was, when the voice talked to me. It was a strange thing. The moment that there was this thing talking to me all of it disappeared and I - sort of - floated in a kind of state, where you are there and you are not there. There is something else there. I have never known anything that was so profound that it made me feel ant like, tiny, absolutely meaningless. One has to be very careful about anthropomorphising one's experience. I know what I was dealing with. I was dealing with a Design crystal bundle. It came from the core of our planet and it came into the cavern that was below my ruina. The Human Design System is not in the world because of me. It is in the world because everybody was seeded with that information in those eight days, the whole planet. We were all receptive to the Neutrino stream that poured through that crystal bundle. The reality is that the energy that I took in was Yin energy, form energy. That was my experience. But to describe it physically is to understand that this was something incredibly violent. I am designed for shock. The only thing that surprises me about any of this is that I survived to tell the tale.

THE MAGIC

In 1987 an extraordinary event took place on this planet. It was seen with the naked eye on a mountaintop in Chile. It was one of the first times in recorded history that human beings witnessed a supernova. A supernova is the death of a star, a vast explosion of unimaginable intensity. That star, now known to scientists as 1987A, bombarded our planet for several minutes with a deluge of subatomic information with its dying breath. When it actually reached us, for fourteen minutes, everybody on this planet received three times as many Neutrinos as normal.

Around the same time on a Mediterranean island called Ibiza, a man had a deep shock experience on January 3 of that year. He described that event as being penetrated by a voice. This mystical experience lasted eight days and eight nights during which he never slept but only listened. He was given immensely detailed descriptions of how universe functions, and out of this he was given the Human Design system. After this experience, he changed his name and became known to the world as Ra Uru Hu. After about a year of trying to bring himself back to reality, Ra begun to experiment with the revealed knowledge and soon realised its power. Since 1992 Ra Uru Hu has been the transmitter of the Human Design System.

According to the voice, the universe started in a different way from how most physicists currently see it. According to the voice, the universe was not born at the big bang; rather the big bang was a conception. That means that the entire universe is one single living entity and it is not yet born. Therefore, there are many things that we cannot know. The voice told the story of creation in its own language. In the beginning there was a cosmic Yin egg, and this egg contained within it all the material of the universe. This echoes the current standard scientific theories that postulate that all the potential material of the universe was compressed into a tiny object about the size of an atom. The voice went on to say that inside this egg was something that could be described as a crystal structure. It is not really a crystal, but the image of a crystal helps us to understand how it works.

There was also a yang seed and within the yang seed there was also this crystal-like structure. Then something remarkable happened. The seed hit the egg at some untold velocity. When the two of them met, those embedded crystals shattered into zillions of aspects, which then spread throughout the expanding universe in patterns known as fractals. A fractal is basically a mathematical figure that divides and subdivides infinitely whilst retaining its original pattern. In other words, the universe is rather like a hologram. Everything that we can imagine, all forms of life on this planet and even inanimate objects, are endowed with crystals of consciousness that came from the original yin/yang crystals.

THE CONCEPTION OF THE BIVERSE

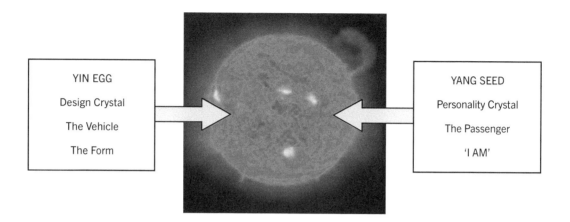

YIN EGG

Design Crystal

The Vehicle

The Form

YANG SEED

Personality Crystal

The Passenger

'I AM'

In a human being these crystals of consciousness have placements within the body. The Personality crystal, an aspect of the original yang Personality crystal, sits up in what we call the Head Centre. In the illustration, you can see that this is the centre at the top. This Personality crystal manifests who you think you are.

The Design crystal, an aspect of the original Yin egg, is located in what is known as the Ajna Centre, the second centre from the top. This Design crystal manifests your biogenetic vehicle, in other words, the body.

The voice mentioned also a third component known as the Magnetic Monopole. This sits in the sternum in what we call the G Centre. The magnetic monopole has two different functions. The first function is that it holds us together in the illusion of our separateness. In other words, it makes us believe we are separate entities from each other. Secondly, being a 'mono-pole', it acts like a magnet with only one pole; that is it only attracts. It exerts a pull from outside of us that guides us along our path or geometry, which we call our destiny. It is responsible for drawing certain people into our lives and for moving our bodies through life. The name we give it is Love.

THE CRYSTALS OF CONSCIOUSNESS

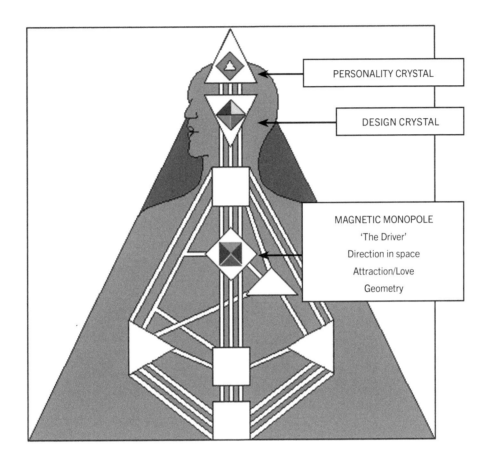

Imagine that we have a limousine. This limousine can be compared to the Design crystal, our body. In our limousine, we each have a driver. The driver knows precisely how to drive the vehicle, he knows the roads, he has the maps and he knows where to go. The driver is the magnetic monopole. It knows exactly where it is going. It knows exactly what the geometry is and it drives the vehicle along that path of geometry.

The Personality Crystal, which is only who we think we are, is neither the vehicle nor the driver. The Personality crystal has no idea where it is going. It is the passenger in the back seat of the car. And you know what a good passenger is supposed to do?

Look out the windows and enjoy the ride …

… But leave the driver in peace!

A MONOPOLE MEDITATION

Think about what all this really means. Imagine for a moment that you were given a pair of sunglasses to put on. These are not normal sunglasses, however. These sunglasses allow you to see neutrinos. They allow you to see the subatomic world...

Close your eyes and put the sunglasses on.

The world around you is alive. Everywhere you look you see energy vibrating and moving in swirling patterns. Look down at your own body. There is no body. Just a condensation of the swirling patterns around you. Look down at what you once thought were your feet. Every cell of your body is a tiny crystal. There are so many in your single foot that you cannot comprehend it, and they all seem so busy! In every second crystals are leaving your foot and moving down into the earth. In every second trillions of new crystals are emerging from the earth and coalescing in your foot. Your entire body is breathing like this with the earth. In every nanosecond your body is dying and being reborn. You are bleeding out into the red sea of creation.

Look again at the crystals moving in and out of your body. These are cells dying and growing. Every single crystal seems to know exactly what it is doing. It seems to move in coordination with all the other crystals, alone and yet separate. It reminds you of a flock of birds wheeling in the sky, totally moving as one. Go now with your imagination down into the depths of one of those crystals. Enter into the cell itself. It's so busy in there! Trillions of other crystals are at work, building and maintaining the cell. These are the proteins and amino acids, the workers of the cell, and the genes that are issuing the instructions, telling everything where it's supposed to go. The inside of the cell is huge, stretching almost to the horizon. But like a huge galaxy, there seems to be a centre around which everything wheels. This is the nucleus of the cell, a hub from where everything is held together.

Move into the centre of the nucleus. Now you are in the subatomic world, a world of protons, electrons and neutrons, spinning around the central core of the cell. Keep moving towards the centre. Allow yourself to be drawn into the awesome presence of that centre. Let go and surrender as the unseen force catches you in its whirlpool and sends you spinning in ever decreasing circles, into the vortex of darkness at the centre of the cell. All around you a terrific noise is building, like the wild winds unleashed in a hurricane. Even though you feel disoriented, there is no need to be afraid. The force-field that you are caught in is in fact what we in the outside world call Love. It is here right at the core of every living cell in your body.

Finally, you have come to a standstill. You are right in the heart of the cell itself. It is utterly silent here. There is no pressure whatsoever. You look out and around you the entire universe seems to be softly turning. Everything is revolving around YOU. You are at the centre of your own universe. You are in the magnetic monopole of a single cell.

Looking out from your cushion of quietness deep within your cell, you see other cells blinking like stars in the distance across the infinite expanse of your subatomic body. They too are softly turning. Everything seems to be going somewhere. Curious to know more, you jump instantaneously into the nearest star you can see and find yourself within another monopole, at the heart of another tiny galaxy. You soon realise that even though you are at the centre of your own little cellular galaxy, you are in fact part of a wider picture. All the monopoles are turning in a vast arc around some distant point. You jump into another star, then another and another….

You are moving through the energetic cellular structure of your own body, monopole by monopole. You are astonished that every part of your body, down to the tiniest microbe, has its own monopole that seems to know exactly where it is going. It is as though there is some master program that runs through the entire body of your universe that holds everything together in an amazing pattern. Even what you had previously thought of as invading viruses, you now see also have monopoles that fit perfectly within this pattern. As you travel from star to star through the different organs and functions of your inner universe, you become more and more certain that everything is revolving around some other kind of great inner galactic hub.

Now let go. You can feel the force again. This time it is so powerful that it frightens you. It seems to be pulling you towards itself. You look around yourself for a reference point, but everything else is being pulled into that same awesome place. You know what it is, and in a split second, you remember that you cannot fight its power. In that fraction of a second you just let go into your whole being. Leave the Driver in Peace! You surrender your control over your life, and from the moment you relax, you realise that what you were afraid of is in fact Love. Your body is held together by love.

Now you are not fighting, you are moving with love. You are not dizzy, even though you cannot see where you are going. You feel like a leaf swept along on the breeze, or a cloud floating majestically through the skies of your being. Finally, almost without your realising it, you find yourself home. You have arrived at the centre of centres, deep within the sternum in your ribcage. From here, you can see the entire universe of your body turning around you. The silence is exquisite. The acceptance you feel for who and where you are is absolutely total. You remember this place. It is the place where you know your own perfection. You are at the centre of your own universe. You are in the Prime Magnetic monopole of your body. Take your sunglasses off, open your eyes when you are ready, take a few nice deep breaths, and smile a knowing smile to yourself.

4. SYNTHESIS

4.1 THE HUMAN DESIGN WHEEL

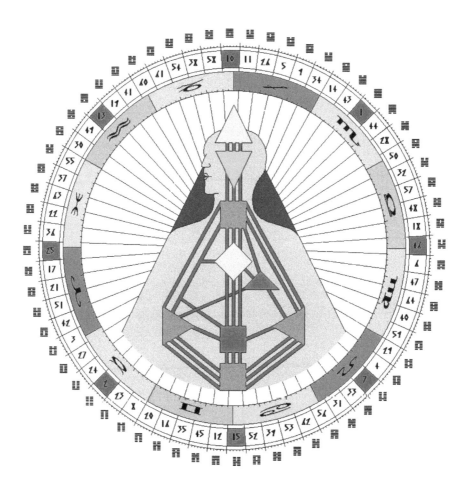

The illustration above shows the Human Design Wheel that lies at the heart of this whole system. The wheel is an ancient spiritual symbol used by many cultures to describe the inner workings of the universe. This wheel is literally a synthesising mandala for all life, and as you can see, it is made up of various parts. In this chapter, we will discuss both the inner wheel and the outer wheel, as well as their relationship, and for the first time we will introduce the Bodygraph, the graphic in the centre of the wheel. As a synthesis, the Human Design System brings together many different aspects from many different cultures and times.

THE INNER WHEEL: THE MACROCOSM

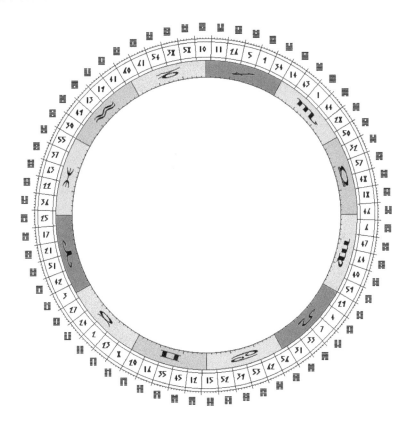

If you take a look at the illustration above, you will see that running around the rim of the inside of the wheel there are 12 symbols. These represent the twelve signs of the Western zodiac, Aries, Taurus, Gemini etc. Astrology is just one of the components that makes up the Human Design synthesis, and there is something important to understand here before we go any further. As a synthesis, Human Design is much more than the sum of its parts. It is not a hotchpotch of different systems someone has just thrown together. It is the mystical revelation of how those systems are designed to interlock with each other. It has come into the world now because the time is right for humanity to begin its next great leap in consciousness. The Human Design Wheel is the completion of a millennial jigsaw puzzle. We are currently entering an age of synthesis. Those of us used to working with a single system, whether left-brain or right brain oriented, may have to adapt our thinking to accommodate this natural evolution.

As you read the pages of this manual, remember that you are entering brand new knowledge. Human Design rides on the shoulders of many other systems, both mystical and scientific, and in doing so, it can see further than most. Because all Human Design calculation is founded upon birth-time, it is often mistaken for a new form of astrology. It is not astrology, although it owes much to that ancient science. Human Design does however use astrological calculation, and here is why….

In order to verify why astrological calculation is valid, you have to understand that the Human Design wheel is a graphic that represents the universe. All around us, in every direction, we are surrounded by an enormous star field. It is this star field which generates the neutrino stream that percolates the whole universe. In Human Design terminology, this has been nicknamed the 'neutrino ocean'. Stars radiate neutrinos in all directions, creating a weave of rippling subatomic information that floods space.

Now think about the planets of our solar system. Imagine the planet Mars for example. It gets caught in the neutrino stream like a fly in a web. In other words, as Mars orbits around our sun, it gets in the way of the neutrino stream before it reaches us here on earth. The moment Mars gets in the way of the stream, then that neutrino stream has to go through Mars. Because the neutrino stream is material, it bears an infinitesimal mass, and this mass is going to interact with the material of Mars.

If you have a black car and a white car, and they bang into each other, you will get a little black paint on the white car and a little white paint on the black car. This is more or less what happens when the stream goes through Mars. The neutrino stream is actually changed by Mars, and after being filtered by Mars, the stream comes through all of us here on earth. As you will see, the same cosmic program influences us all, but we each manifest that program uniquely. The way in which we do this is through these crystals of consciousness that are within us. To understand how these crystals work, imagine two diamonds that are cut differently and have different shapes and facets to them.

If we take these two diamonds and we put the same source of light through each of them, what emerges from the other side are two totally different patterns. That is how we work. We all live in the same neutrino program and we are all being affected in the same way, but we each translate that program through the crystals within us in a totally unique way.

This is why we need the astrological wheel. As we shall see, knowing the positions of the planets at two very specific times will allow us to see our own unique imprinting within the neutrino stream.

THE OUTER WHEEL: THE MICROCOSM

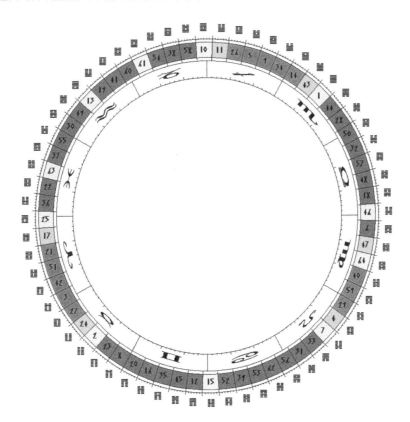

The outer wheel is full of numbers. You can see that it is divided into 64 sections. This division into 64 relates to two things. Firstly, it relates to the ancient Chinese wisdom known as the I-Ching, or the Book of Changes. The I Ching is a rather extraordinary ancient text that has been popularised as an oracle. However, the I Ching, as anyone who has studied it in depth knows, is much more than an oracle. Its originators had hit upon a very profound pattern. What makes the I-Ching so extraordinary is certainly not what it says, because it is actually rather dated, its language being patriarchal and sexist. What makes it so extraordinary is its mathematics. It is based on a binary mathematical model that centres on the number 64.

The I-Ching is a metaphor for life, told in symbolic form. It consists of 64 symbols called 'hexagrams', each made up of six lines. These hexagrams are woven into a certain order that reflects the cycles and seasons of life. Simply put, a hexagram is basically an archetype of information. It is like a mini-dictionary. In Human Design, the 64 hexagrams are stretched out around the wheel, their 6-line structure acting rather like the degrees of a circle. Thus this circle has 384 lines. The sequence of how the hexagrams follow each other on the arc has been revealed. It has not been made up.

The second association to this division of the wheel into 64 is in the field of genetics.

DNA is made up of two strands of nucleotides, one strand being a perfect reflection of the other. This basic binary is also the foundation of the 'Yin' and 'Yang' of the I Ching. Our genetic code is also made up of four 'bases' which are arranged in groupings of threes. Each of these chemical groupings relates to an amino acid, and forms what is known as a 'codon'. There are 64 of these codons in our genetic code. Similarly, in the I Ching there are only four basic permutations of yin and yang (known as bigrams), which are also arranged in groups of threes, known as 'trigrams'. In the same way that the two strands of our DNA reflect each other, each trigram of the I Ching has a partner, and together these two symbols create the hexagram; the basis of the I Ching.

THE 'GENETIC CLOCK' WITH ITS AMINO ACID COMBINATIONS

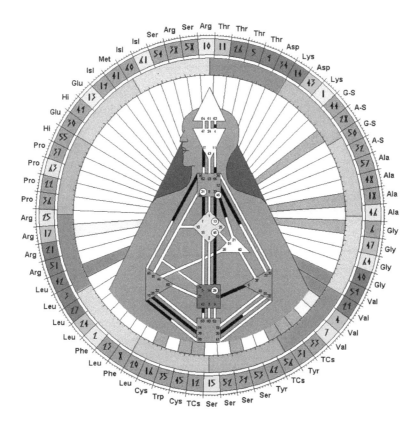

In other words, when Watson and Crick discovered the principle of the genetic code in the late 1950's, although they didn't know it, what they found out was that the genetic code has exactly the same mathematics as the I-Ching, discovered more than 5000 years ago.

Thus the Human Design Wheel is literally the stringing out of our genetic code. It is like a planetary genetic clock that we can use as a tool to read the design of anything that is alive, from a man to a plant, so long as we know when it was either born or created.

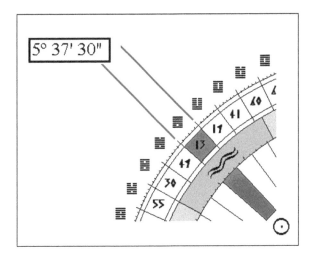

This illustration above shows you that every hexagram has a specific place and measurement of arc in the wheel. The wheel is a circle of 360 degrees and each hexagram therefore covers a space of 5 degrees, 37 minutes and 30 seconds of arc.

THE RELATIONSHIP BETWEEN THE INNER AND THE OUTER WHEEL
Transferring the macrocosm into the microcosm

This is where we see the magic of Human Design at work. As we have seen, the orbiting planets impact on us through interfering with the neutrino stream from deep space. We use the inner wheel to locate their positions in the macrocosm and then we transfer those positions into the outer wheel (the hexagram wheel). In the illustration above, we have an example of a calculation. We can see somebody who was born when the sun was moving across the zodiacal constellation of Aquarius, represented by the symbol made up of two wavy lines.

We can also see that the corresponding division in the I-Ching wheel is the 13th hexagram. Beyond that, we do not use the astrological wheel because we are not looking at aspects of angles around the wheel like astrologers do. Human Design is about pinpointing this information directly in the body. Once we can see these same patterns within ourselves, we can literally see our cosmic genetic imprinting. This final piece of magic is done by means of a further matrix known as the Bodygraph.

4.2 THE BODYGRAPH AND ITS COMPONENTS

At the centre of the two wheels, we can see another graphic made up of nine centres connected by a network of channels. This is the Bodygraph. The Bodygraph is perhaps one of the most important parts of the Human Design revelation. It is a human body graph. The voice that revealed the Human Design System referred to the Bodygraph as a Rave, which was its own word for human. The Bodygraph allows us to translate the neutrino information directly into the body so that we can see how we are imprinted.

The Bodygraph is made up of three different components from three different ancient sciences. It is the synthesis of these components and is thus greater than the sum of its parts.

THE CENTRES

The first component you notice are these shapes known as the nine centres. These centres are based on the Hindu-Brahman tradition where they are known as 'chakras'. In Indian yogic tradition, the chakras are seen as hubs of subtle energy within the body. In Human Design, we call them centres, and unlike the Indian tradition, there are nine instead of the traditional seven. Please understand that Human Design is not the chakra system anymore than it is astrology. It is a synthesis. We will discuss the relevance of each of the nine centres in depth in Part 2 of this manual.

Each centre has a different function.

THE NINE CENTRES, THEIR BIOLOGY AND FUNCTIONS

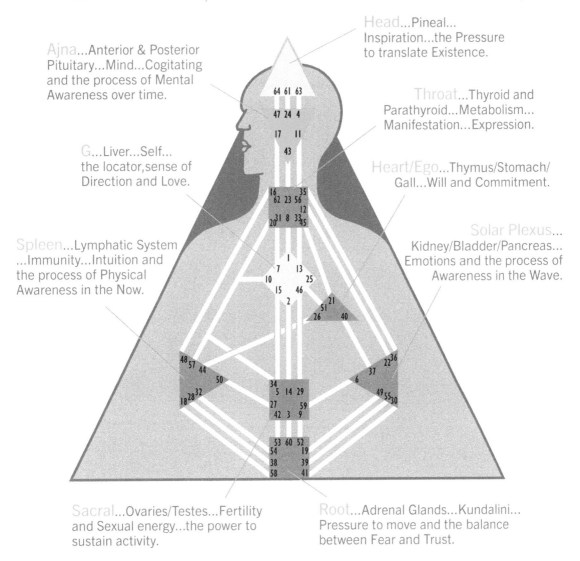

Head...Pineal...
Inspiration...the Pressure
to translate Existence.

Ajna...Anterior & Posterior
Pituitary...Mind...Cogitating
and the process of Mental
Awareness over time.

Throat...Thyroid and
Parathyroid...Metabolism...
Manifestation...Expression.

G...Liver...Self...
the locator,sense of
Direction and Love.

Heart/Ego...Thymus/Stomach/
Gall...Will and Commitment.

Solar Plexus...
Kidney/Bladder/Pancreas...
Emotions and the process of
Awareness in the Wave.

Spleen...Lymphatic System
...Immunity...Intuition and
the process of Physical
Awareness in the Now.

Sacral...Ovaries/Testes...Fertility
and Sexual energy...the power to
sustain activity.

Root...Adrenal Glands...Kundalini...
Pressure to move and the balance
between Fear and Trust.

THE GATES AND CHANNELS

Between these nine centres lies a network of channels. These channels are the second main component of the Bodygraph. The channels are rooted in the tradition of the Zohar/Kabbala tradition, being a development of the Judaic Tree of Life. These channels act as connecting forces between the centres. Basically the channels are about bringing together the energies of two different centres and thus generating something new, a third thing. They represent the quantum principle.

The 64 hexagrams are connected with each other through channels. Each channel has a name and description related to its function.

The third component of the Bodygraph is found in the numbers. At either end of each channel where the channel opens into a centre, you will see a number. These openings are called 'gates' and there are a total of 64 of them. The gates relate to the 64 hexagrams of the outer wheel. In other words, what we are looking at is a simple number coded system that allows us to translate the neutrino information directly into the body.

Let's look at an example to see how this works. In the example below, you can see the sun in the middle of Aquarius, in the 13th hexagram; we can now take that information and see where it belongs inside the Bodygraph. All we have to do is find the corresponding position to the 13th hexagram in the Bodygraph, in other words, the 13th gate. The 13th gate happens to be in the yellow diamond shaped centre, known as the G Centre. Now we have a way of locating stellar neutrino information deep within the chemical processes of our bodies.

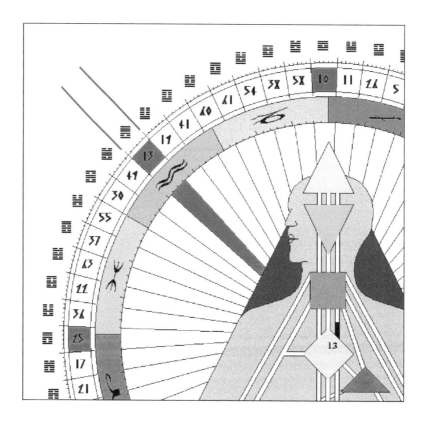

THE KEYNOTES

In addition to their traditional names, all the gates and channels have keynotes. Keynotes are one of the most important ways of learning Human Design, and as you journey deeper into this labyrinth of knowledge, you will discover deeper layers of keynotes.

Don't worry that you don't understand what they mean at this stage. You can examine and learn more about the keynotes in my other book Circuitry.

THE NAMING OF NAMES

To the newcomer, Human Design can often seem like learning a whole new language. You hear all these strange new terms. Some names come from scientific fields, others from the realm of the esoteric; some are Eastern, others Western. Many of these names seem to come from behind some kind of veil. In other words, they are new. Have you ever wondered where names come from?

Indulge yourself for a moment. You are after all reading this, and as the words spill across your mind they are having a deep effect on you. Words and names are like spirits that have a life of their own. Stripped of their pretensions and meanings, they simply exist as pure vibrations in the ether.

In Sanskrit they have a word, 'maya'. It means many things, but above all it means illusion. The Eastern mystics have often spoken of our world as a 'maya', an illusion. Interestingly enough, the root of the word 'maya' comes from 'ma', which means 'to measure'. We humans are measurers… That is why we are here. We are here to measure the illusion. We are here to give everything around us a name.

A name is thus a vibration. It is the sound that something or someone makes. It is the crystalisation of an object or a person into sound. That's the interesting thing about names, that they already exist before we find them. In a sense, they let us find them. Naming is really about unveiling. It's all a matter of waiting.

Working with Human Design is really not about study and knowledge. It's about playing with Truth. There is absolutely no guarantee that you will 'get' it. The deeper we go into our designs, the more we will see that life is about letting go of being in control. It makes no difference whether you understand any of these words. You cannot study to be yourself. You can only 'be' yourself. There are no techniques that ensure you will be yourself. There is nothing you can DO about any of this. What this course will perhaps show you is what is not you. You see, you can't 'become' who you already are. You can only remove what you are not. And it's not as if you have to do anything to remove your conditioning either. There is no therapeutic technique in this. It's purely a matter of understanding. For all you logical minds, we are sorry, but over on the red side, things just sort of happen…Shit happens.

The only thing you need is a spirit of play. If you find your mind full of questions, have a laugh at yourself. You are not here to understand words. You are here to understand Being. Words words words. Human design is filled with words. But just like the Bodygraph, they are not the territory. They simply point the way. It takes the body seven years to learn a new language, a new pattern. Don't get caught up in the black writing. Be in the red writing. It takes seven years to forget your mind. Just take the words in through your body. Breathe them in. That is enough. You don't have to make sense of them. Let time work its magic. Listen to the words as though you were listening to a piece of music, or the song of a bird. Travel lightly through this new world. You are going to discover secrets within your body. Your mind simply shows up alongside. Your mind cannot know Truth. Your body contains all Truth. The answers you seek lie in your blood. They are to be found in the mystery of the red.

'In design information, we have a treasure map. The map for each individual is accessible and available yet it requires study in order to understand its structure. In learning to read your own map and to follow its path, you embark on a journey into the core of your being at a true cellular level. Over a period of time you begin to see the changes that living truly who you are brings. It is the adventure of life and a journey we all are here to make. Enjoy the ride.'

Ra Uru Hu

5. THE INDIVIDUAL CALCULATION

This section is about explaining how a calculation is done. There are two different calculations necessary to set up an individual design. One is called **the Personality calculation** (black colour) and the other is called **the Design calculation** (red colour). This is where we first see this interplay of the conscious and unconscious in our lives.

TIME OF BIRTH

In order to calculate a Human Design chart we must have a person's time, date and place of birth. Many of us are uncertain of our birth time, so we need to be rather careful in approaching this knowledge. There are various techniques such as astrology, dowsing and muscle testing that claim to discover a person's correct time of birth, but even these should be approached with care. If you are unsure of someone's time of birth, the best thing to do is contact your nearest professional Human Design analyst and ask their advice. Sometimes a Design may change very little in a whole day, at others; a few seconds may make a world of difference.

The Human Design System is knowledge for our children. The more accurate the birth time, the more accurate and penetrating the chart. In the future, by getting our birth-time to the second, we will be able to probe the very deepest recesses of our genetic makeup. This is possible by means of a highly advanced branch of Human Design knowledge known as the Global Incarnation Index.

For Human Design purposes, the exact moment of birth is taken as the moment that the baby's body has left the mother entirely. It is not when the umbilical cord is cut. We recommend that birth times be recorded as close to the second as possible. Clocks should be tuned to the atomic clock, available over the internet.

THE PLANETS

The planets in Human Design have a fascinating impact on our design on account of the neutrino stream. Because we use the Earth to represent the primal Yin quality in Human Design, many of the traditional archetypes ascribed to the planets by astrology have mutated and evolved as we humans have evolved. Planetary imprinting is a very profound subject, and is one outside the scope of this present training. However, below is a simplified table of some of the Keynotes ascribed to the planets in Human Design.

PLANETARY KEYNOTES

⊙ SUN - Personality Expression

⊕ EARTH - Grounding/Balance

☾ MOON - Drive

☊ NORTH NODE - Direction (future)

☋ SOUTH NODE - Direction (past)

☿ MERCURY - Communication

♀ VENUS - Values

♂ MARS - Immaturity

♃ JUPITER - Law/Protection

♄ SATURN - Discipline

♅ URANUS - Unusualness

♆ NEPTUNE - Illusion

♇ PLUTO - Truth

THE PERSONALITY CALCULATION

Below is an illustration of how we calculate an individual Bodygraph. This is where Human Design diverts from traditional astrology because as you can see, we are looking at 2 wheels rather than one.

The wheel on the right side with the black colour coding is the wheel of your personality crystal. In other words, this is the neutrino information that was imprinted in your nature at the exact time of your birth. This is a calculation that an astrologer would use in order to create your horoscope.

The other wheel on the left with the red coding is the wheel of your Design crystal, which we will discuss below.

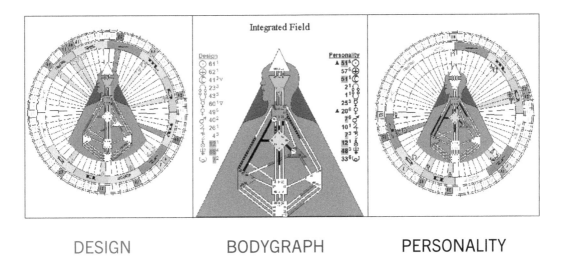

DESIGN   BODYGRAPH   PERSONALITY

In the wheel over, you can see the positions of the planets, the earth and the lunar nodes plotted in the wheel. The coloured spokes represent the hexagram numbers that correspond to the specific planetary positions.

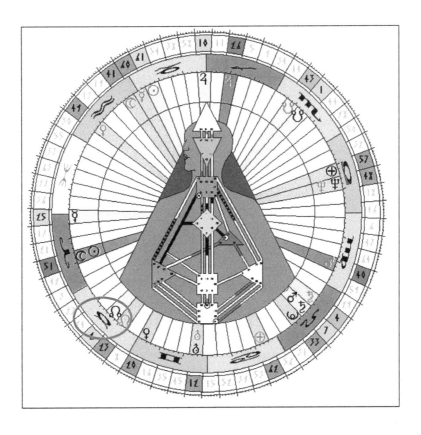

You can see that the natal North Node is in the middle of the zodiac sign of Taurus and its corresponding hexagram is the 2nd hexagram. The first thing you may note is that all this information is coded into the Bodygraph by colours and numbers. It is in fact, a very simple and graphic system. Everything from the personality wheel is coded into the Bodygraph in black. So this North Node in the 2nd hexagram gets coded to the 2nd gate, which we find in the centre in the middle of the Bodygraph known as the G Centre (see below). You will also notice in this instance that although the 2nd gate is coloured in black, the entire channel is not coloured in. That is very important. The North Node activation of the 2nd hexagram can only affect one side of the channel. The other side of the channel (the 14th gate) is left white because there is no planet that activates it. You can double-check this by looking back to the wheel again and finding the 14th gate (in Scorpio). You will see that there was no planet in this position to impact the neutrino field. Thus we only colour in half of the channel.

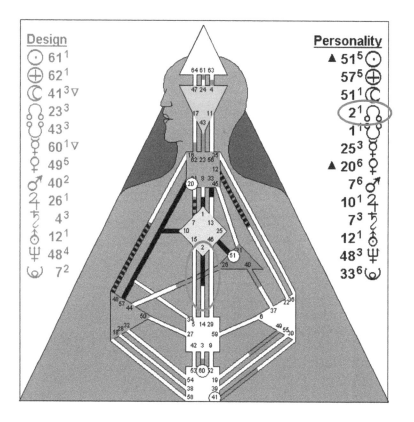

THE DESIGN CALCULATION

Astrologers, like the scientists, only have half the story. We have a second wheel. This is a prenatal calculation because it is made while we are still inside our mother's womb. This calculation is made exactly 88 degrees of the sun before our birth.

That is approximately 88 or 89 days before we are born. We always arrive at the design calculation by travelling 88 degrees backwards from the time of birth, so it does not matter whether you are a full-term baby or premature. In the case of premature births, the foetus' neo-cortex will simply develop more rapidly than usual.

Here is how it works:

A Design crystal (with its magnetic monopole embedded within it) detaches itself from the earth's core and enters the man in preparation for fertilisation. Certain couples can 'sense' the presence of this crystal before they even conceive. Next, a single sperm carrying the Design crystal enters the egg during copulation. It isn't necessarily the fastest swimmer that gets the prize. It is simply the one carrying the goods! (In other words, the Design crystal). Once the Design crystal is inside the egg, it takes the neutrino information at that moment and starts to design the body of the foetus. It will continue to work on this body until the neo cortex - the very special brain facility common to all humans- is completed.

Metaphorically speaking, the neo-cortex is the back seat of our limousine, which means that this is our capacity to look out in a self-reflected universe. When the Design crystal has built the neo-cortex, the foetus and its magnetic monopole send out a signal, which brings the Personality crystal into the body. Because the Personality crystal incarnates from above, as it were, man has given it many names; here in the West, we know it as the 'soul'. This incarnation always occurs 88 degrees of the sun before birth. This means that our personality has approximately three months to adjust to the vehicle before birth.

THE MYSTERY OF THE 88 DEGREES

Many people ask why the Design calculation is done at this specific period of 88 degrees before birth. The answer is both complex and very simple. The complex version, which is also the logical version, is only covered during the Advanced Rave Cartography Training.

However, in a nutshell, the 88 degrees between the personality and the design creates a geometry in the wheel that insures that all life goes on evolving. The simple version is that this was the information that the Voice gave. The number 88 also has a symbolic archetypal resonance, being a representation of the double genetic helix, as well as the traditional number for infinity.

The design calculation is done in the same way as an astrological calculation except that it is done for this particular prenatal moment. In the same way as the personality calculation, the positioning of the planets is coded into the Bodygraph, although this time they are coloured in red. In the example below, you can see the planet Jupiter in the 26th gate. You will find the 26th gate in the Heart Centre and you can also see that half of this channel is coloured in red.

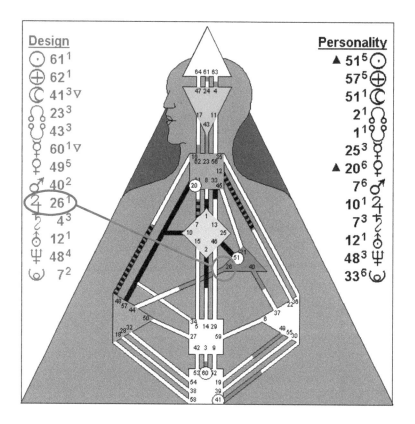

THE BLACK AND THE RED

These two sets of information are different in terms of their values. The personality wheel and all the information in black is what you have conscious access to; in other words, you can work with this information. Having conscious access is like sitting on the side of a hill and looking down at a road in front of you. You can see the traffic on the road and the people in the cars, as well as the direction they are going in. In other words, you can participate in the process. The personality data is what is familiar to you. It is who you think you are.

The real magic of Human Design is to be found in the information coded in red. This allows us to see behind the veil of the unconscious. Everything coded in red operates at an unconscious level within us. It represents our genetic inheritance. This is what you have inherited through your blood as a theme from your parents and your ancestors. In fact at the genetic level, we have more in common with our grandparents than we have with our parents. Thus this information in red is something that you have no conscious access to. Being unconscious, these themes operate as though we were in a tunnel. In other words, you don't know what is going on inside the tunnel. You have no idea whether there is traffic in it, or which way the cars might be moving. Neither do you know whether these cars will come out of the tunnel or not. You can only wait and see. Your unconscious will always be a surprise. These are aspects of your nature that you only come to recognise with age.

For example, if you have the 'Channel of Struggle' defined as part of your design, then you probably don't think of yourself as someone who struggles. The older the person, the more they recognise their unconscious.

WHO YOU THINK YOU ARE

The juxtaposition of both Personality and Design in the Bodygraph is one of the most revealing aspects of any design. Essentially, the Personality, being conscious, represents who you think you are, whilst the Design represents how you are genetically programmed.

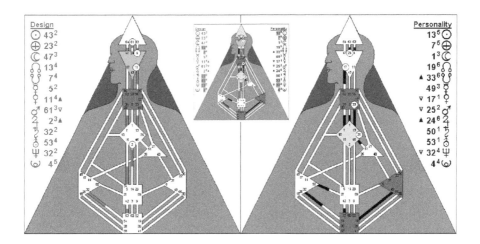

In the above example, we can see a Rave chart split into both its Design and Personality aspects. Looking at the Personality activations in your Design allows you to see who you think you are, so this person thinks that they are both a good listener (channel 13/33) and very sensitive (channel 19/49). However, when you look across at the Design activations on the left, you will see the other side of the story. We do not readily identify with our Design activations, thus, what this person does not know about himself is that despite thinking he is a sensitive listener, what actually happens in his life is that his mouth is always open and he's always talking. When you look at your own Design in this way, you will often see such jokes.

In the example below, you can also see that there are activations that are coloured both red and black. This means that a gate is being activated from both the conscious personality information and the unconscious design information. Such activations tend to oscillate between being conscious and unconscious. Sometimes we are aware of that part of our nature and sometimes we are not. There is always a potential gift in such activations because it is the one place in our design where we also may glimpse the unconscious as it becomes conscious.

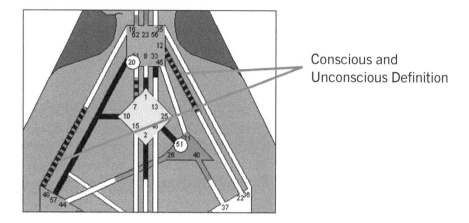

Conscious and
Unconscious Definition

CONCLUSION

In conclusion then, these two great wheels represent the two crystals of consciousness within us. Every human being is in this sense a bi-incarnation. We are made up of two very different sets of forces that are held together by a third, neutral force, the magnetic monopole. When we die, these two crystals of consciousness within us will go their separate ways. The Personality crystal can be accessed consciously, but the Design crystal is something you can only react to.

Finally, the Human Design Bodygraph is the integrated field where we can read both streams of information as a synthesis.

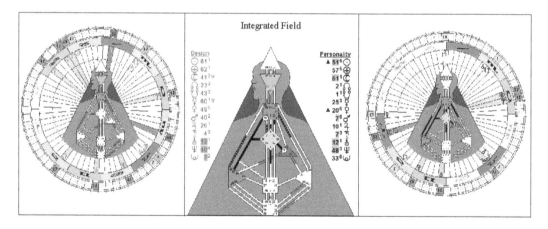

Integrated Field

6. DEFINED AND UNDEFINED CENTRES

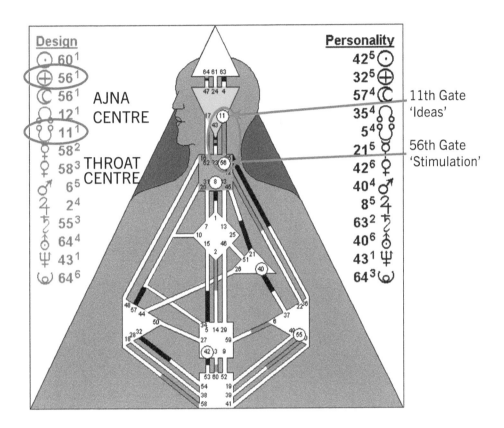

6.1 DEFINITION

The first thing that most people's eyes are drawn to when they look at a Bodygraph is the colours. No matter how deeply you study Human Design, always remember this: these colours tell you everything you need to know about a person.

Having taken the two calculations and integrated them into the Bodygraph, the first thing that we are looking for in Human Design is where gates are activated at either end of the same channel. This means that the whole channel is coloured in AS WELL AS the adjoining centres at either end. This is called definition. In the above illustration we can see how this works:

The green centre (known as the Ajna Centre) is connected to the brown Throat Centre by a single channel (the 11/56) known as the Channel of Curiosity. You can see that both gates at either end of this channel (the 56 and the 11) are activated from the design information in the red column on the left. This is an unconscious definition because it is coloured entirely in red.

So what is definition? If you imagine that the Bodygraph is an electrical circuit board, then whenever you see a channel that is coloured in, energy is always flowing along that pathway between those two centres. Definition represents an absolute consistency in our nature. It is an energy that will always be functioning within you, every second of every hour of every year, until you are dead. This is why definition is the one and only thing in your life that you are ever going to be able to rely on. This is not to say that you can rely on it to be good or bad. You can simply rely on it to be you.

Definition is the great chance for you to be yourself. This information is vital to you. Since it does not change, it is the only thing within yourself that you can consistently rely upon to make healthy decisions in your life. Wherever you see colour in your chart, it represents a part of your nature that was fixed at birth. Definition is the core of who you are.

Let's look at the example to understand how definition works.

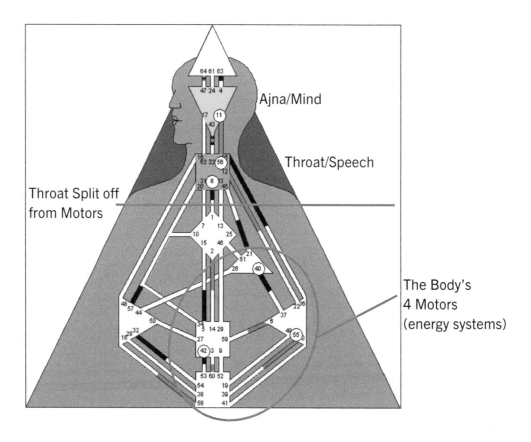

Here is somebody whose mind (the Ajna) is always connected to their Throat. Therefore this is somebody that will always speak their mind.

The connection is made through the channel 11/56 which is called the Channel of Curiosity, a design of a searcher or a seeker. The 11th gate is the gate of ideas and the 56th gate is the gate of stimulation. Transferred to the example this means that this person always has ideas that they want to share in order to stimulate others. Both the 11th gate and the 56th gate are coloured in red. This means, if you recall our earlier metaphor, that their ideas come out of a tunnel. In other words, this is someone who just opens their mouth and out pours all kinds of ideas that they didn't even know they had. With this kind of design, every dinner party is a success because they can talk to anyone and keep everyone stimulated.

However, if you gather together all of this person's friends and you ask them to comment on them, they will all say at the same time: 'Ah! He always has lots of ideas but he never does anything with them'. This person knows that he never turns his ideas into action and is probably deeply frustrated about this. The reason for his dilemma is simple. The circuitry stops at the Throat Centre, the centre of communication. If the Throat Centre were connected to one of the body's four motors (the Root, Heart, Solar Plexus or Sacral) then this person would have the possibility to turn communication into action by acting on his ideas. It is not as though it is his fault that he is caught in this dynamic. There is no connection or definition to the body's energy systems. If our friend understood his design correctly he would know exactly how to deal with this dilemma. In fact he would not be in a dilemma at all. He would be rather relaxed. He would understand that he is not meant to do anything with his own ideas other than share them and inspire others to action.

Definition is who we are. It is what we are designed to live out. The person above can always rely on their ability to express their ideas, even though they do not know why they always have so many ideas. You can't tell such a person to stop expressing his ideas. That is who he is. It is in fact, the only thing that is truly consistent in his nature.

TYPES OF DEFINITION

Apart from Reflectors, who have no definition, there are four possible configurations relating to Definition. Generally speaking, the different types of split definitions have a greater need for other people in their life in order to bridge the splits and give them a sense of integration in life.

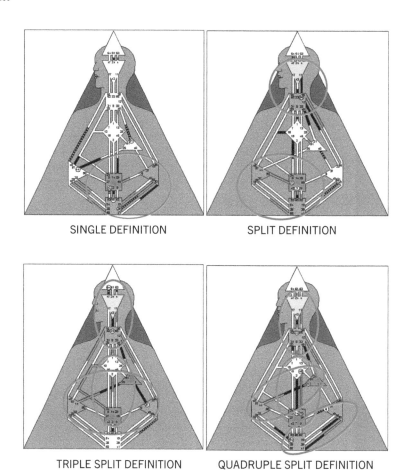

SINGLE DEFINITION   SPLIT DEFINITION

TRIPLE SPLIT DEFINITION   QUADRUPLE SPLIT DEFINITION

LACK OF DEFINITION

When you look at any Bodygraph you can also see that there are places that are undefined. There are undefined channels and usually there are undefined centres. We are a binary of defined and undefined areas. These centres and channels in white represent our conditioning field. They do not operate consistently and are therefore unreliable. Below on the left we can see the design of Mozart, and on the right we can see his conditioning field. In his case, his greatest conditioning was in his Throat Centre, which is his expression.

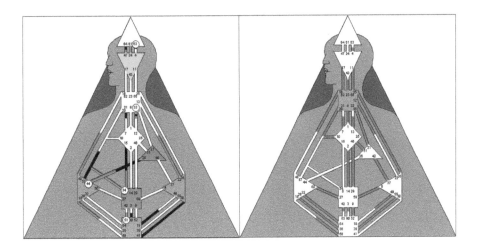

Wherever you see a centre, channel or gate that is not coloured in, you are looking at something that is deeply attractive to you. There is a simple reason for this. Our genes demand that we are attracted to our opposite. In fact, with Human Design, one could go one step further than this and say that our very chemistry is magnetised towards our conditioning field. The white centres are what we long for in life. In Mozart's case, we can see that the only thing he could not be in control of in his life was his expression, and this is what he longed for the most, to express his genius. As we all know, this was also the cause of much of the pain in his life.

Because undefined centres are inconsistent, they tend to become themes that we chase after in our lives. Thus they are the main reason why most human beings do not live their design. We have this false assumption that living out the open centres in our design is what we are supposed to do. The result of this is usually frustration and failure in life, because it is rather like chasing after one's tail. If it isn't meant to be consistent, then it is best understood that way.

6.2 CONDITIONING

Many thousands of babies are born each minute with the same design, and yet still they turn out to be very different from each other. The reason is conditioning. Consider your design chart for a moment. You are looking at a frozen moment in time; an imprint, like a photograph. But although the imprint doesn't change, the conditioning field around it does. In other words, every gate, channel or centre that is not defined in your design is constantly open to fluctuations from the environment.

There are two main sources of our conditioning. The first is the planets. Remember that the planets are constantly moving around the wheel affecting the neutrino field as it streams through us. As the planets move, they open and close the gates that they move through.

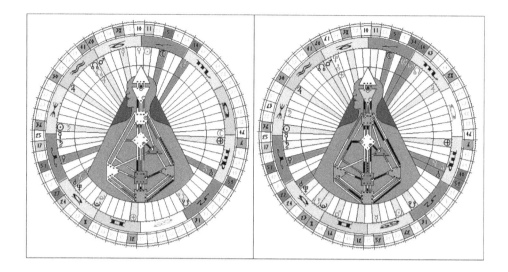

In the example above, we can see a normal Bodygraph within the wheel on the left. Now look at the Bodygraph on the right. You can see the positions of the planets (in blue) at another given moment during the life of this person. You will also notice that during this particular planetary transit, all of this person's undefined centres are in fact defined. In other words, the planets have activated gates in this person's design, even though they don't have those gates defined inherently.

We are all in this sense mirrors for the celestial bodies that are constantly invoking a deep ongoing genetic program inside us. This is why people often experience similar patterns in their lives at similar times. Tracking and understanding planetary conditioning requires an accurate ephemeris and is a fascinating and rewarding subject that is offered as a separate training. Planetary transits can literally condition our behaviour patterns and lure us down all kinds of inappropriate roads. At this moment in time, the most important thing for us is that we grasp our own design and begin to follow its Strategy. This is the only thing that will protect us from being a victim of planetary conditioning.

The second source of our conditioning is the people around us. In order to understand how human beings condition each other, we have to comprehend what a human aura is. These days, the word aura is something of a buzzword in new age circles. The aura we are talking about here is the measurable electromagnetic field that all human beings emit. A human aura extends about as far as twice your outstretched arm in all directions. Thus if you are within 6 or 7 feet of someone, you are effectively conditioning each other's design. This is what we know as the 'chemistry' between two people.

Prior to Human Design, the 'chemistry' between people has been a nebulous affair. Now, by overlapping two Bodygraphs, we can see an exact map of the chemistry between any two people. Thus we can have a deep insight into the power of attraction. As we have seen earlier, we are always attracted to what we are not, in other words, the white areas in our design. We all seek those people who will define a channel and bring colour into our design.

Below is an example of what happens when two people come into each other's auras.

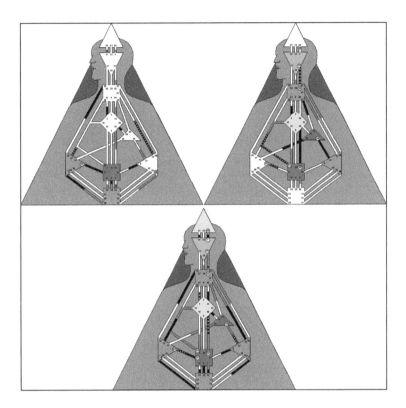

Think about what conditioning really is: when you come into the world, your design is constantly in the aura of your mother, your father and your family. Thus you get deeply conditioned to all those things that you are not. By the time you are seven years old, that conditioning is locked into your behaviour patterns.

So when you start looking at the designs of your family members and of people close to you … your friends, lovers and colleagues, you will often discover that you still have the same energies in your life. You will see that you have been automatically drawn to people who make the same chemical connections as your parents. This is why certain people can seem so familiar to you even when you don't know them. They are bringing you the same energy connections as your parents.

In seeing what is open in your design, you can trace back where you have been conditioned. You can clearly name your soft spots, where you are open to be influenced by others. Thus you are able to see where unhealthy conditioning took place in your early life. It is important to understand that we cannot escape conditioning. It is everywhere. Any life form - animals, plants and even inanimate objects - can connect to us and influence our nature and our body chemistry.

SEVEN YEARS

The first step in freeing yourself from your old patterns is to see where you are conditioned, and then you have to start the process of not identifying with these forces. This can lead to great wisdom and a deep sensibility, but it is a task that takes time. You cannot be there tomorrow. You cannot be truly free of your childhood patterns until the knowledge of who you are gets under your skin and reprograms the actual cells in your body. This is a process that takes seven years because this is the time span for your body to be physically renewed.

Let's see how the person in the example below is being conditioned. Let's see what they are most attracted to in life and what they long for. Mechanically, all we have to do to see this is look at the open centres, find out their names and look for their keynotes. We can refer to the graph on page 28 showing the centres and their functions. In this example, we can see four open centres: the Head Centre, the G Centre, the Heart Centre and the Solar Plexus Centre. Therefore this person has four places in them that they are under pressure to try and fulfil, even though they can never rely on these four places to be themselves.

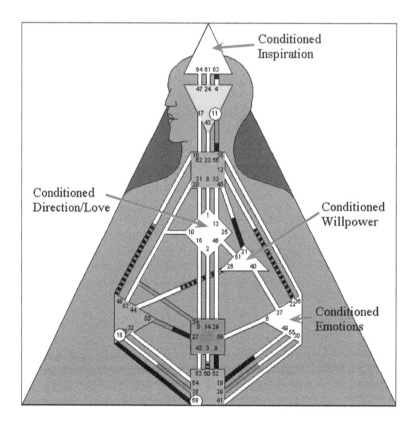

The open Head Centre tells us that this person is attracted to inspiration but experiences that he cannot control when and where it comes. What they are inspired by is totally dependent on who they are with. Their potential gift is actually to know who is inspiring.

The open G Centre is an indication that this person is constantly trying to find their direction in life. Through this centre they will probably try to hold onto love to give them a firm sense of identity. They may feel lost and don't know if they can find their way. Due to their openness, this person will never really know who they are, although this is not a handicap. Love and direction will always remain inconsistent for such a person. In other words, who they are is conditioned by whom they are with. They will be something of a chameleon. Their potential wisdom is to know which way is correct for them by sampling many different ways and directions in life. In this way they will also learn to taste many possibilities of love in their life.

The open Heart Centre shows that this person is also conditioned to be willful. This is someone who constantly makes promises he cannot keep. Whenever this person tries to be willful in their life they will damage their health because it is not natural for them. Their potential wisdom lies in knowing who does have the willpower to get things done on the material plane.

The open Solar Plexus Centre tells us that this person constantly tries to make emotional decisions. They are constantly taking in the emotional energies of those around them and probably feel deeply disturbed by identifying with them. Because of this, they will constantly be torn between hope and pain, expectation and disappointment. Their potential wisdom is to know how emotions work and to maintain an emotional coolness and balance in all situations.

THE DEFINED/UNDEFINED DUALITY

Many students who get in touch with Human Design are inclined to think that definition is superior to lack of definition. This is not true. Defined / Undefined is simply a duality, like day and night. The value of definition is that it is reliable and fixed, but at the same time it is like a very limited thin line. What is undefined is vulnerable to conditioning, and it is this that makes students believe that definition is somehow better. The undefined open areas in our chart have an enormous potential for experience and wisdom. An undefined centre is neither empty, nor broken nor does it need fixing. Definition shows you what kind of a student you are, and the undefined areas tell you where you will go to school in life. The undefined areas are like the courses we will take at the university of life. Remember then, that these open centres are the only place we can finally graduate!

There is also another analogy for the duality of defined/undefined. Definitions are like transmitters. In living out our definitions we send our energies into the world. The open centres are like receivers. Through the open centres we soak in the energies of the world around us. In fact, the open centres in our design do not only reflect the chemistry of those around us, they also magnify it. Thus an undefined Solar Plexus Centre will magnify the emotions of those around us, whether that is joy, anger or sadness.

Because of the inconsistency of the open centres in our design, they are never of value for our personal process in life, but their huge potential makes us very important for other people.

6.3 THE PURPOSE OF HUMAN DESIGN

The purpose of Human Design is to show your uniqueness. The first step to knowing yourself is seeing your definition. The first step in being yourself is relying on that definition. The next step Human Design takes you to is to see what is open in you, in order that you can recognise where you have been conditioned. Becoming yourself requires that you stop identifying with the open centres. It takes seven years to clean out the conditioning. These seven years are a journey in which the awareness of who you are gradually begins to overcome your old conditioned behaviour patterns. The last thing to give up trying to be in control of our lives is the mind. Once the pattern of who you are is set in the cellular structure of your body, only then can you let go of your mind. Everybody can become themselves, but it takes seven years of hard work on yourself and for yourself.

The reward that comes in recognising your own nature is worth the effort. Knowing and understanding your design protects you from being a victim of your conditioning. To be yourself is to be fundamentally healthy.

If you are yourself and you get ill, you only get the diseases that your body can manage. When you do not live your design, you are far more likely to get ill because you constantly confront yourself with energies that you are not genetically equipped to handle. Human Design is a tool that can tell you how your body is designed and how it is meant to run properly.

Mystically speaking, Human Design has the potential to show you that you are a tiny cell moving through a vast body. When you stop interfering with your life, then you allow life to move you in the way that is best suited to you. This not only brings you utter fulfilment, but also allows you to transcend your own design. Ironically, it is only by surrendering to our limitation that we can finally find our freedom.

It is obvious that hearing about your unique design and living it are two different things. To live according to your nature takes great courage. You can learn to understand your design intellectually, but living your design can only be learned from life itself. Human Design is a logical system and logic requires repeated testing to verify the truth of the pattern. It is wonderful that you don' t have to believe any of this. You can see for yourself that it works.

Human Design knowledge is of great benefit to children and parents, since knowing a child's design means that they can be guided in the direction of their nature rather than being driven away from it. Children can thus grow up with a feel for their own true nature. For most of us adults, the road back to our true nature is difficult due to a lifelong conditioning. It takes courage to stay with the process.

Having outlined the origins of Human Design and its components, we will now move on and take a detailed look at each of the nine centres. We will discuss what it means to have them both defined and undefined.

MAPS OF CONSCIOUSNESS

OK.

Put away your logical brain for a few moments and come over to the other side. Think of the moment when you first saw a picture of your own Bodygraph. That is actually quite a moment in your life. It is not every day that someone holds up a map of your inner being. Think about how you found this knowledge for a few moments, or how it found you. If you begin to truly experiment with living your design, it could utterly change your life. This is a revealed knowledge. It works on many levels. Look at your own Bodygraph now. Look at it as though you were a child. You can see clearly that it follows an outline of your body. Don't try and understand it. Simply feel your way into it.

Half close your eyes so that your Bodygraph becomes a little hazy. Notice where the colours are and where they are not. Those colours represent YOU. How are you responding to this image? Did you realise that you are actually responding according to this image? How much does this image feel like you? Is there anything you do not like about your Bodygraph? Is there some area where your attention is drawn? The Bodygraph is a map. It is not the territory. You are the territory.

Look again at the white places in your Bodygraph. Do not forget to look at the white channels and gates. Notice how few gates are actually coloured in. Allow your eyes to see only the white places. This is the backdrop of consciousness behind your life. This is what you can never be in control of. This is what you will one day die into...

Now focus your eyes and your attention only on the colours.
This is YOU.

Unmistakable and absolutely reliable as YOU from the moment you were born to the moment you die. This part of you will never change. It may fluctuate within itself, but it will never change. Feel the anchor of that. Feel the solidity of those colours sitting in the constantly shifting backdrop of whiteness. That's what this course is all about. It's about staying in those colours. It's about being only YOU and nothing else.

Once you can be only YOU, then the door of Magick can open. Then, all things become possible. Take a deep breath. Feel the excitement of what it might mean to be YOU at your highest potential. It will take time. It will be a journey of many twists and turns. It will be painful at times. But over and above it all, remember, now you have a map, and before, you never had this map. From now on, things will be a whole lot easier...

Relax.
Allow life to unfold.
Realise how lucky you are to have come to this knowledge.

PART 2: A GUIDE TO THE NINE CENTRES

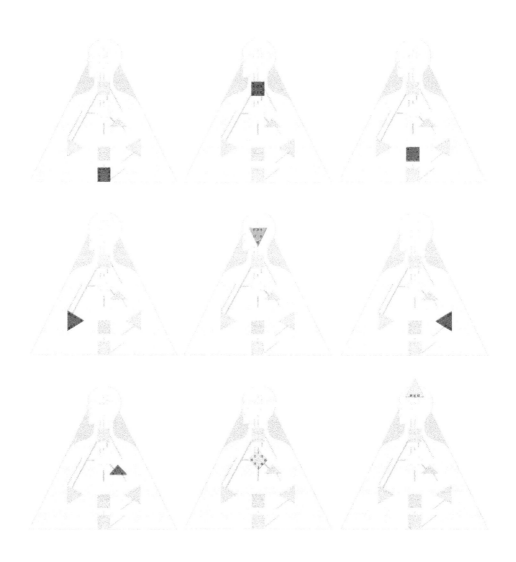

THE NINE CENTRES

1. ENERGY

THE ROOT CENTRE:	THE THROAT CENTRE:	THE SACRAL CENTRE:
Pressure	*Metabolism*	*Vitality*

2. AWARENESS

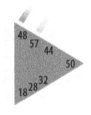

THE SPLEEN CENTRE:	THE AJNA CENTRE:	THE SOLAR PLEXUS: CENTRE:
Body	*Mind*	*Spirit*

3. DIRECTION

THE HEART / EGO CENTRE:	THE G CENTRE:	THE HEAD CENTRE:
Form	*Love*	*Consciousness*

A NOTE ABOUT THE RED

In both Part 2 and Part 3 of this book, we have deliberately left out the majority of the sections in red that represent the unconscious process of awakening.

The reason for this is to encourage you to write about your own experiences of each of the centres as you encounter them in yourselves and others. Listen out for stories and revelations from others, and watch the centres and their themes playing out in the people around you. In learning Human Design, there is no substitute for real life experience. We have included several stories at various places within the manual as examples of the kind of revelations you may have. These are some of the experiences of others who have studied Human Design and we hope you may find them inspiring.

1. INTRODUCTION TO THE NINE CENTRES

One very dark spring night in the latter part of the eighteenth century, a man set up his homemade high magnification telescope and gazed up at the stars. The date was 13th March 1781, and it was a date that would change that man's life. Indeed, even though he never knew it, it was a night that would change the lives of every human being for centuries and centuries after he had died.

His name was William Herschel. A musician originally born in Germany, he lived in Bath, England where he struggled to make his living as an astronomer. In the year 1781 however, all that changed, as he found himself gazing for hours on end at an uncharted object shining faintly in the night sky. At first, he had taken it for a comet, but after tracking it all night, he became increasingly certain that he was looking at an uncharted planet. He wrote to the Astronomer Royal the following morning, and it was soon confirmed that he had in fact discovered another planet in our solar system, outside the orbit of Saturn and invisible to the naked eye. He had discovered the planet Uranus.

In traditional astrology, the discovery of a new planet marks a shift in the consciousness of humanity as a whole. Indeed, the end of the eighteenth century was in many ways a seeding time for the world we see around ourselves today.

Electricity was discovered, the industrial revolution was in full swing and the world was opening up to all kinds of technological advances in communication, science, travel, health and education. It was the height of the so-called Age of Enlightenment. It is not that the discovery of Uranus set all these things in motion, but rather that it stands as a symbol of the paradigm shift that humanity was going through at that time. In fact, we are still very much going through that shift. The discovery of Uranus hinted at an expanding of humanity's limit of vision. Indeed, it was William Herschel who advanced our understanding of nebulae, the hazy clouds that surround dying stars. He even went on to be the founder of stellar astronomy, the study of the region beyond our own solar system. Our modern sense of a galaxy's shape is very similar to what Herschel proposed hundreds of years ago. Uranus, the great Roman sky god, had brought radical change to the world.

In the cosmology of the Human Design System it was the discovery of Uranus that symbolically marked the next great step in humanity's evolution as a species. It was, said the voice, the beginning of the last great mutation. The graphic representation of this consciousness shift is seen in our change from being a seven-centred being to a nine-centred being. From this moment on, all systems that looked at humanity though the traditional Saturn-based paradigm were past their sell-by date. It was not until very recently however, that we have had a truly updated version of ourselves. Human Design has often been referred to as a 'Uranian system', as it is the new map, the synthesis built out of the old systems, which shows us the kind of creatures we are becoming. According to the Voice and its unusual language, we are about to make the biogenetic leap from Homo Sapiens to something known as a Rave.

WHAT IS A RAVE?

A Rave is the revealed name of a new kind of human being. The prefix 'Ra' comes from both the Sanskrit and Native American Sioux meaning 'fire' or 'heat'. The word 'rave' comes from the Latin 'rapere', meaning 'to seize by force'. The coming changes to our world and the way in which the human body will mutate are not in our hands. It is our genes that will seize us by force. However, until 2027, the Rave does not technically exist. In the same way that a physical genetic mutation brought about the metamorphosis of Neanderthal man into Cro-Magnon man, another mutation is about to spread through the human race. Even so, the mutation is present in the genes of every human being on this planet, which means that at some level we are all expecting this event. The human tendency is always to anthropomorphise such things, thus we give the mutation names like The New Age or we see it as a coming Ascension to some higher plane.

FROM SEVEN TO NINE CENTRES

If you look at the traditional seven-centred Hindu chakra system and then you compare it to the nine-centred Bodygraph, you can see that it is rather like moving from a two dimensional map to a three-dimensional map. Whereas the old systems tended to see evolution as a ladder that we climbed, the Bodygraph functions rather like a hall of mirrors, or a labyrinth where energy flows in all directions simultaneously. As one learns in the advanced Rave Cartography training, the Bodygraph encapsulates a knowledge that is truly multi-dimensional, containing secrets within secrets.

The first thing to have clear in our minds at this point concerns the nine centres themselves. Many people still refer to these centres as chakras. This is no longer an appropriate terminology. The Bodygraph is not so much a meditation tool as a map that describes an individual's uniqueness, role and direction in life. The nine centres act as information hubs within the body itself. At all times, we should remember that the Bodygraph is only a map. It is not the territory. The nine centres exist as a multi-dimensional grid that describes the inner workings and interconnectedness of all human beings. It is our personal experience of these centres that brings the knowledge alive.

THE SYMBOLISM OF THE COLOURS

A fairly frequently asked question in Human Design concerns the colours of the nine centres themselves. Why are the centres coloured in the way they are? Unfortunately, there is no simple answer to this question, as we were not given this information as a part of the Human Design revelation. However, there may be some insights we can glean from a closer observation.

The four centres in brown are the Root, the Spleen, the Solar Plexus and the Throat. These four centres represent the structure of life itself. The Root is the pressure to stay alive, whilst the Spleen and the Solar Plexus filter this pressure through individual survival and group interaction. The Throat ensures that the pressure to be alive is metabolised through these two types of awareness.

The two centres in red are the Heart and the Sacral and both share a theme of surrender. The Heart represents the surrender of the individual ego to become a part working within the whole, and the Sacral represents the greater surrender of all beings to life itself.

The two centres in yellow are the G and the Head, and these two centres share a common mystical theme. The G is evolution through Love and the Head is our evolution through Consciousness.

Finally, standing out alone is the Ajna Centre in green. This is truly the colour of humanity, for it represents the fertility of the human imagination and is the essence of what we really are. We are a mental species living in a mental 'maya'. Green is after all, the colour of our planet.

2. ENERGY

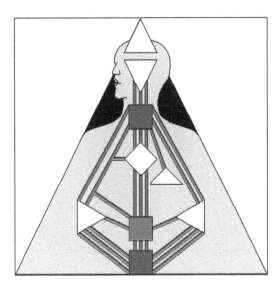

The Bodygraph is essentially an energy map. It shows us how energy flows in our lives, as well as where it comes from and how and when it motivates us. One of the great revelations of Human Design is the incompleteness of the definition in our Bodygraph. As individuals, no one person is ever complete. It is this fact that drives us to seek wholeness in the outer world, whether that leads us to love or drugs or God or any other thing that might bring us some sense of being whole.

The irony is that we are designed to be incomplete. We are designed to be incomplete because like the cells within our bodies, we are designed to move as one totality where every cell is interdependent with every other cell. As we journey through our seven-year cycle of deconditioning, we are essentially moving from a state of co-dependence to the reality and freedom of our true interdependence.

THE FOUR MOTORS

In the Bodygraph there are 4 energy centres, known as 'motors'. These centres are the Sacral, the Root, the Ego/Heart and the Solar Plexus. It is in fact the individual 'wiring' of these four motors that ultimately divides human beings into the four Types that we will study in Part 3 of this manual. Each of the motors has its own set of very different qualities and functions within the Bodygraph, and we will look at each in the context of its functionality. However, it is always important to remember that these four centres do have an underlying fundamental relationship – they are each a source of energy in our lives.

2.1 THE ROOT CENTRE: PRESSURE
WHY ALL THE STRESS?

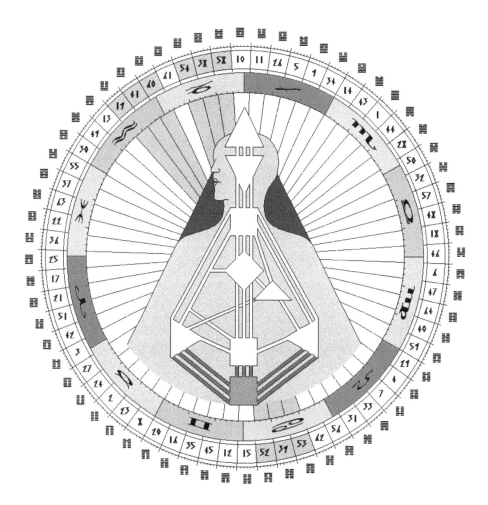

We begin at the Root Centre because it is the centre of beginnings. It is represents the very pressure of existence. According to the physicists, before the Big Bang, all the material of the universe was compressed into a space the size of a tennis ball. That is a great deal of pressure. In microcosm, the Root Centre causes a similar pressure – that is, it forces us to live, grow and evolve. If we are to live and survive, we have no choice but to submit to this pressure.

All life begins with this stress. Stress is the foundation of who we are, just as the Root Centre is the foundation of the Bodygraph. At the very top of the Bodygraph is the Head Centre and at the very bottom of the Bodygraph is the Root Centre. These two centres have a deep connection to each other because they are both pressure centres. In other words, being a human being is rather like being in a pressure sandwich.

Whilst the Head Centre brings mental pressure in the form of doubt, confusion or inspiration, the Root Centre is a very different kind of pressure. This is the pressure to evolve and adapt to the world and to life. It is the very fuel of evolution and is the purest and most powerful energy within us.

The ancient Hindus had a name for this energy; they called it Kundalini, the 'serpent power'. For millennia, many yogis have attempted to harness this power through meditation techniques and yoga. Many have gone mad, as the same pressure that can make us healthy can also destroy our bodies and minds.

BIOLOGICAL RELATIONSHIP

Biologically, the Root Centre is associated with the adrenaline system and with our stress hormones. Stress in life is something that you have to take advantage of rather than something that you have to suffer from. Stress cannot be avoided. Stress is an important fuel, which actually helps us to master difficult situations. You cannot fight against this vital fuel, and when you do, you can find yourself easily depressed, in particular through the gates that connect the Root to the Sacral Centre.

As we have seen, the Root is a motor, and it is the only one of the four motors in the Bodygraph that has no direct access to the Throat. The moment a motor can connect through definition to the Throat, the energy of that motor can be expressed and manifested. The energy in the Root is far too strong to be directly connected to the Throat.

If you look at the Bodygraph, you will see that the only way that the pressure from the Root Centre can reach the Throat is if it is 'processed' through another centre or centres. Thus, stress in itself is merely a 'fuel' that energises certain deep biochemical processes within us. How we cope with stress in our lives is always connected to our own unique Root Centre and the way in which its gates are defined or undefined.

THE THREE FORMAT ENERGIES

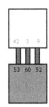
Between the Root Centre and the Sacral Centre are three channels known as the energy formats. These three channels generate three great archetypal energy frequencies that operate through our bodies and our lives. We have cyclical, developmental processes through the Channel of Maturation (53/42), logical and focused processes through the Channel of Concentration (9/52) and unpredictable, mutative processes through the Channel of Mutation (3/60).

THE NINE PRESSURES OF BEING ALIVE

Below are represented each of the gates of the Root Centre and the themes of their pressure in the world. The understanding of gates and channels is very profound and is outside the scope of this present training. All the channels, gates and circuits are studied in one of the author's other Human Design book, *Circuitry*.

58 – To Correct

38 – To find Purpose

54 – To Rise up

53 – To Begin

60 – To Mutate

52 – To Focus

19 – To Need

39 – To find Spirit

41 – To Desire

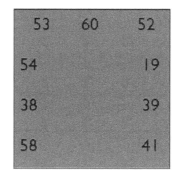

HEALTH AND SPIRIT

The two other centres that directly process pressure from the Root Centre are the Solar Plexus Centre and the Spleen Centre. The Solar Plexus processes this as three types of emotional pressure – the pressure of need (Gate 19), the pressure to find spirit (Gate 39) and the pressure of desire (Gate 41). In the Spleen Centre, the same vital energy from the Root Centre creates the pressure to stay healthy through its connection to our immune system. This also manifests in three potential ways – the pressure of ambition (Gate 54), the pressure to find purpose (Gate 38) and the pressure to perfect (Gate 58). It is interesting to note that it is these last three primal pressures that ensure we humans stay healthy and alive – we have to be materially successful, we have to have a sense of purpose in life and we have to continually improve our lives. One only has to look around oneself in life to see the truth of this in human beings.

JOY AND STILLNESS – THE GOLDEN RULE OF THE ROOT CENTRE

Because of the hexagram structure within the nine gates of the Root Centre, two themes emerge as the essence of this centre. These are the themes of Joy and Stillness, and they are related to the 58th and 52nd Gates respectively. It is one of the many paradoxes within the Bodygraph that it is in the centre of Stress and Pressure that we find the source of Stillness and Joy. These two themes whisper a secret to each of us about the nature of stress – as long as we begin something either out of stillness or joy, then no matter how stressful our endeavours, we will remain grounded in the Root Centre. We are either able to remain inwardly still through potentially stressful times or we rise to the occasion and meet the challenge with joy. This is the Golden Rule for the Root Centre – do not begin anything in life, unless it is rooted in either a place of stillness or a sense of joy.

CONDITIONING THROUGH THE UNDEFINED ROOT CENTRE

Like the undefined Head Centre, the undefined Root Centre can be placed under great pressure. Remember that when a centre is undefined (when it is white), it is not only vulnerable but it will also magnify any connection to it. Somebody with an undefined Root Centre can end up appearing to be deeply hyperactive as a result of conditioning, with predictable consequences.

There is nowhere where Human Design has greater relevance than in understanding the mechanics of a family relationship. Let's take the example of a child with an undefined Root Centre. Remember also that we are always attracted to our opposite in life (the undefined or open centre is always attracted to the defined). So little Billy invites one of his new friends over to tea. The moment that friend comes over and hooks up Billy's undefined Root Centre, the resulting magnification of his Root energy can be explosive. These two children are going to be highly energised together and this can easily appear to the parents to be a problem.

In a classroom environment, the collective aura will ensure that all nine centres are continuously defined, and this is the kind of arena where a child with an undefined Root Centre is going to be under enormous pressure and stress. This will usually result in a high level of restlessness, which can so easily be misread by parents and teachers alike and is often even punished. Such a child is usually accused of being unable to concentrate and sit still. Furthermore, it can be assumed that the child needs some special kind of help or therapy, which will result in them feeling even more helpless and humiliated.

There are an enormous number of children who have no motors defined. So many of these children are put on courses of drugs or suppressants. They are falsely diagnosed to be hyperactive and unhealthy. This is simply not true. When they can be educated in the nature of their design and how to live with it, then they will no longer identify and give Authority to energy that does not belong to them. They can take advantage of it, but they do not have to be ruled by the conditioning nor out of control in it. Conditioning is not the enemy. Ignorance of conditioning is. Any conditioned field can bring positive impact. It is however always going to be inconsistent and as such is not reliable.

ADRENALINE AND STRESS

Under conditioned pressure, the undefined Root Centre can often manifest unusual behaviour. The other response that can often be experienced is the opposite to hyperactivity – in other words 'stage fright'. People with undefined Root energy can often 'freeze up' in tense and stressful situations. They can actually be frozen by the strong adrenaline energy rushing through them. An undefined Root Centre is either going to love a crowd or be terrified by a crowd. They will either rise on the surge of adrenaline that is magnified through their chemistry, taking advantage of the surplus energy, or they will tend to avoid the crowd for fear of being overwhelmed. Many singers who perform on stage have undefined Root Centres and enjoy the adrenaline energy of the crowd.

What is essential to grasp about all conditioning is that we cannot afford to give Authority to what we are not. In other words, somebody can pressurise us at the mental level (through the undefined Head Centre) to think about a certain dilemma that has to be resolved. But if it is not our dilemma in the first place, then it is not our responsibility to carry that unresolved burden. The same thing is true for the undefined adrenaline system. One does not have to get lost in the pressure. One can either take advantage of it or avoid it. The key is to recognise what belongs to you and what does not. In recognising what you are not, you can eliminate its pull over you. The net result is a great potential for wisdom.

The person with an undefined Head Centre who does not suffer from the conditioned pressure of that Head Centre, has the potential wisdom to recognise which inspiration is really of value. Their gift is to see who can truly be inspiring. In the same way, someone with an undefined Root Centre can understand better than anyone else the nature of stress and how it operates. There is a great advantage in these undefined centres when we can escape being a victim of their conditioning. When we can use Human Design knowledge in this way, we can really transform our lives:

'In my own design, I have an undefined or open emotional system. And for over a decade now, I have been teaching people about the emotions. Through my open Solar Plexus, I have experienced the full emotional spectrum. For so long in my life before I understood my mechanics, I gave Authority to emotions that did not belong to me. It brought chaos into my personal life and chaos into my professional life. In understanding my own mechanics, I no longer give Authority to what I am not. I am healthy for that. Along with this understanding has come wisdom about the emotional plane and how it operates.'

Ra Uru Hu

This dichotomy within us of having centres that are defined and centres that are undefined is our greatest challenge, yet it brings the greatest rewards. It brings valued knowledge. This is knowledge that is of value not only to oneself, but also to others in our lives. We have now seen through the Root Centre that human beings are always under stress by design. We are under stress to stay alive and be healthy and communicate with each other. This is what it means to be human. It is the fundamental pressure of life.

EXAMPLE OF AN UNDEFINED ROOT CENTRE: STING

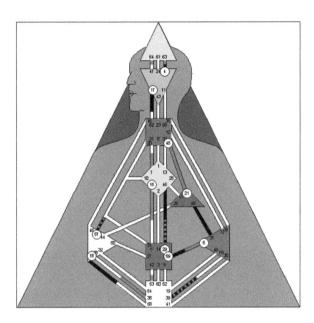

In the example above, we can see the Rave chart for Sting. As you can see, he has an undefined Root Centre. This means that he can easily be overwhelmed by other people's stress. People with undefined Root Centres always have to be careful about allowing other people to put them under pressure. Sting needs to be very wary of making a rushed decision in life because someone else is feeling stressed and is pushing him, for example, to meet a certain deadline.

His undefined Root Centre will amplify another person's stress and over the long term can be very destabilising to his health (note the only other undefined centre is the Spleen, which represents the body's immune system). As long as he gives himself enough physical space from other people, as well as not identifying with their stress, he can enjoy both the calm of having an undefined Root Centre, and the rushes of adrenaline he obviously gets when he performs before large audiences.

EXAMPLE OF A DEFINED ROOT CENTRE: BRAD PITT

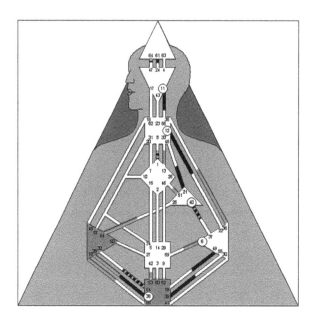

In the example over, we can see that Brad Pitt has a strongly defined Root Centre (strongly because there are also several gates defined other than the definition itself). Brad is someone who actually thrives on adrenaline and stress. As his only definition, and being connected to the Spleen Centre, we can see that adrenaline is healthy for him because it is actually the only consistent theme in his life. He is someone that will always love high-energy environments and situations in life that push his limits and make him feel excited.

Whenever you see connections in the Bodygraph between the Root Centre and the Spleen Centre, there is a biological need in that design to pump the adrenaline through the immune system. In other words, these are people that need regular exercise in life, and they can feel very stagnant if they are locked in situations that do not excite them. They are not the kind of people who like to sit behind desks for hours on end. Like Brad, such people feel at their best when they are up against the odds.

	THE ROOT CENTRE	
	DEFINED	UNDEFINED
NATURAL STATE WHEN ALONE	Pressure to be productive.	No pressure.
HEALTHY STRATEGY OF THE AUTHENTIC SELF 'THE GIFTS'	Ability to release and process stress in particular ways. Comfortable with its own needs. Uses stress constructively as fuel for creative processes and endeavours in the world. Knows how to use its pressure around others without overstressing them.	Never allows itself to be pressured or hurried into making a decision. Can enjoy the rush and adrenaline of stress, and can deal with pressure without being overwhelmed by it. Doesn't succumb to pressure to do things more quickly. The more it is pressured, the less it responds. Always able to withdraw into its original stillness.
UNHEALTHY STRATEGY OF THE NOT SELF 'THE TRAPS'	If the pressure is repressed, and therefore not released in an effort to please others, severe health and or emotional problems can result. Expects others to be capable of dealing with the same pressure, totally overpowering and overloading them, and ultimately driving them away.	Tries to get things done as quick as possible in order to release the pressure. Makes hasty decisions under pressure from others. Tendency to go hyper or get carried away by the rush, then eventually buckles under the pressure of running off other people's stress. Unable to take time to discharge and unwind. Judges itself for being lazy.

SUMMARY OF THE ROOT CENTRE

Components:

- The Root Centre is a pressure centre and a motor.
- Its biological attribute is the adrenaline gland.
- The theme of the Root Centre is pressure to be, to evolve, and to adapt in the world.
- The defined Root Centre has a fixed way of dealing with stress and the pressure to be alive in the world.
- The undefined Root Centre experiences stress as something coming from others.
- The Golden Rule for the Root Centre is – do not begin anything in life, unless it is rooted in either a place of stillness or a sense of joy.

2.2 THE THROAT CENTRE: METABOLISM
WHERE DOES YOUR VOICE COME FROM?

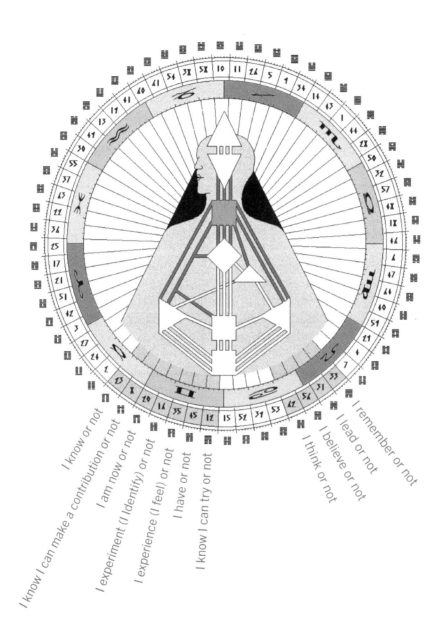

I know or not

I know I can make a contribution or not

I am now or not

I experiment (I Identify) or not

I experience (I feel) or not

I have or not

I know I can try or not

I remember or not

I lead or not

I believe or not

I think or not

It is astonishing how little human beings know about their own nature. Take for example the human voice. Where does it come from? If you ask somebody where their voice comes from, they are probably going to tell you that the words that come out of their mouth originate somewhere in their mind. We tend to be mind oriented. We tend to assume that what we say has been nurtured mentally. But we know very little about the actual mechanics of our voice.

The Throat Centre is the primary focus of the entire Human Bodygraph. If you imagine that the Bodygraph is a map of a town, then the Throat Centre would be the centre of the town. It is the most complex of all centres, having a total of eleven gates, and every single one of these gates has a voice. The eleven voices and their themes can be seen in the example above.

In the Bodygraph, all the energy flow is under pressure to get to the Throat. Having begun with the Root Centre, we have seen the primal forces that drive us. Now we see how energy is actually metabolised and transformed within the body itself. In looking at the Throat Centre, we are looking at the essence of what it is to be a human being, and everything about being a human being is about manifesting.

BIOLOGICAL RELATIONSHIP

The Throat Centre is our centre of manifestation and metamorphosis. Biologically, this is where the thyroid and the Para-thyroid glands are located. These glands are endocrine glands and act as metamorphic agents in the body. They govern our metabolism - how we break down our food, how we burn energy, whether we are fast or slow, whether we digest quickly or not, whether we are big or small, skinny or fat. All these things are rooted in the thyroid system. The fact that the Throat Centre is related to the thyroid glands means that any metamorphic process can only be initiated through the Throat Centre. It is thus the centre that brings change into our lives.

Because the Throat Centre governs so many vital biological processes in our bodies, if we do not honour the Strategy of our Type, it is here that things first begin to break down within our bodies.

TWO ASPECTS OF MANIFESTING: COMMUNICATION AND ACTION

The Throat Centre is the apex of manifestation. Manifesting has two essential aspects: verbal manifestation and manifestation as action. In other words, in the Throat Centre we find both the capacity to communicate in language and the capacity to manifest activity.

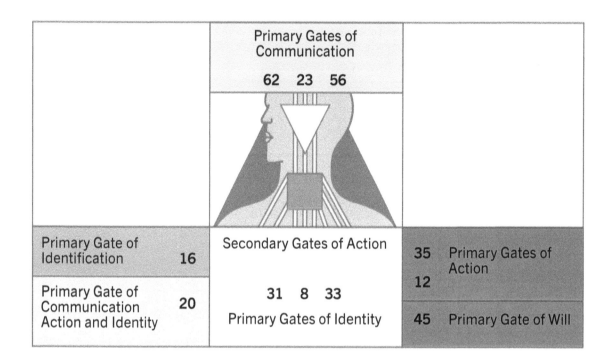

	Primary Gates of Communication	
	62 23 56	
Primary Gate of Identification 16	Secondary Gates of Action	35 Primary Gates of Action
Primary Gate of Communication Action and Identity 20	31 8 33 Primary Gates of Identity	12
		45 Primary Gate of Will

PRIMARY FUNCTION: COMMUNICATION

The primary function of the Throat Centre is communication. This is verbal manifestation, and it is the special gift human beings have of articulating in language. There is nothing more quintessentially human than our ability and indeed our necessity of sharing our unique experiences of life through language. It's important to understand that communication is not about telling people what to do. Neither can the Throat Centre tell oneself what to do. The whole business of 'doing' has its source in the four motors in the Bodygraph. The Throat is not a motor. It is rather like the gearbox in a car. That is, on its own, it cannot set your car into motion, but it still has a deep relationship to the engine.

Communication and action are two themes that are thus deeply linked with each other. Communication ensures us that we are not here alone, since it is the only tool we have to logically express our nature to each other. Through communicating before acting, we can see beforehand what is viable in our lives and what isn't.

SECONDARY FUNCTION: ACTION

The secondary function of the Throat Centre is action. Whenever the Throat Centre is connected to one of the four motors in the Bodygraph, there arises the possibility of action and the ability to 'do'.

The body has four motors: the Sacral Centre with its generative capacity, the Root Centre (adrenaline and stress), the Heart/Ego Centre (the ego and will-power) and the Solar Plexus (the emotions). The second function of the Throat Centre is to physically manifest, to act rather than speak. When the Throat is connected through definition to one or any of the four motors, then you have somebody who is a doer.

However, even if doing is possible, the law of the Throat is: Speak before you act. Communicate first. Somebody who has a defined Throat Centre can always speak, and someone with a defined Throat Centre connected to a motor can always do. Usually, such people speak too much and 'do' too much.

What the mechanics of a defined Throat tells you is: be careful about how and what you use your energy for. Don't talk about everything, and don't give your energy away to every impulse in life. If you speak at the wrong time, you won't be heard and if you act at the wrong time, you will meet resistance.

THE DEFINED THROAT CENTRE

In a defined Throat, the words can come from six different areas. As we have seen, most of us think that we speak out of our minds, but this is an important misunderstanding. We are conditioned to communicate from the mental plane. Design shows us that there are five different places where our words can come from, and the mind is only one of them. Now, let's return to the first function of the throat and think about where our voice actually comes from.

The Throat Centre is there to manifest speech, and it acts like the diaphragm of your stereo speaker. In other words, depending on which centre the Throat is connected to, that centre will speak 'through' the throat.

1. THROAT TO G CENTRE

Example: Tony Blair

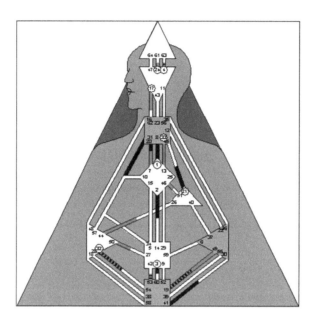

If you have the G Centre or Self connected to the Throat, then your identity is going to speak. Anybody who has this kind of configuration in their chart needs to realise that whenever they speak it is coming from their true identity, and thus they can be very vulnerable to criticism. When you criticise them, they tend to take it very personally and can feel deeply hurt because they speak out of their very identity. Such a person may be also be very uncomfortable with what they say and how they express themselves because their voice is not coming from their mind, and thus it may not always agree with their mind.

A person that has the G Centre - the self - connected to the Throat but no defined Ajna has a mind that is always trying to write a script. Let's say this person has a problem with their friend and wants to talk about it. Their mind will immediately go to work on the problem, trying to figure out what to say and when to say it. Finally they come to the point where they say to themselves: 'Right, I know exactly what to say to them and I understand what the problem is'.

However, when they actually meet this friend of theirs, they get a big shock because they open their mouth to resolve the whole issue and it is their self that speaks, not their mind: 'Hello, you look great. Let's go out and have dinner.' All the time, their mind inside is racing: 'Why did I tell them that? Why don't you tell them what's wrong? What is the matter with you? Are you sick? Are you afraid? Do you have a problem?' This kind of dilemma exists because people think that their words come from their mind and in this case they don't. They come from the Throat Centre.

2. THROAT TO HEART CENTRE

Example: David Beckham

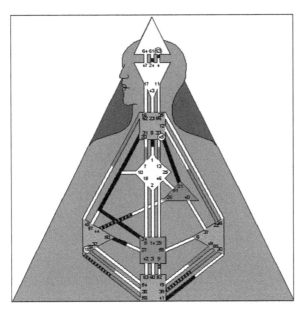

If you have the Heart Centre connected to the Throat, then your ego is going to speak. A person with the Heart Centre connected to the Throat will always begin their sentences with 'I', 'Me' or 'Mine'. With such people, even though it can seem that they are always talking about themselves, you cannot tell them to stop because that is their nature. You can begin to see now that there is no choice in the way in which we speak. It is all down to what is connected in our circuitry.

CONDITIONING

The general response to people with this 'ego voice' is resistance and projection. The kind of things they are used to hearing from others is: 'Why do you always have to talk about yourself?' or 'Why do you have to be so selfish?' and 'Why are you such an egoist?' If they are not clear about their voice, these people will be conditioned strongly by others into thinking that there is indeed something wrong with them. But there truly isn't anything wrong with them. This is simply where their words come from. When these people articulate, they do so from their will power, their ego power.

The moment they take those comments and projections seriously, and they try to suppress their ego voice, yielding to the conditioning, is the moment that they get into physical problems. If you suppress a part of your nature, you will damage the associated organ systems in the body. Thus, such people can experience ongoing problems and disturbances with their heart and their stomach, because these are the organs associated with the Heart Centre. If the person knows that they speak out of their Heart Centre and that certain people may feel uncomfortable, they are no longer made to feel guilty or ashamed. They can trust their ego voice, because that is their way of speaking, and they can learn to refuse to listen to people who try to condition them to be something else.

3. THROAT TO SPLEEN

Example: Adolf Hitler

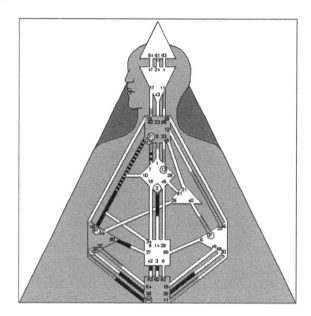

When you have the Spleen connected to the Throat, your words come from your intuition, your taste. This is a very spontaneous voice and these people articulate how they are feeling in the now. If they do not know that, they can suffer from frustration because they cannot say what they want to say. What actually comes out of their mouth is never what they expect to come out, and this gives them a sense of inadequacy about the way their mind works.

However, this sense of inadequacy and fear of what they might say is only because all human beings are conditioned to expect their mind is going to do the speaking. A person with the Spleen connected to the Throat is always going to give you a running commentary about how their body is feeling, and particularly so when they are feeling uncomfortable!

The other great potential of the Spleen Centre is spontaneously clarity. Thus, when the Throat is connected to the Spleen, instinct can be immediately expressed and the body can actually talk. It is important to understand that this kind of configuration in a chart is based on that individual's lymphatic system expressing a spontaneous truth based on their own body's survival mechanism. It can emerge out of fear or out of the body's cellular memory of an event in the past. Above all, the Throat to Spleen connection is the only place where our bodies can actually communicate through language.

4. THROAT TO SOLAR PLEXUS

Example: George Bush

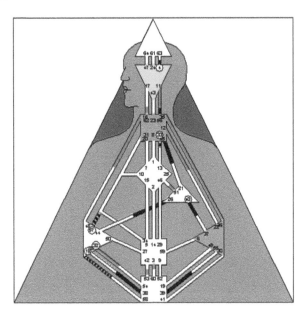

If you have the Solar Plexus Centre connected to the Throat, you have somebody who is always going to express their feelings and emotions. There is often a sense of emotional drama in their words. Sometimes their words are full of hope and sometimes they are full of despair. The conditioning they hear from others is to stop being so emotional. Everybody tells them: 'You have to control yourself. You cannot talk so emotionally.'

As we have seen, you cannot change the way you are designed, and you cannot tell these people to be different, because they speak out of their emotional wave, which is sometimes up and sometimes down. If they try to suppress their emotions, there is a risk to their health. Such people usually succumb to the conditioning pressure, and they literally give up hope of ever being themselves.

5. THROAT TO AJNA

Example: John Cleese

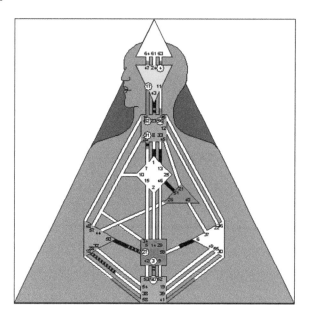

When the Throat is connected to the Ajna Centre, to the mind, then the mind will speak. Only those people who have this kind of configuration talk directly out of their minds. They verbalise their thoughts and mental concepts and they fit into the cliché of someone who can always speak their mind.

There are so many people whose Minds are not connected to the Throat or whose Ajna Centres are open and undefined. They are often frustrated throughout their life that they never say what they want to say, and they usually end up thinking that there is something wrong with them or that others never seem to listen to what they say.

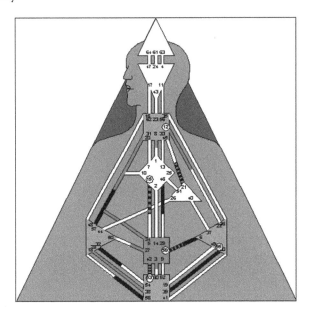

6. THROAT TO SACRAL

Example: Sean Connery

When the Throat is connected to the Sacral Centre, it is our life force that speaks, but it only speaks naturally in response. This last connection between the Sacral and Throat is a unique one because the Sacral also acts like a diaphragm in a similar way to the Throat (you may notice that these two centres are in certain aspects, a mirror of each other). Whereas the Throat speaks through whatever it is connected to, the Sacral responds energetically through whatever it is connected to. In this instance, there is only one channel that links these two centres together (known as the Channel of Charisma). Thus we have words that often rush and bubble out of the Sacral Centre because they are literally charged with its vitality, or lack of vitality.

Knowing where your voice comes from makes an incredible difference in your life. You can express yourself as you are and not feeling guilty in doing so. It takes a burden off your shoulders. An intrinsic honesty goes with that, because you are allowed to be yourself. For example, if you are an egoist, and you speak through your 'I', that is all you can do. It is simply your nature to be that way. We have vast generalisations that are at work in our civilisation. We are full of prejudices and judgments, because we try to change people's nature all the time, telling them to be different. Seeing where your voice comes from enables you to recognise that we cannot fix people and that we do harm to them by not respecting their voice. The first thing to understand is that it is the Throat that speaks and not the Mind. This is the first step in breaking prejudices about what is morally right or wrong. Don't be a victim of somebody else's oppression – of somebody else telling you what is right or wrong. Human Design is not moral. It has no inherent prejudices and no dogma. Human Design is about showing people their uniqueness and giving them the dignity to be themselves. The fact that it is the Throat that speaks takes you to a neutral ground. Whatever is going to be connected to it will speak, and you cannot change, fix or erase that fact.

THE UNDEFINED THROAT CENTRE

The Throat Centre is very complex. It has eleven gates, which translate into eleven different potential voices. Think about what it is like for somebody whose Throat is open and undefined. We know the defined Throat is going to speak depending on what it's connected to. However, the undefined Throat is turned on by conditioning and is therefore inconsistent. If you're at a dinner party, and there are five or six people with a defined Throat and one person with an undefined Throat, it is the undefined Throat that is usually doing all the talking. They're blabbing all night. Their Throat is under enormous pressure from everyone else, and when they get home that evening that throat of theirs can be physically sore.

People with undefined Throats always wants to speak but are so often frustrated, because it is not up to them what they say, or when they say it. Obviously, if they do not understand their own design, this can be very confusing and disturbing for them. Undefined Throats are uncertain about their ability to express themselves. They have to know that their Throat Centre speaks inconsistently. The undefined Throat often has the experience that it seems so easy to speak to some people, whereas with others, communicating clearly is far from easy. In the end however, it's all down to the individual chemistry between the two people.

UNDEFINED THROAT AND HEALTH

Someone with an undefined Throat has a thyroid system that is under pressure from their environment. This means that their metabolism is physically put under pressure by the presence of certain people. This is not to say that such people are unhealthy for the undefined Throat, but that if an undefined Throat speaks without awareness through such conditioned pressure, it will eventually damage the delicate hormonal balance of the thyroid. A typical result of this is a gain in body weight.

The most important thing to understand if you have an undefined Throat is that you are designed to be silent. That is the natural state of an undefined Throat, because it is not designed not to speak. It is designed to be silent until the moment that it is necessary to communicate, and until it can respond to communication from another. The moment that someone with an undefined Throat is trying to control their speaking they are going to get ill.

Unaware people with undefined Throats can have many difficulties in terms of articulation. They can develop speech problems or speech impediments. Here you find people who have problems with their tonsils, their larynx or their vocal chords. They can experience regular sore throats and can suffer from hoarseness. It is healthiest for them to have important conversations in public places where they can be private, for instance in a restaurant or a cafe. There they have people around them, many who can connect up the circuitry of their Throat, but that do not want anything from them. The reality is that the undefined Throat is essentially vulnerable and if you have an undefined Throat, you need to recognise the nature of that vulnerability. The other thing is that the undefined Throat always has to come to grips with the fact that anybody who has a defined Throat who is in their life is conditioning their speech pattern.

Please understand that conditioning is not a negative. You cannot escape it. It is everywhere. Human beings are even conditioned by other life forms - animals, plants, and even inanimate objects! Human Design is not about escaping or fixing the conditioning. It is simply about seeing it, and in seeing it, no longer being a victim of it.

UNDEFINED THROAT IN RELATIONSHIPS

Think about the nature of the undefined Throat in a partnership. Your partner has their Throat defined, and they have it defined in a specific way. Let's say for example, that they have it defined through the channel between the Throat and the Ego (21-45). In such a case, the Ego will speak through the Throat and its language will be possessive in expression - 'I have' or 'I don't have'. If you have an undefined Throat, and your lover has this whole channel, then every time you have a conversation together it is always through that channel. Not surprisingly, whether you like it or not, the conversation is always about what you have and what you don't have, and it's always materialistic because that is the nature of this channel. But this is not your voice. This also means that the other ten ways that you would have as an opportunity to be able to express yourself are not available to you. Not only that, but you also become conditioned to seeing everything with your lover in terms of what you have and what you don't have, which is not natural to your nature together but is simply the result of conditioning.

It is not just a question of not knowing where your voice comes from. In not knowing your Design and your mechanics, you don't know how others are conditioning you verbally. Neither is it a case of anyone doing anything wrong or bad. When someone conditions you through their chemistry, they don't have any choice in the matter, whether they are aware of their design or not. The Throat Centre is where we manifest and where we articulate. To recognise how things work within you takes a vast burden off your shoulders. It means that you don't have to be what you're not. Thus, you can learn to recognise when the forces and people around you are unhealthy for you, because they do not allow you to be yourself.

UNDEFINED THROAT BETWEEN PARENT AND CHILD

A child with an undefined Throat may learn to speak very late. They have to be allowed time to learn to speak. There is no need to be nervous about this, nor is there reason to panic. Such children do not need therapeutic help. However, there are things that a parent can do to help encourage such a child in their developmental process. The first thing is that they have to be patient and not put the children under pressure by forcing them to speak. A child with an undefined Throat will develop their skills only if you don't put any pressure on that Throat: 'Speak now. Say it properly. Say it correctly', these are the worst kind of things that such a child can hear. When a child with an undefined Throat begins to speak, they can experience difficulties in articulating because there is this pressure on them to try to get the words out. It will take them some time until they get into gear. It takes such a child much longer than normal to adjust to verbal patterns. At the same time, they can have an incredible gift for mastering languages if they develop at their own pace.

Children with open Throats are not natural 'doers' in life. Correct actions for such children have to be learned because they are not inherent. They need a sensitive touch from parents who understand how to encourage the gifts of the undefined Throat. So often, these children end up being compared to their brothers or sisters who have defined Throats and put under huge pressure from their families.

Whether children can develop their potential or not, depends on the nurturing that they get, and that nurturing is dependent on awareness. It is so humane to understand somebody's design, and in particular between parents and children. When the child with the undefined Throat becomes comfortable with speaking, it is because their parents have loved them and just helped them to go through their process without undue pressure.

POTENTIAL OF THE UNDEFINED THROAT

One of the gifts of an undefined Throat is that these people can easily pick up different kind of accents or dialects. They are at ease with all kinds of different ways of speaking because their speech pattern is always being conditioned by who is around them. There is absolutely nothing wrong with having an undefined Throat. It is simply a mechanical fact, and as such you can learn a great deal from it. With an undefined Throat, you can immediately know how you are being conditioned by the quality, tone and expression of your voice. Because the Throat also governs manifestation, it also rules our actions, so if you have an undefined Throat, others are also conditioning your actions. This is a deep, deep truth for you to learn. The undefined Throat should never be in a hurry to speak and act. You have to find out what you can rely on inside yourself, because you certainly cannot rely on your Throat - that is your actions or words in life. It is impossible.

However, this does not mean that you cannot take advantage of having an undefined Throat. It simply means that you can only rely on your Throat to speak inconsistently. The dichotomy of defined/undefined is just the two sides of the same coin. One is no better than the other. A defined Throat is reliable, but also very fixed in its process of communicating. It is limited to the defined aspect in the Throat – in other words, they have a fixed way of talking for their whole lives. If you have an undefined Throat, you can become very wise about the nature of communication. You can recognise who can talk clearly and who cannot. You can recognise who gets things done and who can't get things done. You can experience all the different voices of the Throat Centre because there is no limitation for you. This is the real gift of an undefined Throat. Every undefined centre is a window on wisdom. You become wise through what is not defined in you rather than what is defined.

NO GENERALISATIONS

It is very difficult to know somebody's chart by simply watching them. We have been discussing the way in which different people talk out of defined and undefined Throats. However, there are often many dynamics at work in someone's design. If for example, somebody in a group is dominating the talking, it could be someone who has the Ego motor connected to the Throat - the Throat is defined and they are talking out of their Ego and thus they control the environment.

It may equally be someone with an undefined Throat and an undefined Ego, which is pumped up by everybody around them, and is blasting out an endless stream of words. The only difference is at the end of the evening. At the end of the evening, the defined Throat feels okay, because that is the nature of the defined Throat, to be able to release speech naturally. But by the end of the same evening, an undefined Throat most likely will end up suffering from a sore throat or a difficulty in digesting their dinner. Remember, the Throat Centre is all about metabolism – it is about how we digest life – how we move energy through our bodies and transform it into action or words.

Just like the science of genetics, Human Design is not a cut and dry affair. There are so many possible variations that go to make up an individual design. There are people with undefined Throats who are brilliant speakers. Bill Clinton is a classic example of that. He is a master speaker and debater. Someone with an undefined Throat can be enormously capable of articulation simply because they recognise how the whole process of speaking works in others, and they learn from that. They can have great language skills and very powerful voices. There are a lot of famous singers with undefined Throats: Elvis Presley, John Lennon, Luciano Pavarotti.

This illustrates that it is never easy to judge a design from the surface. Another example in this vein is a person with a defined Throat where the connection that defines the Throat is unconscious (coloured in red) in which case they do not speak consciously at all. They may find it very difficult to articulate, and are always surprised when their words come bubbling to the surface as though they have just emerged from a tunnel. They can be very surprised by what their unconscious says, and it almost always disagrees with their mind. This can be both amusing and very destructive to the personality. Such people may become very uncomfortable with the words coming out of their mouth and they end up never trusting their voice. They may even refuse to speak. If you are looking for a mute, you are just as likely find one with a defined Throat as you are an undefined Throat.

COMMUNICATION

People so often complain that there is a lack of communication in the world. Ironically, this is untrue. It is simply that the communication itself lacks clarity, because people are unaware of the nature of their Throat Centre. If you don't know where your own voice comes from, then you really never know how to trust the design of your own Throat. If you are not talking in your voice, you are not properly able to share your experiences in life, because you are never talking as yourself.

TIMING – THE GOLDEN RULE OF THE THROAT CENTRE

Because the Throat is so complex, the most important element in allowing it to operate correctly is your Type and Authority, both of which we will study in Part III of this manual. Only by following the mechanics of your Type and your Authority can you ensure that your words and actions will emerge correctly. So many people speak and act too soon or too late. The Golden Rule of the Throat Centre is –follow your Type and Authority and the timing will always be perfect.

	THE THROAT CENTRE	
	DEFINED	UNDEFINED
NATURAL STATE WHEN ALONE	Able to speak and/or act.	Silence.
HEALTHY STRATEGY OF THE AUTHENTIC SELF 'THE GIFTS'	Consistent and reliable tool for communication. Knowing where its true voice comes from means it can speak its own truth. When connected to a motor, it has the capacity to act and the satisfaction of moving forwards in life.	A versatile, spontaneous voice whose capacity to speak depends on who it is with. It communicates best when given space. Can experience all the different voices of the Throat Centre. Comfortable with silence as its natural state. Waits to be initiated to speak or act by others.
UNHEALTHY STRATEGY OF THE NOT SELF 'THE TRAPS'	Can speak or act too readily or inappropriately, talking too much and thus losing its impact. Because the verbal style is fixed, it can seem overwhelming to others, especially if Strategy is not being followed. if not connected to a motor, makes claims but is unable to follow them with action.	Tries to be verbally dominant, speaking without invitation, inappropriately or at the wrong time. Fears it won't know what to say and tries to rehearse conversations rather than allowing for spontaneity. Tries to initiate and ends up suffering from exhaustion and severe health problems. Always tries to attract attention to itself.

SUMMARY OF THE THROAT CENTRE

- The Throat Centre is the centre of manifestation (speech and doing).
- Biologically, it relates to the thyroid and the Para-thyroid gland and thus its theme is metabolism.
- The Throat is the most complex of all the centres, with 11 gates.
- All energies lead to the Throat Centre to manifest in words or in action.
- The primary function of the Throat is communication.
- Communication leads to doing when the Throat is connected to one of the four motors.
- The Throat Centre is not motor. It is a gearbox.
- A defined Throat can always speak and/or act but is fixed in its communication/doing.
- An undefined Throat speaks inconsistently and has their speech pattern conditioned by others.
- The Golden Rule of the Throat Centre is –follow your Type and Authority and the timing will always be perfect.

2.3 THE SACRAL CENTRE: VITALITY
SEXUALITY AND POWER

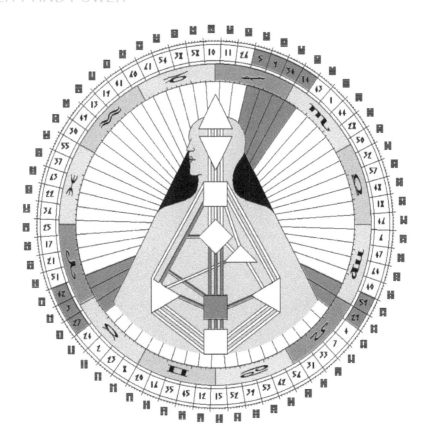

The Sacral Centre is the second most complex centre in design, after the Throat. It has nine gates. In many ways, the Sacral is in fact a mirror of the Throat Centre. It generates a frequency, which leads to what appears to be doing, and it also has the capacity to speak, although without articulation. Like the Throat, the Sacral operates like a diaphragm, but instead of speaking according to whatever centre it is connected to, the Sacral generates a burst of life force that can only emerge as a response. This vital response that comes from the Sacral can emerge in three main ways:

- It can come as language, but only when the Sacral is directly connected to the Throat.

- It can take the form of sub-vocal sounds and grunts. The classic Sacral sounds are the 'Ahuh' and the 'Unun', which are the Sacral Centre's way of saying yes and no respectively.

- It can take the form of an inner commitment as the life force within one's body surges towards a certain decision that one is confronted with. If the Sacral response to a certain decision is 'no', then there is no surge of positive energy.

The Sacral speaks by making noises and sounds, and it is this spectrum of sounds that vibrate through the Sacral Centre that adds to its profundity in our human life. The main difference between the Sacral and the Throat is that the Throat is a gearbox for all the energy systems in the body, while the Sacral is the most powerful energy source in the body. The Throat is not a motor, whereas the Sacral is the prime motor in the body. In the image above, you can see that the Sacral activations in the wheel create the impression of an energy vortex operating in a spiral in the body. The Sacral Centre represents the life force energy itself. It is literally a Generator of life, and once turned on, it is never turned off. It is turned on when we are born and it is turned off when we die. However, the Sacral does require phases of regeneration and rest in order to recharge its batteries, otherwise its generating capacity turns into de-generating, and exhaustion is the result.

It is through the Throat that metamorphosis can take place. But the Sacral Centre is an energy font; it is an empowerment field for life itself. Within it lies the nature of our sexuality, our genetic imperative to reproduce, find intimacy and nurture. At the same time, the Sacral moves us. Any being that honours the nature of their Sacral is at the pinnacle of power.

BIOLOGICAL RELATIONSHIP

The Sacral Centre is the root of human fertility and is related to the ovaries in a woman and the testes in a man. Because of this, the Sacral Centre is different from any other centre in that it is the only centre that operates differently for women than it does for men. This has to do with its capacity to generate. What it generates is life itself, and having done so, it begins a slow degeneration into death. In a man, the peak of generation is around 18 years of age and in a woman it is between 33 and 34. There is an obvious difference in the peaking of Sacral power. In women it comes much later than in men. Because the function of the Sacral Centre is to power life itself, it empowers our survival in life. In essence, it is a fertility centre and unlike all the other centres, it does not really need to reach the Throat Centre. It can propagate life on its own. Thus its main themes are sexuality, fertility and vitality.

THE DEFINED SACRAL CENTRE

Anyone with a defined Sacral Centre has an enormous power at their disposal. Such power can either work generatively and creatively or it can become degenerative and destructive. It all depends on that person's understanding of how their Sacral Centre functions. Somebody with a defined Sacral Centre can always be involved with activity, although this activity does not necessarily have anything to do with manifesting activity. A defined Sacral generates a constant energy buzz in the body, and that humming energy has to go somewhere. It is often experienced as a restless motion like walking and not knowing where to go, or the need to just burn energy by moving along and being active. It often generates the need to be involved in repetitive activity such as shuffling papers all day or cleaning the house over and over again without being able to stop. The bottom line is that Sacral people can find it difficult to sit still until they have exhausted their generative reservoirs, which usually happens at the end of the day.

THE SACRAL FREQUENCY AND THE THEME OF FRUSTRATION

If you hand a Sacral person a tennis racket and a tennis ball, they will probably start hitting it. They keep on hitting it out of their Sacral frequency until they get totally exhausted. The important thing for a defined Sacral is to know when they are involved in the right activity. They always have to go through a barrier of frustration, and if they do not make it through that barrier, but give in because of the frustration, then the activity is not right for them. When a Sacral being moves through the frustration barrier and continues in the same activity, then their true power begins to emerge.

In the tennis analogy, this person keeps on hitting the ball but they do not get any better. At a certain point, they get a trainer for suggestions of how to improve their play. The trainer gives them advice and when they are back on the tennis court, they hit the ball in the same way as before but they still do not seem to really improve. If they do not like tennis, they throw the racket on the ground and swear not to do it again. It's usually at this point that they give up altogether. If they really love tennis, they stay with it the process, and they discover that at a certain point, their game suddenly makes a quantum leap and they get better, all because they waited for the point of metamorphosis. If Sacral people are committed to what they do, they have the energy to endure the time of frustration and they have the patience to wait for the metamorphosis to come.

The Sacral person never realises when this point of metamorphosis happens. It just happens. The time of being stuck in the Sacral frequency can be very short or very long. But when metamorphosis finally does happen, they shift to a whole new level of skill or competence until they get stuck on that level, and the same process occurs all over again. This Sacral process of getting stuck is really the road to mastery. All defined Sacral Centres are here to master something. That is their tremendous gift. The nature of the Sacral frequency is to keep on feeling as though it gets stuck. This is because the Sacral being generates. It does not manifest. There is no metamorphosis built into being Sacral because that can only come through the Throat. A Sacral person needs to understand that their periods of getting stuck are a vital and natural part of their life, so that they do not get caught up in the frustration.

THE SOUNDS OF THE SACRAL CENTRE

The other way for Sacral people to avoid frustration lies in the recognition that the Sacral speaks. Anything that is connected to the Sacral, the Sacral will speak for. Just as words come out of the Throat, sounds come out of the Sacral. Whatever is connected to that Sacral always has the potential to release that information through sounds.

As we discussed earlier, the Sacral Centre is rather like a lower mirror of the Throat Centre as you look at them in the Bodygraph. Indeed, before the Throat Centre was fully developed in humans, it was the Sacral that was our only means of expression and communication. The mutation that took place in the larynx of our ancestors finally allowed man to begin to manipulate sound into language. However, before this stage in our evolution, man relied entirely on the Sacral Centre for survival. In other words, before we could talk in language, we spoke in grunts and sounds.

Thus, Sacral beings need to be introduced to this concept that the daily sounds that they hear themselves making are in fact coming from a place of real power and truth within them. Obviously, this does not mean that all people with defined Sacral Centres (70% of humanity incidentally) have to communicate in grunting sounds! But it does mean that they should pay respect to such sounds.

The other revelation that comes from this comes in the form of a little joke, which is that it's impossible to begin a conversation with a grunt! This is actually a rather profound statement because it says something about the Sacral Centre that is very important to understand. What it says is that the Sacral Centre cannot initiate, and this is the biggest difference between the Sacral and the Throat: the Throat initiates communication, whereas the Sacral responds.

SACRAL RESPONSE

As we have seen, Sacral people need to pay attention to the sounds that they make. They often speak in sounds like groans, sighs, and growls. Most importantly however, is that they allow themselves to respond rather than initiate. The true Sacral voice only functions in response, and it will always tell them what to enter into and what commitment is right for them.

Because of this tremendous generating frequency inside them, Sacral people are always waiting for the opportunity to respond, so that they can know their own truth. Their primal life force sounds are always a barometer of their energy level. The essential thing for a Sacral being is to understand that their power only really functions in response. Thus their mantra in life is: Do not initiate. Never take the first step. The moment that they try to initiate, they lose all their power.

Whenever a Sacral person is asked something from the Throat, it is being offered manifestation. Perhaps the hardest thing for Sacral beings to accept is that their Sacral response is not aware. In other words, they are putting their trust in their life force, rather than any of their awareness centres. If you ask a Sacral person: 'Do you want to go out for dinner?' and you hear them answer: 'ahunh' then that is their truth coming out of their Sacral Centre. If a Sacral person is in a partnership with a Throat person and their partner says to them: 'Let's go out for dinner.' and the Sacral person says: 'Unun', then their Sacral is telling them not to go out for dinner! The Throat person will probably want a reason for their response but the Sacral person has no way to counter that. This is one of the reasons that others so often manipulate Sacral people – because they do not trust in this impulse within them.

All Sacral people have to know that anybody that has a right to be in their life has to respect their response in sounds. The Sacral does not have that articulated vocabulary, so it cannot ever give a reason for a decision it makes. Sacral people often describe this process as life making a decision 'through' them, which is exactly what is happening. The Sacral response is so pure that it bypasses all awareness altogether. It doesn't matter what you think or feel, the life force knows what is right for you.

The Sacral is very powerful in response. As long as the Sacral is making its commitments through their sounds, the energy will be there to reach metamorphosis. When somebody asks you: 'Do you want to play tennis? - and the Sacral person says: 'Unun', then that is their truth and they should not do it because the energy to do it is simply not there. They will not have the commitment to move through the different levels of feeling stuck in order to attain a level of mastery. Others are always manipulating Sacral people because they do not listen to their life force but instead give their decision over either to their mind or their emotions.

1. SACRAL CONNECTED TO THE THROAT

When the Sacral Centre is connected to the Throat, either directly or indirectly, you have generative force that is ready to manifest. These people often witness their responses as physical movement rather than sounds. In other words, you might ask such a person: 'would you like to come out for lunch?' and their immediate response is to physically stand up. That is how generative power is immediately converted into the potential for manifestation. At other times, the response may emerge as words, but the words will always carry the enthusiasm or disinterest of the Sacral life force. What is interesting for such people is that they have to learn to respond to their response. In other words, they may hear themselves say 'yes', but then their real response emerges and either confirms or denies their 'yes'. In other words, they often have to allow themselves to change their mind.

2. SACRAL TO SPLEEN

Remember, the quality of the Sacral truth will always be dependent on which centre the Sacral is connected to. If the Spleen Centre is connected to the Sacral, it is the existential awareness that will come out in sounds. Sacral beings are at their best when they have been asked something, because then they can respond and then they will experience the power of their Sacral: 'Do you like this?' they may hear, and if they hear themselves respond 'Unun' or make a sound that is uncertain or not affirmative, the Spleen Centre is telling that person that it is not healthy for them to do this. Thus, when the Sacral is connected to the Spleen, this is someone who is constantly responding to life from deep within their immune system. The Sacral sounds in such a person always indicate what is or is not healthy for them in the now.

3. SACRAL TO G

When you have someone with a defined Sacral connected to the G Centre, you have a person that responds through their identity. The three channels that connect the Sacral to the G Centre are known as the 'tantric' channels. They act as conduits for the life force of the Sacral to empower the identity. People with these channels actually 'identify' with their energetic responses to life. In other words, the Sacral Centre empowers them with a sense of life making a decision or commitment through them. The theme of these people is to surrender to the life force that moves them without the need for awareness to guide them. These people can have a unique experience of surrendering to a greater force than themselves.

WAITING — THE GOLDEN RULE OF THE SACRAL

Sacral people are the great quitters in the world. They so often find that they cannot stay with things, because they rarely answer with their Sacral. Because the Sacral is such a very powerful motor, other people feel that and want to take advantage of their Sacral power. So many Sacral people make commitments that end up being a torment for them. Their main disease is frustration with their life because they don't feel fulfilled.

The root cause of these problems is that Sacral people do not know how to trust in their Sacral. Trust for a Sacral person is always about waiting. They are not here to initiate, so they have to wait and see what life brings them. It is so easy for Sacral beings to give away their energy to the wrong things and people because they do not know how to wait. Sacral people are designed to wait, and if they do not learn to let things come to them in their own time, they will miss hearing their response and miss the entire purpose of their lives. This is in fact the Golden Rule of the Sacral, whenever it is defined – Wait, Don't Initiate.

THE UNDEFINED SACRAL

The undefined Sacral is always open to Sacral conditioning. The person with an undefined Sacral is always going to be interested in how life actually works. Whereas the defined Sacral is the most industrious power on the planet, if you really get to the bottom of an undefined Sacral, you will find that they don't really want to work too much in life. They will love to just relax and let others do all the hard work. However, when you look at someone with an undefined Sacral, this is not usually what you will see, because this is one of the most easily conditioned of all the centres.

THE RIGHT PEOPLE

The undefined Sacral is extremely sensitive to the energy levels in both people and places. People are the key to a healthy undefined Sacral. The undefined Sacral can never rely on their sounds telling them their truth. What they do is simply mirror the truth of the Sacral person in their aura. Thus they have to be very careful, because their vitality is dependent on the people around them. Ignorant of their mechanics, they always run the risk of having their power sapped and burnt out by simply being in the presence of the wrong people.

It is very easy for someone with a defined Sacral to end up running around on the 'borrowed' energy of someone in their aura, whether that might be their child, friend or lover. Because their Sacral system is much more sensitive than the defined Sacral, they are not biologically equipped to handle that kind of energy consistency pumping through their bodies, and they pay the price through breakdown and exhaustion. If you have an undefined Sacral, you have to remember that you are putting other people's fuel into your own system, so you had better ensure that their fuel is the right kind for your vehicle. If you put petrol in a diesel engine, it will seize up, and then you will need help.

SEXUALITY

The undefined Sacral is fascinated by relationships and sexuality. It is very easy for these people to become ill or depressed through entering into the wrong relationships. Both their sexuality and their fertility are conditioned, which means it depends entirely on whom you are with. This causes the most harm to teenagers with an open Sacral because they do not understand how their Sacral Centre works. What usually happens is that they are conditioned by their first sexual experience, and they end up thinking that that is what sexuality is always like. The undefined Sacral Centre has to be very careful in early relationships. They will need to experiment to avoid being unnaturally conditioned.

It is teenagers above all others who need to know that their sexuality depends on what their partner offers them. In other words, it can be a totally different experience if they change their lover. They need to know that sexually speaking, they can be conditioned into any role, from being totally asexual to being completely promiscuous. This is always a deep revelation to them because they will always meet certain people with whom they feel overwhelmed by the sexual chemistry. In such cases, they can realise that it is simply the aura of the other person that is conditioning them, and they don't necessarily have to do anything about it.

Knowing about the nature of your undefined Sacral also leads to the avoidance of being caught up in self-judgment and plagued by guilt or shame. There is nothing more innocent and beautiful than an undefined Sacral. It is a window that reflects the nature of sexuality itself. If a person with an open Sacral Centre is told by their partner: 'You are a terrible lover', they can just relax in the clear knowledge that it is not their fault, because they can only mirror what their partner is sexually.

Human Design is a wonderful tool in deconditioning the nature of an individual's sexuality. But by far its greatest gift for an undefined Sacral is that it enables you to always find the correct relationships in life. Knowing your design, you can see which partner is correct for you, and accept the conditioning of that partner without being identified with that conditioned field. Partnership and sexuality is one of the most essential aspects to the human experience. It is sad to recognise that most of the pain that comes with partnerships is the result of 'Not Selves' choosing other 'Not Selves'.

EXAMPLE OF SACRAL CONDITIONING IN A RELATIONSHIP

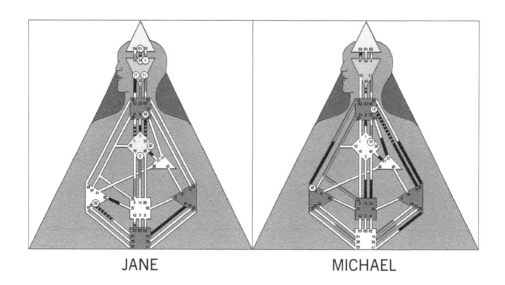

JANE   MICHAEL

THE RELATIONSHIP

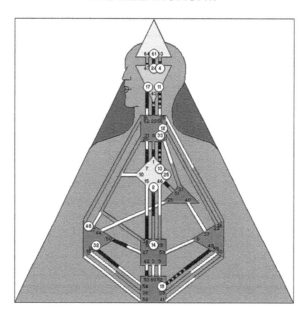

In the example above, we can see two people, Jane and Michael, and the combined chemistry of their relationship together. Here we can see a classic example of Sacral conditioning. Jane's undefined Sacral Centre is immediately defined by Michael's Sacral.

First of all, this is a deep attraction for both of them. However, Michael's defined Sacral will dominate the energetics of this relationship. We can see how his Sacral is connected to both his Spleen and his emotional system via the Throat Centre. Jane takes in all his waves of emotional energy as well as his level of health. Added to this, both the Heart and Root Centres are defined and connected. That is an enormous amount of conditioned pressure and vitality that is going to pour through Jane's undefined Sacral system. If she is not clear what is going on, she will rise and fall on the tides of Michael's life force, which is so connected to his emotional state. In other words, when he's in a bad mood, she can feel polluted and sapped by his presence.

The only problems in relationships come when we identify with the conditioning. If Jane moves away from Michael whenever she feels his Sacral energy becoming sluggish, the chances are they won't get into a fight! Remember that the undefined centres in our design mirror and amplify the conditioned field. Jane will feel the low wave coming long before Michael does because her undefined Sacral is essentially a barometer of his energy levels. Defined Sacrals are tremendously powerful as we have seen, but they need time to regenerate when they are tired, and this usually means they need to either sleep (preferably alone) or be left alone entirely.

If you do not know who you are, it is not possible to enter into a relationship correctly. Neither is it possible to either grasp or accept the nature of the sexual bond that you are entering into. If you cannot find the correct partner, your relationship is going to end up being built on trying to change each other, rather than a truthful acceptance of each other. It is only when you enter into a relationship as yourself that you are going to get the rewards of that relationship.

	THE SACRAL CENTRE	
	DEFINED	UNDEFINED
NATURAL STATE WHEN ALONE	Pure creative potential waiting to be put into action.	Silence.
HEALTHY STRATEGY OF THE AUTHENTIC SELF 'THE GIFTS'	Has consistent, reliable access to energy, released through response. Has tremendous staying power to see something through once the Sacral responds positively. Can relax in the knowledge that it never has to initiate, surrendering to its own response Strategy. Patience even when frustrated.	Ability to surrender to the buzz of the Generator world without getting involved in it. Allows others to vitalise it, letting life flow through it, knowing when to withdraw and discharge. Ability to step back and allow others to do the work it doesn't want to do. Enjoys diversity of sexual roles without identifying with any particular one.
UNHEALTHY STRATEGY OF THE NOT SELF 'THE TRAPS'	Can get so stuck and frustrated waiting that it forces the issue prematurely, thus losing its power. Can exhaust itself through trying to initiate its own direction in life. Has the tendency to quit things entered into incorrectly. Through lack of patience, compromises its power and ends up doing things it hates with people who do not initiate it.	Tries to take on too much and over-commits, unable to say No, especially when influenced by a defined Sacral. Puts itself under great pressure to work, becoming frequently overwhelmed and exhausted by other people's energy. Once away from that energy, cannot sustain workload, loses confidence and crashes. Either represses sexuality or identifies with sexual conditioning from others, leading to neediness and confusion.

SUMMARY OF THE SACRAL CENTRE

- The Sacral Centre is the most powerful motor of the life force.
- This centre is different according to gender.
- The themes of the Sacral Centre are sexuality, fertility, vitality, movement, and persistence.
- It has a special frequency: it gets stuck, moves on to another level, and gets stuck again.
- The Sacral speaks: it makes sounds.
- The defined Sacral has to wait to respond.
- The undefined Sacral has no fixed sexual identity.
- The Golden Rule of the defined Sacral is: Wait, Don't Initiate.

3. AWARENESS

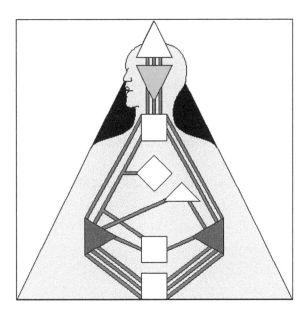

THE THREE AWARENESS CENTRES

There are three awareness centres in human beings. These are the Spleen, the Ajna and the Solar Plexus. These are the only centres within us through which we can actually be conscious of what is going on around us. Only these three centres actually allow us to experience life as a self-reflective awareness, and each of them has the capacity to guide us through life. Each of the other six centres are purely mechanical.

These days in the 'New Age', there is a great deal of hype about the importance of awareness as a goal of the enlightened. Through Human Design, we can see the mechanical truth written in our genes. In order for someone to be awake, it is not necessary to even be aware. It is necessary only to live according to one's Design, following the Strategy of Type and Authority.

Whether someone is aware or not depends entirely on their Design, and as we know, that depends only on when and where we are born. Seen through Human Design, awareness is simply a lens that functions through our individual Design. There is no goal. There is only you, perfectly designed the way you are.

3.1 THE SPLEEN CENTRE: BODY
THE IMMUNE SYSTEM

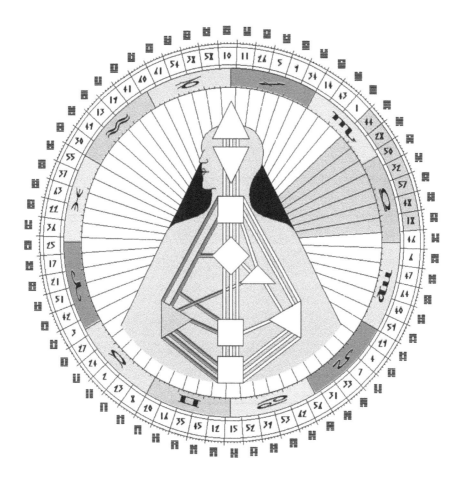

The Spleen Centre represents our body consciousness. It is our primary of awareness, and is a form of awareness that we share with all other forms of life. Essentially, it is our existential awareness. However, despite its importance, this existential awareness is fundamentally weak.

Each of the three awareness centres has a frequency. The mind, the Ajna Centre, has a frequency over all time. The Solar Plexus, being emotional, has a frequency that is a moving wave that continually oscillates back and forth. The Spleen Centre is fundamentally weak because it can only speak once. It can only speak in the now, because it is a spontaneous response. It is what we call intuition, gut instinct or the hunch. The Spleen is the source of our capacity for spontaneous judgment of what is correct or not. Because the Spleen Centre operates in the now, it never repeats its first response. If you do not listen to your instincts immediately, then you will miss their warning, and their warnings are always rooted in survival.

HISTORICAL BACKGROUND

Human awareness has evolved over time, and each awareness centre represents a different phase in the evolution of our awareness. The Spleen Centre is in fact the oldest awareness centre. In this centre we find the beginning of our evolutionary process. We can call it our primary awareness, because we inherited it from our animal beginnings. If we take a look at the design of plants, mammals, birds and insects in the graphic below, we find that they all have the Spleen Centre as their only potential to guide their lives. All of these life forms are guided by the existential awareness of the Spleen Centre, the centre of awareness in the 'now'.

THE DESIGN OF FORMS

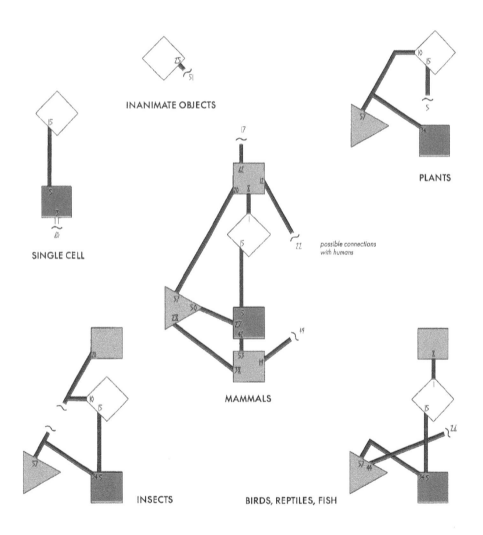

INANIMATE OBJECTS

PLANTS

SINGLE CELL

possible connections with humans

MAMMALS

INSECTS

BIRDS, REPTILES, FISH

THE HIERARCHY OF AWARENESS

As we have seen, of the three awareness centres, the Splenic awareness is the weakest. The Ajna/Mind is twice a strong as the Spleen and the Solar Plexus is twice as strong as the Ajna/Mind. The Spleen is the core of well being and survival. It is about life and death, and the fact that it is the weakest awareness centre shows us how fragile life truly is.

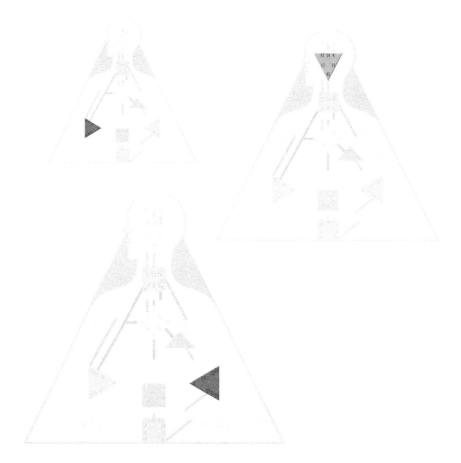

BIOLOGICAL RELATIONSHIP

The Spleen Centre represents the body's immune system as it operates through the lymphatic system, the spleen itself and the spleen cells. Comprising around eighteen percent of all the cells within our bodies, our lymphatic system is vast. The lymph cells are in fact rather like little ears, noses and tongues, which are all over the body. Their job is to constantly listen, taste and smell in order to ensure that everything is balanced and healthy within our body, and if it isn't, they immediately warn us. If something arises in our body that disturbs the lymph cells, such as an invading virus, they immediately spring into action, activating the body's defence system. We can compare the lymphatic system to a washing machine that cleans out all kinds of dirt in our bodies. At another level, our lymphatic awareness also alerts us to negative vibrations coming from other people's auras.

AWARENESS AND FEAR

In truth, all awareness is rooted in fear. Because the three awareness centres each operate at different frequencies, they each manifest different patterns of fears. The frequency of the Splenic Centre is the now, and it is always fear that is related to survival itself. Each of the seven gates of the Spleen manifests a different fear.

THE SEVEN FEARS OF THE SPLEEN

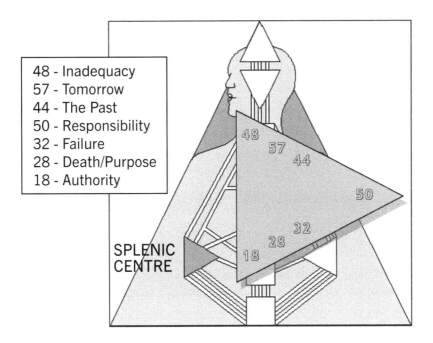

48 - Inadequacy
57 - Tomorrow
44 - The Past
50 - Responsibility
32 - Failure
28 - Death/Purpose
18 - Authority

SPLENIC CENTRE

THE DEFINED SPLEEN AND HEALTH - THE FEELGOOD FACTOR

People with defined Spleen Centres can often be people who take their health for granted in life. The defined Spleen brings a consistency of feeling good within one's body. Because the immune system of a defined Spleen is basically strong, when such people do become ill, it means that the disease has overloaded the Splenic system and they could be in danger. Having a defined Spleen does not preclude that you will always be healthy. The fact of the matter is that the defined Spleen is often so strong that it can prevent you from recognising that there is something the matter with you. Therefore people with defined Spleens should ideally have regular medical check ups done, to make up for their defined Spleen masking potential problems.

TYPES OF SPLEEN

There are essentially three types of defined Spleen - manifested Spleens, projected Spleens and generated Spleens.

MANIFESTED SPLEEN

Example: Peter Sellers

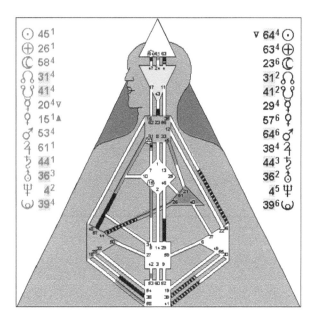

If the Spleen is connected to a motor (other than the Sacral) which is in turn connected to the Throat Centre, you have a manifested Spleen. These are people whose immune systems are extremely powerful. They can literally eat or ingest anything and their immune system will protect them. Such immune systems generally require equally strong medicines, such as antibiotics, should the body become ill.

The down side of having a manifested Spleen is that being so powerful, it is not particularly sensitive and usually does not give any warning if the body is overloaded. Thus, these are also people who can seem extremely healthy until they suddenly drop dead!

PROJECTED SPLEEN

Example: Bhagwan Shree Rajneesh

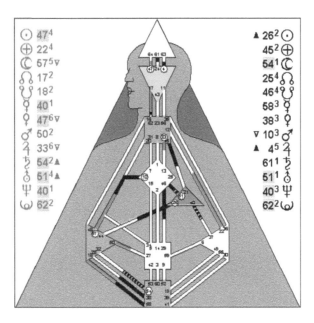

If the Spleen is defined but neither connected to a motor and the Throat or the Sacral Centre, then you have a projected Spleen. The projected Spleen is the more sensitive of the three types of defined Spleen, but its health depends entirely upon working correctly in conjunction with the right people.

If a defined Spleen succumbs to the conditioning of one of the other awareness centres in the design, such as the emotions or mind, then in all likelihood, disease will be the result. Projected Spleens neither generate health through response nor manifest it naturally. Health for the projected Spleen depends on being recognised by the right people. Only then can the particular quality of the channel or channels linking the Spleen be correctly lived out.

For example, if you have the Channel of Struggle (28/38) in your design, then you need people around you that don't try and make things easier for you. Such people will actually prevent you from following your nature, which will eventually make you ill.

GENERATED SPLEEN
Example: Nicole Kidman

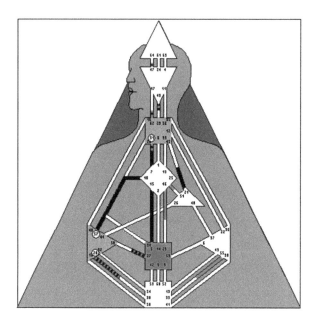

If the Spleen is connected to the Sacral Centre, no matter what else is in the design, you have a generated Spleen. If the Sacral is also connected to the Throat (as with Manifesting Generators), then you still have a generated Spleen, although this type of immune system is more akin to the manifested Spleen.

Generated Spleens operate at optimal health when they are responding to life. Because over 70% of this planet is peopled by Generators or Manifesting Generators who do not follow their Strategy, but instead try to live like Manifestors, the general health level among humanity is not nearly as high as it should/could be.

Generated Spleens literally generate a 'feel good' energy when they are following their Strategy in life. As long as there is no defined emotional centre in the design, the defined Spleen will always know instinctively which medicine and/or diet is correct for it, but only in the moment that it responds. As a general guide however, defined Splenic systems that are cut off from the Throat may often find that homoeopathy is one of the healthiest medicines for them.

SPLEEN CONNECTED TO ROOT

Example: Brad Pitt

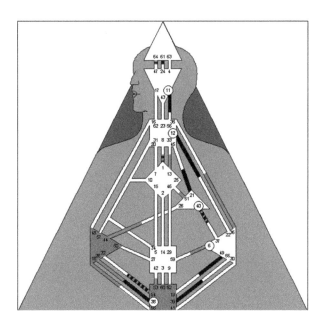

When the Spleen Centre is connected to the Root Centre, there is always a deep need for the immune system to be literally pumped with the adrenaline from the Root. Thus all three channels between these two centres are under pressure to physically exercise. People with definitions here always need to push their bodies physically in order to remain healthy. These are people who will feel good when they are physically challenged as long as they rise up to meet that challenge with acceptance and joy.

SPLEEN CONNECTED TO SACRAL

See example under Sacral Centre (page 83).

SPLEEN CONNECTED TO EGO/HEART

Example: Bodygraph of unknown person

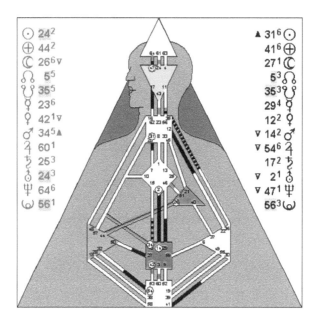

As with the Spleen to G, there is only a single channel that directly links the Spleen Centre to the Ego/Heart Centre, the Channel of Surrender, a design of being a Transmitter (44/26). People with this definition in their design have an instinctive gift of understanding the needs of the community.

When the Spleen is backing up the Ego, you have someone whose individual health is directly connected with how successful they can be at working with other people. Here, an individual's health is directly connected to their material success.

SPLEEN CONNECTED TO THROAT

See example under Throat Centre (page 70).

SPLEEN CONNECTED TO G CENTRE

Example: Freddie Mercury

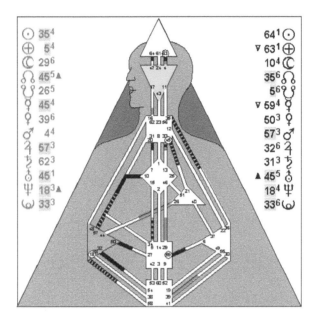

When the Spleen Centre is connected or defined to the G Centre, we find something rather fascinating. Since the G Centre is about our direction and identity, when it is directly connected to our immune system, the result is someone whose very identity is rooted in survival. There is, in fact, only a single direct channel that links these two centres, the channel 57/10, known as the Channel of Perfected Form.

These are people whose direction in life is always rooted in their intuitive, spontaneous behaviour. Since the Spleen Centre is only interested in individual survival, such people are designed to act only for themselves, and as long as they trust their bodies and their immune system, their behaviour will always be correct.

SPONTANEITY AND HEALTH

The hospitals of the world are full of people who didn't trust their hunches. Being a spontaneous awareness that exists only in the moment, the defined Spleen Centre demands spontaneity in return for survival and health. If you do not know that your intuition is a part of your mechanics, and that your very survival depends on it, you are going to miss it. There are so many people with defined Spleens that are sitting in the accident wards of clinics and hospitals telling the person that is fixing their broken leg or arm: 'I just knew it, I just knew it was going to happen, I don't know how, but I simply knew it'. They had a hunch, or an instinct, but they didn't honour it because they didn't know that they could trust in it. Such hunches are rooted in the defined Spleen Centre.

The truth is that human beings are not unaware of their own nature. Every human being experiences the various aspects of their design. However, what we do not recognise nor understand is which part of our nature is truly consistent and reliable. The moment that you know you have a defined Splenic centre, and that you know you can rely on your awareness in the now, then and only then are you protected in life. Knowing this about yourself means that you avoid the common trap of allowing your mind to talk you out of listening to your instincts. Remember, your mind does not have inner Authority, and it is so easy for it to overwhelm your immune system.

The mind and the immune system do not understand each other. Imagine somebody with a defined Spleen is walking down the road and they pass in front of a shop window. In the window there is a sign indicating that there is some kind of lecture about to start on the inside. Our friend stops there for a moment to read the sign when a man in the doorway says to him, 'are you coming in?' In that split-second, our friend's defined Spleen Centre, his immune system, has a hunch not to go inside. Then the conditioning begins. The person in the doorway turns to our man, saying, 'look, it's free, you'll find it interesting, and if you don't like it, you can always leave.' This all seems very reasonable to the mind, thus our friend decides to ignore his immune warning, and enters into the lecture.

As we saw earlier, the Spleen Centre is the weakest of the three awareness centres, but this does not mean that it is wrong. It is weak in terms of the conditioning we receive through the other two awareness centres, the Ajna and the Solar Plexus. Whereas our emotions can overwhelm us and our mind incessantly talks to us, our immune system only whispers to us, and because its frequency is only in the now, it only whispers the one time Thus in the case of our friend in the above example, if he doesn't listen to the funny feeling that tells him not to go into the lecture, he will undoubtedly pay the price, so he ends up catching the flu from the person he sits next to and it takes him three weeks to get over his illness. All the time he is lying there in bed recovering, he is thinking to himself: 'I knew it, I just knew I shouldn't have gone in there'. The energy that it took to recuperate, and the time disturbed, all of that was unnecessary.

If you have a defined Spleen Centre and it is the Authority in your design, it is of great value to know that there is an awareness within you that is always reliable and trustworthy. The awareness of mechanics frees you. It frees you to be yourself, and the by-product of you being yourself is being healthy.

THE UNDEFINED SPLEEN

Example: Florence Nightingale

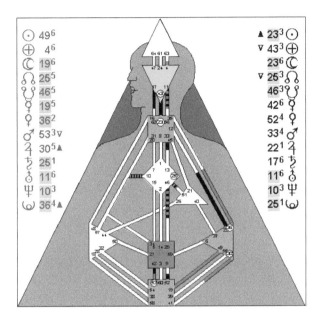

Like all undefined centres, the undefined Spleen has its gifts and its handicaps. It has a huge potential as a place of victimisation, and a profound potential as a centre of wisdom and sensitivity. There is nothing or no one more physically sensitive than an undefined Spleen. Such people have an immune system that is essentially open, and like a sponge, they soak up the general level of physical health and wellbeing wherever they go. There is a Human Design joke about undefined Spleens, which is that they make wonderful doctors but lousy nurses. The joke hides a profound truth about the nature of an undefined Spleen because being so open, it is a natural barometer of health in others, thus its great potential is diagnostic rather than soothing (a benefit of a healthy defined Spleen). The other side of the undefined Spleen is that it soaks up ill-health as well as good health, which means that eventually it becomes ill itself if it remains in an environment that is unhealthy.

THE UNDEFINED SPLEEN AND FEAR

Whenever you see an undefined Spleen Centre, you know two things about these people. They do not consistently feel good and they are naturally full of fear. The undefined Spleen is here to process and learn from fear. It would be true to say that their whole life process is tested by fear, and as long as they accept this, they can become wiser and stronger. A person with a defined Spleen is not without fear, but it is under control, because due to the frequency of the Spleen Centre, which is about being in the now, the fear is constantly counterbalanced. However, undefined Spleens have to learn to see fear as their ally rather than their enemy. They also have to understand that in addition, they take in and magnify other people's fear.

Thus if they deal with fear in a healthy way, they have to confront every single fear they have, going through them one by one, so that they become less and less afraid until the fear is gone. Each fear that they have mastered makes them stronger and they can reach a point, eventually, where they are totally fearless. But first they have to honour their fear without trying to either suppress or fix it.

THE UNDEFINED SPLEEN AND CONDITIONING

1. THE TRAP OF FEELING GOOD

One of the greatest places of conditioning in Human Design is through the undefined Spleen and its inconsistent pattern of feeling good and feeling bad. Because of this vulnerability, people with undefined Spleens can spend a lifetime being conditioned to feel good and bad by the energetics of others. If you have an undefined Spleen this doesn't mean that you will never feel good. What it means is that you will have to go through all the things in life that do not feel good, in order that you then learn about all the things and people that do make you feel good. With an undefined Spleen, you can become very sensitive to your environment, because you gain a vast amount of experience by taking in the ill health (mental, emotional or physical) of others. The golden rule of Human Design is: all human beings always seek out what they are not. For the undefined Spleen, feeling good can be the greatest trap of all, because whoever or whatever makes you feel good may not be right for you.

Imagine for a moment a woman with an undefined Spleen. This woman grows up feeling uncertain and fearful about her environment. Her husband has a defined Spleen and also happens to be an alcoholic. Thus every time the husband comes back into the house, through conditioning, the woman immediately begins to feel safe and good about herself again. However, the husband is a drunk and over time becomes abusive to that her. Naturally this relationship is unhealthy for the woman but because of the conditioning to her undefined Spleen, she cannot escape the vicious circle. The very person that abuses her also gives her the illusion of stability and feeling good. Life is filled with such examples of co-dependent relationships, and the majority of them are because one partner has an undefined Spleen and the other has a defined Spleen. In such cases, it is typically the partner with the undefined centre that becomes the most needy.

2. SPONTANEITY CAN KILL YOU -
THE GOLDEN RULE OF THE UNDEFINED SPLEEN

All human beings seek out what they are not. There is nothing more attractive to someone with an undefined Spleen than the idea of being spontaneous. And there is nothing more dangerous to their well being than being spontaneous. This is a basic mechanical truth for the undefined Spleen, and it is their Golden Rule. These people simply are not designed to be spontaneous. They can never trust the now. An undefined Spleen ignorant of their own mechanics is so attracted to spontaneity in order to find the feel good factor and make their fear disappear. But they pay a high price for that. In order to decondition an undefined Spleen, you have to first of all overcome the drive and temptation to be spontaneous in life.

THE UNDEFINED SPLEEN AND HEALTH

People with undefined Spleen Centres are invariably interested in own their health or the health of others. If you have an undefined Spleen, your immune system is by nature vulnerable. However, being vulnerable does not mean that it has to be unhealthy or is in any way weak. It is very important again to remember that these undefined centres always carry within them a potential for wisdom; in this case to be wise concerning one's health and well being. If someone with an undefined Spleen is living according to their design, they will be naturally cautious about what they eat and about what kind of medicines they use. They may tend to be much more holistic in their approach than someone with a defined Spleen. For instance, they are far more likely to have a greater tendency towards being a vegetarian, or towards homeopathy or alternative medicine.

THE GIFTS OF THE UNDEFINED SPLEEN

The great gift of the undefined Spleen is sensitivity. This is not emotional sensitivity, but sensitivity through the body. Because they are open, these people can eventually become very clear about what kind of energies they are filtering. Many professional healers have an undefined Spleen Centre. When they step into somebody's aura, there is a spontaneous recognition that takes place through the connection. They can actually experience another person's illness. The undefined Spleen has the sensitivity to tell whether someone is healthy or ill, thus they are a kind of barometer to ill health in others. However, such wisdom and clarity only comes when they do not identify with what is not them. In other words, they have to understand that they are absorbing and experiencing the ill health of others, and by taking it in, they can read it and thus either offer help or learn to avoid those very same people.

If people with an undefined Spleen try to identify with whatever they are feeling, they can easily become hypochondriacs and end up being paranoid about being infected by others. They often assume they are constantly ill. People with undefined Spleens have to make sure that they stay in the aura of sick people for only a short time. If they spend too much time around sick people, they themselves are likely to become ill.

THE SPLEEN CENTRE IS NOT A MOTOR

As was mentioned above, the Splenic system can be compared to a washing machine. You may fill it with dirty clothes, but if you don't plug it in, it won't wash anything. It is very important to understand that the Spleen is not a motor and therefore it cannot behave like one. However, the moment it is connected to a motor, it is immediately energised and begins to clean our dirty laundry! Thus if you have an undefined Spleen Centre and it is suddenly defined by a planetary transit moving through your design, instead of feeling good, what is more likely to happen is that you may get ill. As soon as the process has passed through your system, you will have access to the feel-good. It is because of such planetary transits that undefined Spleens have regular natural clean-outs, becoming sick at almost the same time each year.

THE IMMUNE SYSTEM
Defined versus Undefined – An example

Below we can see two examples of different Spleen configurations in children. It is often by watching children that we can learn the most about these centres and how they work. Child B, with the undefined Spleen begins life with a far more vulnerable immune system than child A, who has a manifested Spleen. Child B will get most of the childhood diseases: the mumps, the measles etc. If there is anything going around, this child will catch it. These are the first children in the class that come home with a cold.

CHILD A   CHILD B

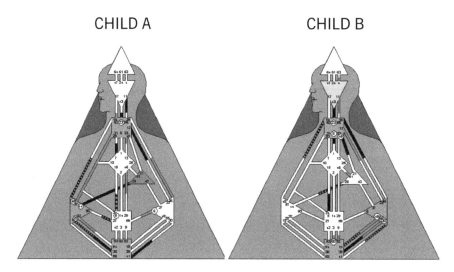

Assuming child B is fortunate enough to have good health care and proper shelter, love and a proper diet, and if they are allowed to recuperate fully, their immune system will grow stronger from each experience. One of the most important things to remember about children with undefined Spleens is that they should not be sent back into the world, sent back to school for example, until they have really healed from a sickness. This is not the moment that their nose stops running. You always have to give them a couple of extra days.

It is very important for these children. Only if they are allowed to heal properly will they build up a healthy defense mechanism. For example, child B catches a cold. The cold is one week coming, one week staying and one week going. But the moment that the one week of staying is over and the basic symptoms are gone, this is not the time to send the child back to school. This advice drives many parents crazy, because they don't want their children under their feet. They have to go to work. They are so glad that their children go to school so that they can have a quiet day at home and do their thing. They don't want to have their children running around the house when they seem to be okay. However, this advice of allowing their child a couple of extra recovery days is vital for their long-term health. If the parents send them to school again too early, they will only come back a few days later, even sicker with the next illness, and this will really hurt their immune system.

Once an undefined Splenic system deals with a virus successfully, that virus never has a chance again. In going through the healing process, the immune system develops a memory and a capability to handle that same virus again. This is the same premise as vaccination. We infect children with the virus so that their immune system recognises it and learns how to defend against it. Thus child B has the potential to live deep into old age as long as they are allowed to develop their immune response properly. In fact, child B has the kind of system (being undefined) that can actually allow him to get more and more healthy as he grows older. The extent of this possible old age is of course dependent on him not being spontaneous. It is dependent on him honouring the mechanics of his design.

Child A has a manifested Spleen Centre. You can see that the Spleen is connected to two motors (the Ego and the Root), which are in turn connected to the Throat. This is a very strong immune system that can take a lot of punishment, but that is not at all sensitive. Child A is less likely to catch all the childhood diseases, or get sick that often, which of course doesn't mean that he will never get sick. However, when he does get sick, he gets very sick. This is the kind of child for example, that will run an extremely high temperature. Since he already has a defined immune system that is consistently working, when he does get sick, it shows that his immune system has really been overwhelmed. It is quite common for somebody with a defined Spleen like this to go through their whole life eating and imbibing whatever they like, without any major illness, until one day, out of the blue, their system reaches a point of overload and they die of a heart attack. The immune system carried the load all of those years, keeping their physical problems veiled, only to finally collapse under the pressure.

Child A will most likely need strong modern medication such as antibiotics if he gets ill, since his body is equipped to handle such things. Child B however, may be better off with homeopathic medicine or herbs, which are gentler on his system. This is not to say that defined Spleens always need antibiotics and undefined Spleens should never take such things. These are simply generalisations that may help the parents of each child attune to their child. Child B with his undefined Spleen may not be able to handle modern medication. His parents should consider carefully what they put into his body. Undefined Spleens are usually very much concerned about their diet, their environment and the quality of the water and the air. Thus, you can see that is often the people with the undefined Spleen Centres that are the healthier people in the long run, because they constantly care about health. By design they can live a healthy life with enough sleep and exercise and with a low toxin intake.

Child A with his powerfully defined Spleen Centre may well grow up with little interest in health education because he assumes out of the way he feels that he is always healthy. One thing is certain; he will never have the kind of empathy with a wide range of illnesses and/or diets that child B has. The important thing to see from the above comparison is that there is no good or bad in Human Design. It is not better to have a defined Spleen or an undefined Spleen. They are simply two different journeys in life. The most important thing of all is to understand the nature of your own Spleen system so that you can take the appropriate measures to safeguard your health. Above all however, health hinges upon us living out the correct Strategy and Authority in our individual design. It doesn't matter how much you know about health, if you don't follow your Strategy, you won't ever be truly healthy.

	THE SPLEEN CENTRE	
	DEFINED	UNDEFINED
NATURAL STATE WHEN ALONE	General well-being.	Sensitivity to well-being in oneself and environment.
HEALTHY STRATEGY OF THE AUTHENTIC SELF 'THE GIFTS'	Has a reliable immune system which maintains the body's equilibrium throughout illness and health. Can trust hunches and intuition in the now, and can act spontaneously if the Spleen is the Authority. Has a fixed way of processing fear, leading to a deep inner sense of security.	Accepts the inconsistency of physical well-being, knowing that it is what makes it sensitive and highly attuned to the body's needs. Adept at diagnosing ill-health and disease in others or environment. Is not afraid of fear itself, but learns to be wise as to its nature by not suddenly reacting to it or trying to fix it. Enjoys aura of defined Spleens without being dependent. Is never spontaneous.
UNHEALTHY STRATEGY OF THE NOT SELF 'THE TRAPS'	A sense of invulnerability can lead to an overloading of the system and sudden serious and unforeseen health problems. Not listening to hunches when the Spleen is the main Authority, or following hunches with a defined Solar Plexus can lead to physical problems, disease and danger.	Constantly chases after feeling good and tries to fix its own inconsistency through diet, therapy, relationships or helping others. Gets caught up in how it feels physically, 'becoming its own problem'. Tries to be spontaneous in order to feel better and make the fear go away. Will sacrifice its own security for the sake of well-being. Becomes dependent and possessive in relationships.

SUMMARY OF THE SPLEEN CENTRE

- The Spleen Centre is our oldest awareness centre, our body consciousness.
- Its frequency is in the now and its fears are about survival.
- The main themes of the Spleen Centre are: health, feel-good, survival.
- Biologically, it relates to the lymphatic system, the spleen and the spleen cells.
- The function of the Spleen Centre is to keep us healthy and alive.
- A defined Spleen has to honour their gut feeling to stay healthy.
- An undefined Spleen has to pay attention to its health. It can never be spontaneous.
- The Golden Rule of the undefined Spleen is: Spontaneity can kill you.

3.2 THE AJNA CENTRE: MIND
WHO'S THE BOSS?

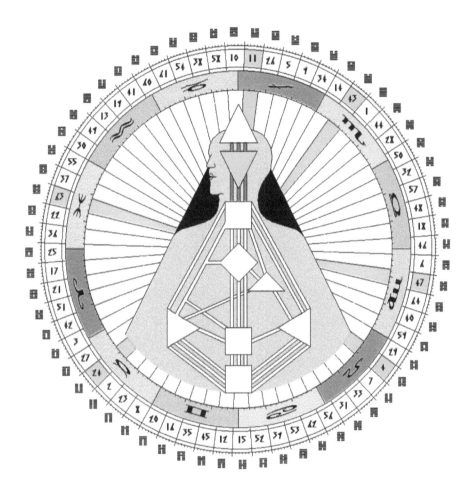

There is nothing more compelling than the human mind. It is our gift as a species to have this capacity to be able to conceptualise the world around us, to be able to give everything a name, to be able to store and communicate the human experience and to be able to enrich our species within an ongoing expanded educational base. The mind dominates our lives and our world, and it dominates our perception of ourselves and everything that surrounds us.

The Ajna Centre is our second awareness centre, and it represents our mental awareness. Fueled by the pressure from the Head Centre, its function is to conceptualise thoughts and express them in language through the Throat Centre.

HISTORICAL BACKGROUND

Between 85,000 and 90,000 years ago our mental consciousness began to evolve. At that time we went through a process that opened up the potential of the Ajna Centre. That process was a physical genetic mutation that changed the function of the human larynx. Before that time human beings had always been able to drink and breathe simultaneously. However, this capacity was lost after the great mutation occurred. In essence, what happened was that the larynx dropped in the Throat, thereby allowing the vocal chambers to open up, leading to the development and articulation of complex sound patterns. That period in our history marked the beginning of our language capability, ending our need to communicate solely through primal sounds such as sighs, groans, and growls. The result of this transition was the rapid development of new areas of the human brain as we learned to communicate in deeper and more complex ways.

BIOLOGICAL RELATIONSHIP

The Ajna Centre is where the anterior and the posterior pituitary glands are found. These are very important endocrine glands because they are the headquarters of the instructions for the whole body. We humans lead a mind-dominated life, because the pituitary glands are in charge of sending out the hormonal information that will be metamorphosed by the thyroid glands. They give instructions both about the maintenance of the inside of the body and the outside world.

THE MIND IS A TIME MACHINE

Mental awareness dominates our lives. It dominates the way in which we perceive the world in which we live. As a species, we take our minds very seriously. Essentially, when we are dealing with the mind, we are in fact dealing with two processes, a collective process, which is visual, and an individual process, which is acoustic. Of the two, it is the visual process which dominates. The other thing to keep in mind is that when you are dealing with the mind, you are in essence, dealing with a time machine. As we have seen, each of the three awareness centres has a different frequency. In the mind, the frequency is across time, and there are three variations: the abstract collective mind is about the relationship from the present to the past. The logical collective process is about the nature of the mind in terms of the present projected into the future. Finally, when you are dealing with the individual process it takes place in a pulse, which we can theoretically call 'the now', because it is experienced as the present. These three aspects make up the time machine we call the mind.

DECISION MAKING AND THE MIND

The mind is not a motor. Thus, we should be wary when approaching the mind, because where there is no motor, there is no need for any kind of manifesting or doing. The Ajna Centre is the only awareness centre that is locked away from the body's energy systems, because it has no direct access to a motor. It is flanked on both sides by the Throat and the Head Centre, which are both non-motors. This is not true for the Spleen Centre, which we have already seen, has direct connections to the Sacral and the Root. It is certainly not true for the Solar Plexus Centre, which is a motor itself.

So what exactly is the mind for? The answer is simple and twofold: communication and research. The mind is there for communicating the essence of what it is to be human. This is why it has the capacity to look at life in many different ways all at the same time.

AUTHORITY – THE GOLDEN RULE OF THE AJNA CENTRE

In Human Design analysis, there is a very important term known as Authority. Authority represents each person's unique way of making decisions in life, and there are two basic categories of Authority. Firstly, there is outer Authority, which is essentially the capacity to be authoritative for others. All minds have outer value to others. Secondly, there is inner Authority. This is the place within yourself where you can always find a reliable 'yes' or 'no'. Inner Authority is related to the subject of Type, which we will explore later. The golden rule when dealing with the Ajna Centre is that, regardless of whether the mind is defined or undefined, it never has inner Authority. It is not up to our minds to make decisions. It is up to our minds to do research.

Since human beings are a duality, the mind is also dualistic. It is dualistic in the way in which it processes information. In other words, it can always show you the advantages and disadvantages of any decision, ranging ahead in time to the possible outcome, and diving into the past for evidence of another possible outcome. It can research that decision in great depth, but the only thing it cannot do is actually make the decision, since it has no capability to judge one side over another.

Essentially, the mind is like a banana republic where some little corporal, whose only purpose is to keep the records and do the research, all of a sudden becomes the leader of the nation. This is when everything falls apart. Our minds are petty dictators. They would like to be in control of our lives. And because of the power of mind, and the way in which we are taught from birth to use our minds to make decisions, these little corporals are in control of our lives. The result is torment, confusion and suffering.

THE POWER OF TYPE OVER MIND

Imagine that you have a problem with somebody and you really want to straighten it out. You want to talk to them about it so that you can get it off your chest. The most important thing to remember is that your mind is only there to look at the duality of what the problem is, and not to decide on a course of action. Let the mind compare all the sides of your argument. When the research is complete, regardless of the personal preference you feel towards one side or the other, understand that this is not the time to jump and pick up the telephone. In the ignorance of your Type, you are unable to know what Strategy will work for you. In ignorance of your true place of inner Authority, there is never proper timing.

One of the deepest experiences possible regarding the nature of the mind can be experienced by anyone with a defined Sacral Centre. Because Sacral people respond to life via their Sacral Centre, which is unaware, they offer a prime example of how the mind plays tricks on us.

For example, when a Sacral person is asked: 'Would you like to go out for lunch?' and they hear their Sacral say 'ahuh', the next thing that might happen is that the mind jumps in with an idea, saying: 'what I'd really like is Italian food.' But, in truth they do not know that. It is simply the mind running away with the Sacral response. If they are then asked: 'would you like to eat Italian food?' and their Sacral says 'uhun', the mind only jumps in again with another idea, and so the game goes on.

The point of the above example is that it shows how fickle the mind can be and therefore how ill equipped it is to guide us in life. Only when we find our true Authority in life, can the mind take its rightful place as servant rather than master. However, the deconditioning of the mind can be a tricky business because we are all so conditioned from birth to make decisions with our minds. Any time you attempt to make a mental decision and turn it into action, the consequences of that decision will haunt you for the rest of your life, because the mind cannot let go. Your mind will always be wondering about the other possibilities of not taking the decision; did I do the right thing? Did I do the wrong thing? What might have happened if such and such had happened?

The only thing that you can rely on the mind for is to be of value to others. It is not that the mind is without value. In fact, it has enormous value. It is a tool for communication so that you can find out for yourself what you think you have experienced in life. It has nothing to do with the decisions we actually make throughout our lives. It is simply there to set up a perspective, to look at both sides of something without saying which side is better. Its essential job is to do the research.

AWARENESS AND ANXIETY

As we saw at the beginning of this Section 3 on awareness, all awareness is rooted in different patterns of fear. The fear of the Ajna Centre is called anxiety. This anxiety is purely mental and it is what makes human beings worry. The anxiety from the Head Centre is about not being able to understand or make sense of our lives. It is the anxiety of not knowing something. The anxiety from the Throat Centre is about not being understood, or about not being able to communicate with clarity. Whenever communication fails, anxiety will rise to the surface and as we know, it can lead to all kinds of problems, both physical and psychological.

When you can see your mechanics, and you can see that your mind can never be your inner Authority, only then is it possible to eliminate anxiety. Each of the 6 gates of the Ajna Centre manifests a different kind of anxiety.

THE SIX ANXIETIES OF THE AJNA

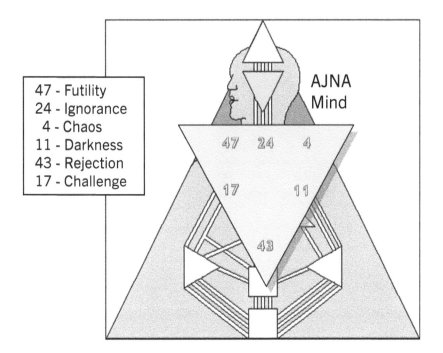

47 - Futility
24 - Ignorance
 4 - Chaos
11 - Darkness
43 - Rejection
17 - Challenge

AJNA
Mind

THE THREE MENTAL PROCESSES

The mind has three possible modes of operating. Two of them are visual and the other is acoustic. The visual processing of mental information is either logical or abstract. Logic is about understanding a pattern and projecting it into the future, while abstract refers to the need to make sense out of what has happened in the past.

The acoustic mental process is rather unique and can be very difficult. Essentially, it is about finding a rationale for a unique awareness, or in other words, it represents the translation of inner knowing into language. However, in the Ajna Centre it is the visual sense that dominates. In the Spleen, the most important sense was smell, and the nose dominates. Here in the Ajna, it is sight that dominates, and thus the eyes become very dominant, for the simple reason that we take in information through the eyes.

THE DEFINED AJNA CENTRE

All defined centres represent that which is fixed in our nature. Thus, if you have a defined Ajna Centre then you have a fixed way of thinking. The way in which you think is reliable and trustworthy (as a research centre), but at the same time, there is a deep limitation in this. You can only think in that particular way.

WILL I EVER STOP THINKING?

If you have a defined mind, this is highly unlikely! You are a mental person by design, and you have a particular kind of neurocircuitry in your brain which demands that you constantly process everything mentally. This is particularly true for people with the Head Centre defined.

You cannot escape who you are. This is one of the great wonders of Human Design. Conditioning targets us in our defined centres as well as our undefined centres. Imagine what it is like for somebody in the so-called New Age, who has a defined Ajna Centre. Their mind is fixed, and they are a truly mental person.

Then one day a friend of theirs shows up, having just come back from a long journey to the East. The friend happened to spend several months with an Indian guru whose main teaching is to drop the mind. The friend happens to have an undefined Ajna Centre. In such an undefined mind, the mind is like a waterfall, with everything just pouring through from all kinds of directions all the time. The experience of 'No mind' is wonderful for them. In fact, it is a truth for them, because they are always open to the mind around them. So, the friend comes back from India and says to the person with a defined mind: 'you know, you should really go and study with this man because no-mind is such wonderful experience'. And so they go and meditate together. However, the person with the defined Ajna Centre naturally is unable to stop his mind, and feels like he is a failure. He can then become obsessed with trying to eliminate what is in fact a very beautiful part of his nature.

You can see from the above example how dangerous generalisations can be. A lack of education in the nature of who you are is mechanically dangerous, not only to your psychic well-being, but also for your physical health.

MIND CONNECTED TO THROAT

If you have a defined Ajna Centre connected to the Throat, you are someone who can always speak your mind. However, the ability to be able to speak your mind doesn't mean that it is something that can do well. Many people with this kind of configuration fall into the trap of talking about things and then never actually following up on their words. This can lead to deep-seated feelings of inadequacy and/or the perception of others that they are hypocritical and 'flaky'. The answer for such people, as always with Human Design, lies in a clear understanding of their own mechanics.

THE UNDEFINED AJNA CENTRE

A person with an undefined Ajna Centre is truly a person with an open mind. Whereas the defined mind is fixed and focused depending on its definition, the undefined mind can be logical, inspirational or abstract. The quality and intensity of their thought process is entirely dependent on whoever is around them.

We always have to remember in Human Design that the open centres in our design are our areas of greatest potential and greatest confusion. The undefined mind is a sign of intelligence in this respect. Such people are intelligent rather than intellectual. Many of the greatest minds in history have been undefined: Freud, Jung, Marie Curie and Einstein (above) are all classic examples of undefined minds. And yet, one only has to look at the personal lives of such people to see how chaotic the undefined mind can be at managing life itself.

So often, people with undefined minds compare themselves to the people around them who have defined minds. They wonder why they cannot easily sustain a consistent thought process when alone, and thus they often end up either devaluing their mind altogether, or trying desperately to be intellectual. Defined minds can be very good at looking as though they are intellectual, studying everything and anything they can get their hands on. They are often collectors of reams of information, books and even objects, but no matter how much they know or have, it never gives them a sense of peace.

Such people are very vulnerable to anxiety, even though they may not show it, and they can have a deep fear of being alone. The reason for this is that they do not understand that they can never fix their mind. The undefined mind is not designed to be consistent, rather it ranges from being totally empty to over brimming with ideas, concepts, details, opinions etc.

The very fluid nature of the undefined mind is the source of its dynamic, ever-changing intelligence. These are people who can hold a conversation with anyone and always adapt their thinking to the other person. They can be logical and factual with one person and artistic and abstract with another. Their mind knows no bounds, and thus can have extraordinary value as an outer Authority for others, but is helpless as an inner Authority to guide them in their own lives. In an undefined mind, the entire process of conceptualising is conditioned by others.

Let's invent an example of how the undefined mind is conditioned: You have an undefined mind and you are sitting in a café, and behind you there is a person with a defined mind who happens to be dreaming about going to Paris for a holiday. Because you are sitting in their aura, a subtle chemistry passes between you, which your mind picks up on. Almost immediately, you find yourself thinking about taking a holiday, and wondering what Paris is like at this time of year! On the way home, you pass a travel shop, book a trip to France and a week later you are on the plane.

Have you any idea what kind of a holiday this will turn out to be? In the first instance, it isn't even your holiday! So you arrive at your destination and immediately everything begins to go wrong: the place is dirty, the weather is awful and you spend the whole time wondering what to do and wishing you were back at home. The final straw is that on the third day there, you fall down the steps and break your leg.

The moral of the story is: if you have an undefined mind, be careful you don't take someone else's holiday. People with undefined minds are forever identifying with other people's thoughts, concepts, opinions and ideas. These are very impressionable minds. The gift of such people is that if they learn to stop identifying with anything they think, they actually become mind readers, not in an esoteric sense (although that is also possible), but in the sense that they can empathise with anyone. They can just sit with someone and watch what their mind does. Whatever crosses their mind, someone in a group will probably say it.

The undefined Ajna Centre is a wonderful processor of mental information. Such minds also store huge amounts of information as memory, even though they cannot necessarily access what they have remembered. Certain thoughts and concepts that they took in at some point in their past are triggered in the presence of certain people, but such memory recall is never in the hands of the undefined mind. They simply have to learn to surrender to the magic of not knowing something until they know it!

An undefined mind can always tell whether someone else is mentally clear or confused. Their role is to share many different ways of thinking with others, and if they let go of trying to make sense of their lives with their minds, they can be totally free of prejudice and mental judgment.

WHO IS THE BOSS?

The Ajna Centre is never the boss. It is the research centre. There are all kinds of generalisations in the world that can be deeply painful. We have already seen the generalisation that leads to people with undefined minds thinking that they should always be able to concentrate their minds consistently. However your mind works, it is perfect, and knowing the design of your mind can show you the nature of that perfection. As for the boss, true Authority is always somewhere else in one's design, and we will discuss this further in Part 3.

▽	THE AJNA CENTRE	
	DEFINED	UNDEFINED
NATURAL STATE WHEN ALONE	Knows only a fixed mental way of thinking.	No consistent thought pattern.
HEALTHY STRATEGY OF THE AUTHENTIC SELF 'THE GIFTS'	Has an inbuilt structure for processing or computing information. Feels very comfortable with concepts, enjoys the 'research', reviewing and organising of information in readiness for communication.	Fluid and adaptable thinking, able to soak up new ideas and concepts, without becoming fixed on any of them. Enjoys having no fixed way of processing thoughts. Enjoys the openness and versatility of intelligence. Accepts uncertainty.
UNHEALTHY STRATEGY OF THE NOT SELF 'THE TRAPS'	Can totally dominate the life, making decisions that override other true authorities. Can create all kind of anxiety from trying to work out decisions mentally.	Tends to worry about not understanding and remembering things. Compares itself unfavourably to defined minds. Tries too hard to be intellectual, holding on to fixed mental processes, concepts or opinions. Needs to be certain.

SUMMARY OF THE AJNA CENTRE

- The Ajna Centre is our second awareness centre. It is our mental awareness.

- The frequency of the mind is over all time and its fear is called anxiety.

- The main theme of the Ajna Centre is the conceptualising process.

- Its biological attribute is the pituitary glands.

- The true function of the Ajna Centre is to do research.

- The mind has no decision-making capabilities.

- The defined Ajna Centre has to trust its fixed way of thinking and processing mental information.

- The undefined Ajna Centre knows many different ways of thinking, but is inconsistent in and of itself.

- The golden rule when dealing with the Ajna Centre is that, regardless of whether the mind is defined or undefined, it never has inner Authority.

101 THINGS TO DO WITH AN UNDEFINED MIND

1. Watch the mind-traffic (this is actually the whole list).

2. Meditate (a focused way of doing '1' – above).

3. Re-arrange your book collection (by subject, size, alphabetical order, etc).

4. Go from room to room in your home and notice all the unfinished things you left 'momentarily' to go and do something else. Turn the bath taps off and call the emergency plumber.

5. Open your wardrobe and consider the clothes you bought that you loved in the shop but find you don't want to wear. Give them to the friend you went shopping with. Make a 'mental' note to shop alone and at quiet times when the changing cubicles around you will be empty and ask the shop assistant to leave you alone. Use your correct authority to decide what you buy.

6. Review how many times you have listened to someone raving about their new hobby, gone out in a burst of enthusiasm to spend a fortune on equipment to try this yourself, kept it (unused) for months and got rid of it at half it's original price. Give your gym club membership to a friend who loves exercise.

7. Realise that when you go upstairs/into a room to do something and forget instantly why you went there this is not necessarily a sign of premature senility and relax as you retrace your steps to retrieve your lost intention.

8. Say something a friend was about to say 2 seconds before they do and enjoy their astonished expression. Consider a career as 'The Great Stupendo' to run alongside your other work.

9. Stop yourself every time you begin a sentence with 'Well, I think'. You will be speaking for whoever you are with. For this reason avoid people with clipboards who button-hole you in the street for your opinions; it's a pointless exercise.

10. Laugh at your list-writing compulsion (examine how elaborate it has become, e.g. the sub-lists and list of essentials extracted from the main list) in a vain attempt to pin down all the data passing through your mind. Ask yourself if you would need counselling if you lost your personal organiser.

11. Avoid attending hypnotist's stage shows unless you want your awful Elvis impersonation to be seen by everyone and not recall one second of just how foolish you looked. If the person inviting you along owns a camcorder be sure that your correct authority says yes before agreeing to go.

12. Notice how often you drive to work/to collect the kids/to the supermarket 'on automatic pilot'. Ring the dentist/hairdresser/vet and apologise for missing your appointment because you just drove to work/to collect the kids/to the supermarket.

13. Write a shopping list, go shopping (having left the list on the kitchen table because 'your mind was elsewhere') and see what you buy. Are you unconsciously shadowing someone else and picking the same items off the shelf, or responding to special offer advertising? When you get home, look at the list you wrote to compare them. Go back to the shop for the 2 essential items you didn't get.

14. Read a medical dictionary and decide, sequentially, that you have each of the diseases listed, and possibly a few more no-one has discovered yet. Lie down until the thoughts have gone away completely.

15. Never, ever, answer the door to anyone selling anything – unless you want to be the only fully triple-glazed, right-wing activist at your local Jehovah's Witness church (no offence intended to any such persons reading this; the example quoted is purely for illustrative purposes). Give thanks for the 'cooling off' period available for all major financial transactions potentially signed in haste.

16. Attend a New Age exhibition (without your credit cards) and see whether you can get through the day without deciding to drastically change your diet/lifestyle/belief system at least once.[Unless you have made the decision in accordance with your correct authority, naturally]

17. See what happens if you have a 'media fast' - no newspapers/TV/internet, etc for as long as you can bear it.

18. Lie awake worrying that you might not be able to find another 83 things to add to your list before someone asks you whether the list is finished. Realise the list is never finished.

Elaine Rogers
Emotional Manifestor

[I would like to deny all responsibility for this article, which was jointly and severally the work of colleagues, friends, people in the library/café/supermarket/park/bus/ street and anywhere else I may have been when I thought I was thinking about ideas for this article.]

DISCOVERING MY BRAIN

When I was about twelve years old I had a very embarrassing educational experience – I had to have Differential Calculus explained to me five times in one maths lesson. No matter how many times the teacher repeated it all, I just didn't get it. For days, even months afterwards, I beat myself up because it seemed I was the only one in the class who hadn't got it, and I came to the conclusion that I was, without a doubt, completely stupid.

In fact I had always suspected I was stupid because I often didn't understand things. I still don't. I don't understand anything that involves complicated relationships between things, logical systems, and anything to do with money. I don't understand the plot in most movies and I usually can't even work out who's the goodie or the baddie. I can't get the hang of road directions, I have no idea why my investments did so badly, and I used to sit in Management meetings at work wondering what on earth they were going on about, praying that no one would ask me for my opinion.

Recently my family had a meeting with our accountant who was trying to explain the UK taxation system. For the tenth time I mouthed the dreaded question 'but I don't really understand the bit about….' both my sisters screaming with frustration, because of course it was as clear as daylight to them. Point proved yet again – I am thick – beyond a shadow of a doubt.

The Revelation

And yet somehow I managed to get a University degree, become a better than average teacher of the English language, and produce ground breaking teacher training videos for the Government of Hong Kong. All this and more with a brain that feels as if it's full of a kind of gungy sludge, mixed with fuzz and coated in slime. Nothing will stick inside my head. There's just nothing solid in there to get a grip on anything.

Well you can imagine my amazement when I saw my chart and discovered I was 'completely blank from the waist up'. Well not quite…I have one solitary little gate in my head and that is the 47.4 unconscious. Pretty much all my definition is 'below the belt'. This explained a lot! All my life I had been trying to 'be brainy' impose logical facts and systems on an abstract mind that only knows how to try frantically to lay out images and desperately piece them together like an artist assembling a collage but with half the bits missing.

So yippee…I can stop panicking. I don't have a brain! What I do have is an incredible ability to focus on something (9/52), insatiably tear it to pieces, get right to the heart of it, and make it clear for everyone else (18/58). I battle with confusion because the clarity when it comes, is like emerging from the clouds into clear blue sky (58/38). I know there is a way of making sense of the sludge, and I know that when I've done it, I can communicate it pretty well (26) if I'm in the mood (39/55).

Now I understand. My undefined mind is really just an open doorway, a portal through which 'stuff' comes in. It slithers through and kind of wends its way down into my guts. This takes time and can't be done quickly or spontaneously. Once the information is down there in the intestines of my design, it gets thoroughly digested. All the sludge and fuzz is pumped and squeezed by the 18/58 and the 58/38, like peristalsis, until it forms into solid bits.

The best bit in my experience is the stillness and focus of the 9/52. I can only describe it as that 'after breakfast and a large cup of coffee' moment, when one has to dive into the bathroom, close the door and seat oneself on the throne. Pants around the ankles, there is that wonderful stillness when the hair stands up on the back of the neck, the whole world seems exquisitely focused, concentration is razor sharp, poised for action…and then the body delivers!

This is how my mind works. I suppose you could say I have shit for brains! So this perhaps is my biggest Human Design revelation so far: discovering my brain. And if you are like me and have an undefined mind, have you discovered your brain? If it's not in your head, where is it I wonder? I'd love to hear from anyone with brains in interesting places!

Judy Dendy
Emotional Generator

3.3 THE SOLAR PLEXUS CENTRE: SPIRIT
THE EMOTIONAL WAVE OF HOPE AND PAIN

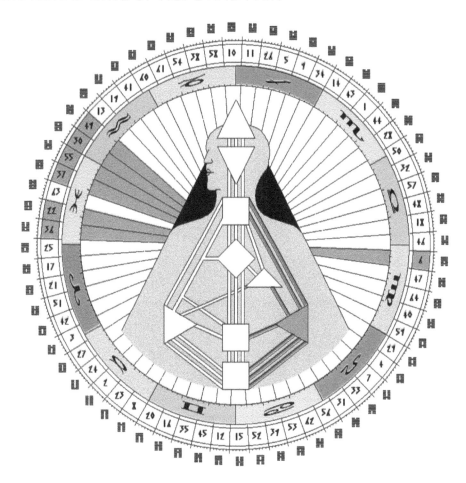

There is no other centre in Human Design that has greater impact than the Solar Plexus Centre. The Solar Plexus is the source of all our feelings, emotions and sensitivities. When you first come into contact with your own design, regardless of whether your Solar Plexus is defined or undefined, the knowledge of how your emotional nature actually operates can be the greatest liberation of all.

We have already seen that in the Bodygraph there are four motors and three awareness centres, but the only centre that has the potential to be both is the Solar Plexus. This is why it is so powerful, in both a negative way and a positive way. As you learn about your own Solar Plexus, many of your oldest emotional patterns will become clear to you. You may understand, heal or let go of old hurt and guilt from your past. Above all, you may learn how to be compassionate towards yourself and others, as you see the awesome power of this centre and the grip it has over the mass of humanity.

HISTORICAL BACKGROUND AND SPIRITUAL IMPLICATION

The Solar Plexus Centre began to evolve as our third awareness centre some time between the birth of Jesus and Buddha. As a species, we are only at the beginning of discovering what emotional awareness actually is. In essence, emotional awareness is about experiencing ourselves directly as one entity, in other words, as a spirit consciousness.

According to the voice, this new awareness will be physically born into the world in the year 2027 as a genetic mutation. After this date, children will begin to be born with what may appear to be a genetic defect within the solar plexus system. In truth, these children will be the first real 'Raves' to be born on our planet, and it will take many hundreds of years for the mutation to spread into the gene pool and for humanity to begin to realise itself as a single entity.

Spirit awareness will be something very special, because it can never exist within a single person. In other words, you cannot attain it in a cave in the Himalayas. Spirit awareness only emerges when two emotional people step into each other's aura and their emotional waves interact with each other. The combined energy field where their waves are in resonance together is where spirit awareness is possible. This is what the two waves of the Aquarian Symbol really mean. The Aquarian Age is to be an Age of mass spiritual awakening. We have no idea what that will be like. We cannot imagine how it feels to share a consciousness with someone else outside of our own body.

It is important to understand that this spirit will evolve when our mental process comes to an end. This means that people have to understand who they are. As long as human beings do not accept who they are, the mind will not let go, because its frequency is over all time. Spirit consciousness is where our future lies, and we are a bridging generation that can help to plant this seed. Our own evolutionary step is to deal with the Solar Plexus Centre as a powerful motor, and fully understand its true design.

BIOLOGICAL RELATIONSHIP

Biologically, the Solar Plexus Centre relates to the kidneys, the pancreas, the prostate gland and the nervous system. People who are unable to deal with their emotional nature are likely to suffer in these areas of their body, or in associated areas. An example might be emotional problems that lead to water retention in the body and weight problems.

THE FREQUENCY: THE WAVE

The frequency of the Solar Plexus Centre neither operates in the now nor does it operate over all time. It operates in a wave. The Solar Plexus Centre releases a wave pattern that we experience as an eternal cycle from hope to pain, from expectation to disappointment, from joy to despair and back again. Furthermore, because we are all moving in space, this wave is really a spiral from which we can learn, rather than a circle into which we are locked.

Our next evolutionary step is to learn to recognise this wave pattern, accept it and eventually transcend it. This is what will lay the foundation for spirit to emerge. Understanding the frequency of the emotional motor is a prerequisite for creating emotional stability. The collective power of all the Solar Plexus waves across our planet literally creates the chaos of the world in which we live today. Thus the most important knowledge of our time is to explain the nature of the emotional system to people so that the planet can find inner peace.

As this knowledge is spread and people begin to become aware of their emotional wave, it will seem as though a huge mirror layered in dust is finally being cleaned and polished. And when the mirror is clear, the whole vibration of the earth will change, and finally we will see our true face reflected in the glass.

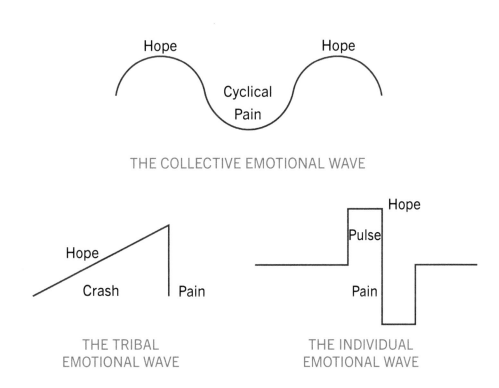

THE COLLECTIVE EMOTIONAL WAVE

THE TRIBAL
EMOTIONAL WAVE

THE INDIVIDUAL
EMOTIONAL WAVE

AWARENESS AND NERVOUSNESS

As an awareness centre, the Solar Plexus Centre has its unique patterns of fear, just like the Ajna and the Spleen. As they move through the seven gates of the human emotional system, these fears are experienced as seven types of nervousness.

THE SEVEN TYPES OF NERVOUSNESS

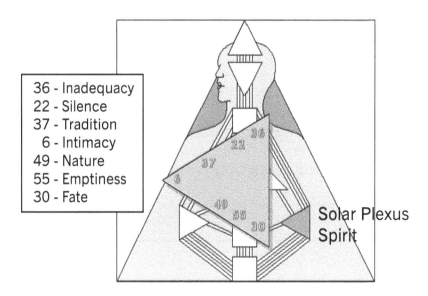

36 - Inadequacy
22 - Silence
37 - Tradition
 6 - Intimacy
49 - Nature
55 - Emptiness
30 - Fate

Solar Plexus
Spirit

These seven fears are very powerful because of the nature of the Solar Plexus as a motor. They are not fears that are static; they operate in waves, which means they can suddenly disappear and then reoccur, as the emotions surge and plummet. Solar Plexus fears are the kind of fears where mountains can become molehills and molehills can become mountains. They are all connected to the nature of the wave itself. What this also means is that Solar Plexus fears are the least trustworthy fears in the moment, but they will reveal the truth in the long run.

AUTHORITY – THE GOLDEN RULE OF THE SOLAR PLEXUS CENTRE

Just as the Ajna Centre has its Golden Rule of having no inner Authority, so too does the Solar Plexus Centre have its golden rule. Whenever you are dealing with a defined emotional system, whether in a person or a relationship, there is no truth in the now. In other words, you have to wait out the wave in order to be clear. Thus all emotional fears are fears that can only be truly dealt with once someone has moved through their wave and come out the other side.

THE DEFINED SOLAR PLEXUS CENTRE

There are essentially two kinds of people on this planet: emotional people and unemotional people. Because of the confusion of conditioning and the ignorance of our own unique designs, this division is often not at all clear. The emotional people have no general understanding of their emotional wave, and the unemotional people are conditioned to think that they are emotional. The result is a planetary frequency of emotional chaos and suffering rather than harmony and clarity. Like all defined centres, the defined Solar Plexus is operating 24 hours a day, from birth to death. Such people are governed by their own emotional nature, whether they realise it or not, and as we have seen, this nature is an emotional wave that consistently washes in and washes out again.

TYPES OF EMOTIONAL CHEMISTRY

SOLAR PLEXUS TO THROAT

When the Solar Plexus is connected to the Throat, the emotions can manifest in language and in action. This is the most volatile and chaotic kind of emotional chemistry. The two potential channels between these two centres have a deep potential anger stored within them and if such people are not waiting to be clear before they express their feelings, the results can be hurtful and inappropriate.

SOLAR PLEXUS TO SACRAL

When the Solar Plexus is connected to the Sacral, the emotions tend to emerge as Sacral sounds, like growls, sighs and groans. This is also the only direct link between our emotional nature and our sexuality, and thus it may come as no surprise that it governs our genetic strategies for mating. All the different variations of the emotional wave are released through this channel.

SOLAR PLEXUS TO ROOT

When the Solar Plexus is connected to the Root, the emotions are under enormous pressure, which is experienced as nervous energy if there is no further definition to either the Sacral or Throat. In this kind of chemistry, the emotions can only be accessed through other people's chemistry or through sporadic planetary transits that may release the emotional pressure.

SOLAR PLEXUS TO EGO

When the Solar Plexus is connected to the Ego, we have the meeting of two very powerful motors; the emotional drive and the power of will. This type of emotional chemistry requires a constant balancing of these two energies; the individual emotional wave and the energy of the Ego to work within the community.

PATIENCE

The great theme of all emotionally defined people is patience. With the Solar Plexus Centre defined, the wave from hope to pain is always operating. The key is waiting out the wave. When these people are emotionally excited and full of hope, they have to wait out the whole span of the wave before they make a decision. They have to understand that hope is only an energy running through their chemistry and not an awareness.

When they are emotionally depressed and feeling the pain or angst of the emotional system, they have to wait out the wave before making any decision. Just like pleasure, pain is simply an energetic that moves through the body from time to time. It has nothing to do with clarity.

EMOTIONAL CLARITY

As we have seen, the Golden Rule for the Solar Plexus Centre is: 'No Truth in the Now'. What this means is that emotional people are not designed to be spontaneous. They can never know something as a certainty because their decision making process is not fixed. It takes time. In order to find any kind of emotional clarity they have to wait for a minimum of three opportunities. As an example, if you are emotionally defined and you meet someone for the first time, you can never really know if you like them because everything will be coloured by your wave. If your wave is down, you may not respond favourably to them, and then when you meet them again a week later, you may decide they are actually rather wonderful, because your wave has come up. The third time you meet the same person, you will have a much clearer picture because you will have experienced them through the different nuances of your own emotional chemistry. Then, you can begin to get a feeling for whether you really like them or not.

It is so common for emotional people to make rash commitments based on being high in their wave. They are feeling good one day, and someone asks them to do something with them tomorrow, and in that moment of feeling good, they say yes. The next day, when they wake up feeling different about the world, they remember making a commitment for that day but they are no longer in the mood to go. Thus they are faced with a dilemma; should I break the commitment and risk the consequences, or go against my will? Emotional people who make decisions too quickly are often facing such situations. The key is to always remember to sleep on it. If you sleep on it, you will avoid the dilemma altogether. Emotional people always wake up feeling differently about things the following day. Thus they have to allow themselves to take time with their decisions, no matter what others say or how much pressure they are being put under.

Even when you have waited long enough, emotional clarity is never a certainty. This is not the absolute Authority of the Spleen Centre, which says yes or no in the now, with no ambiguity. Neither is emotional Authority like the mind, which is totally subjective. Emotional clarity can only ever be about 80% certain, because it never stops changing. Thus, for an emotional person, waiting is the only way to have a sense of whether something is correct or not. Emotionally defined people have to understand that they are not dealing with awareness, because the solar plexus has not yet evolved into this potential. They are dealing with a terrifically powerful emotional motor that wants to jump to action at the least sign of excitement or disturbance.

THE EMOTIONAL AURA

There is a true responsibility that goes with having a defined Solar Plexus Centre in your design. This is to understand the power of the emotional aura. When an emotional person feels good, it is not only you who feel good, but also everyone around you. In other words, you transmit the frequency of your emotional wave out into your environment. That is quite a power; to make others feel good or bad. If you are up on your emotional wave, and you go in for a job interview, your chances are improved. If you're on the emotional low end of the wave, and you go in for the same job interview, it isn't going to work so smoothly. The emotional being thus controls the environment around them.

CONFUSION IN RELATIONSHIPS

Emotional people have a deep need to recognise their nature and understand their wave pattern. Anybody who is close to them also has to accept them when they are up on their wave and accept them when they are down. Emotional people have to be especially careful in taking people into their life. If they want to make new friends or find a partner, they can never trust in a spontaneous coming together. They have to meet people repeatedly, not only to know the other person better, but also to see how the other reacts to their own changing wave.

Emotionally defined people can cause confusion in relationships without even knowing they are doing anything. They have to learn to see that they can make others instantly uncomfortable simply by changing the way they feel inside. The source of all manipulation and guilt lies within the interplay of the defined and undefined Solar Plexus Centres. We have to remember that an undefined centre will magnify the vibration of any defined centre, thus, if you are emotional and happen to be feeling good about someone, they will feel twice as good about you. This can be very misleading, especially when you meet the same person again and your wave has shifted. They may come across in a much cooler way, and if you take it personally, you may end up thinking that they are rejecting you, while all along, it was your own emotional wave conditioning the environment. Emotional people can always know where they are in their own wave by watching the responses of the people around them with undefined emotional centres. In seeing their emotional impact on others, they can learn to treat those people with greater care, and in particular, stop doing harm to undefined emotional people, who have no choice but to innocently mirror their emotional wave.

EMOTIONAL CHEMISTRY AND REASON-MAKING

Given the dominance of the mental field on this planet, human beings are forever making up reasons for everything. This is actually one of the things that human beings do best. Giving reasons to emotional chemistry is one of the greatest causes of suffering on our planet. The tendency is to make up a reason so that one can try to fix, change, escape the wave, or else blame it on someone or something else. We will do anything just to avoid accepting our feelings as perfect.

When emotional people go up on their wave, they generally make up a reason for it. Similarly, when they are down in their wave, they find another reason for it. The reason can be anything: the government, their lover, their job or their friends. Naturally there is no clarity in these reasons because there is no reason in the first place. We give reasons in order to try and change the way we are feeling. If we have a reason, we feel we may be able to do something about it. It is all a matter of human beings being uncomfortable when they are not in control. If you are emotionally defined and are feeling sad one day, people will tend to ask you what is wrong. You can watch this in your own life. Listen to the reasons you want to give in response to that question. In fact, there is no reason. Its all just chemistry. Women understand this at a biological level. Because women go through a regular menstrual cycle in which their chemistry is constantly changing, they are generally less apt to look for reasons for emotions. They know that the changes in their moods are due to a mechanical function of their body. They don't go around saying, 'I have my period so I'm going to quit my job.' In other words, they don't turn chemistry into a reason.

EMOTIONAL MECHANICS: THE UPSIDE AND THE DOWNSIDE

By explaining the mechanics of the emotional system, there may be the assumption that something can be done. This is not true. Knowing how the emotions work does not give you any power or advantage. What it gives you is recognition of the fact that you cannot escape your basic emotional mechanics. Knowledge is not power, nor can the emotional wave be controlled. It is our inner chemistry, and is not meant to be controlled. The only thing you can do is watch the wave curving up and sliding down again. However, being aware of your emotions opens up the opportunity for a different form of experience, because it eliminates the identification with the experience. This is pure meditation in action. The awareness that the high end of the wave soon becomes a low end enables the emotional being not to identify with the peaks of hope and the troughs of pain anymore. Awareness can help to accept the wave pattern as something natural and even transcendent.

Most emotional people live a lifetime of fighting the low end of the wave. People want to be only happy, and if they are not, they assume something must be wrong with them. They are desperate to find the high end of the wave and feel like a failure when they notice that the low end of the wave keeps coming back. It is really a blessing to recognise that this is all only a mechanism that has to be understood and surrendered to. Either end of the wave can be beautiful in the sense that it does not have to disturb one's inner tranquility. That is what awareness is for. Awareness is not about giving tranquility to your nervous system. We are alive and this nervousness drives us. But there is a deeper kind of tranquility. It is deep inside us, and it is rooted in the simple understanding of how one's vehicle works. There is nothing more to it than that. If you accept how your vehicle works, the by-product is inner tranquility.

If emotional people go through the whole spectrum of their wave, their knowledge can be extraordinarily deep, because it includes all the single perceptions at the different points along the wave. Imagine a photographer who wants to understand the nature of a flower. The Splenic photographer goes out, sees the flower and takes one picture spontaneously. For them, it is perfect. But for the emotional person, a single picture can never be enough. They have to take a whole serious of pictures of that flower. They have to stay out there the whole day long, watching the changing light, experimenting with perspective, trying different films etc. By the end of the day, they know how that flower looks in the dawn light as well as the dusk light, and all the different timbres in between. They could fill a portfolio with all those impressions. They even know the fragrance of the flower because they have touched it and smelt it.

Even though emotional people may feel they are at a disadvantage because they cannot be truly spontaneous, they have a different gift in life. The emotional person operating throughout their wave has many, many perspectives upon any subject. It is these collected perspectives, as one moves through the wave, which brings great depth to the emotional being. When you know somebody through your wave, you know them with a great deal of depth. You see various aspects of their nature depending on where you are in your own wave, and by the time you get through the full cycle of that, you have grasped their essence. This is the true gift of the emotional being, and yet none of it is possible unless they cultivate patience.

THE UNDEFINED SOLAR PLEXUS

We have already seen that all undefined centres are open and vulnerable to the conditioning of those centres that are defined in others, or by the chemistry of another undefined centre that happens to complete a channel. We also know that undefined centres act like amplifiers of the defined centres. With this in mind, we can turn to the undefined emotional centre and discover one of the great misconceptions on this planet. This is that the majority of people who think they are emotional or over-emotional are in fact the very opposite. If one were to do a statistical analysis of all the people who are taking up the couches of therapists, psychologists and psychiatrists around the world, you would most likely discover that an extraordinarily large percentage of them have undefined emotional systems. In other words, these people are continually going up and down on the emotional wave of somebody else, magnifying it and identifying with it.

EMOTIONAL INSTABILITY

People with undefined emotional systems are often the great victims on this planet. They have a tendency to suffer from emotional instability, often being chaotic because all of their life they have felt out of emotional control. They usually also suffer from a deep-seated fear of rejection, which is rooted in their childhood. Growing up, undefined emotional people take in and reflect back the chaotic emotional waves of others and at some point they are usually punished for that. They can also be very disturbed because of the enormous pain they store in their emotional system, which they are totally unequipped to handle. They are the most vulnerable people in the world.

It is in the Solar Plexus Centre that we find guilt, blame and shame, and nowhere are these afflictions more apparent than in the undefined emotional system. Emotional people can very easily manipulate undefined emotional people who are unaware of their design, and they often do so, even at an unconscious level. The result is that the undefined emotional centre takes on a great weight of guilt that is actually stored as memory within their bodies. They are not genetically designed to handle these emotional burdens, because they do not belong to them. Thus, they try to get rid of them in seeking out some form of therapeutic help.

When an undefined emotional person understands their own mechanics, it is really a huge relief for them, and they begin to let go of all these patterns that have never belonged to them. Now they can understand why their emotions often seem volatile and overwhelming, and why for example, they can go from being calm to being furious in the blink of an eye. They can begin to realise that there has never been anything wrong with them, but that their emotional state depends entirely on who is in their aura. Just seeing their mechanics takes an enormous burden off their shoulders. Emotionally open people are actually designed to be totally cool when they are on their own, and they need time to be alone to clean out all the emotional conditioning that are constantly taking in. Through the mechanics they also learn that they can never make an emotional decision, because it will never be their own decision unless it comes from a cool place within them. Whenever an undefined emotional person feels uncomfortable in the aura of someone, they have only to remember to simply leave the room, and go away to be on their own.

THE UNDEFINED SOLAR PLEXUS IN RELATIONSHIPS

It is one of the ironies of our genetics that we are only attracted to what we are not. Our genes determine our survival as a species, which means that they have to keep on bringing together unusual genetic material in order to further the possibilities of evolution. In other words, it is the undefined centres in your design that are the most attractive to you in life. Let's think about the implications of this for the Solar Plexus Centre, which is not only the place of emotions, but also the source of pleasure and pain.

If you have an undefined Solar Plexus Centre, you are going to be genetically attracted to emotionally defined people. It is their potential to bring real pleasure into your life that is going to turn you on. The very chemical capacity of their sexuality, whether through need, desire or passion, is what is going to condition you.

Let's say you have an undefined emotional system and you meet someone who is attracted to you and they're emotional. Through the conditioning, you are going to be even more attracted to them. Then imagine how disappointing it is for you to wake up with them the next morning when they are at the low end of their wave. Their low wave is mirrored in you, and thus their discomfort with you is magnified in your discomfort in being with them. The result is chaos and misunderstanding.

Whether we are emotionally defined or undefined, patience is a guiding theme for us when it comes to our relationships. Generally speaking, when most relationships come together, it results in a defined Solar Plexus. Thus, the majority of human couples are emotional in their definition as a partnership and have to recognise mechanically the golden rule of the emotional centre. 'No truth in the now' means that it is essential for us to wait things out in order to find our clarity.

THE BEAUTY OF THE UNDEFINED SOLAR PLEXUS

There are great advantages to the undefined emotional centre, but only when we become aware of it. Like any undefined centre, it holds great potential for wisdom. In this case, the wisdom is about emotions. By taking in other people's emotional wave, the undefined Solar Plexus Centre is a barometer of the emotional health of those around them. They are the only ones who can ultimately tell us whether the emotionally defined are making any progress in learning to be patient. The undefined emotional person has to learn to come to terms with the sensitivity of their emotional system. We cannot escape emotional conditioning.

However, we can learn to surf the waves that are right for us, and undefined emotional people know that apart from pain there is also great pleasure in meeting emotionally defined people. The great pleasures of the Solar Plexus are sexuality, food, passion, excitement, romance, and music. This centre is rooted in quality of life and sensuality.

THE CONDITIONING OF CHILDREN

If you have an undefined emotional system, you need to understand your own childhood. Let's consider the themes of child rearing and abuse. Abuse can be physical, sexual, emotional or mental. Imagine what it is like when you have a child with emotional definition, and you have a father who is undefined emotionally. When that child gets angry with the parent, the parent gets twice as angry with the child. This kind of energy pattern goes on escalating until finally the parent snaps, and something terrible happens.

One of the classic patterns learned by the undefined emotional child is called 'making nice'. To avoid the escalation of emotion in the household, the child becomes the peacemaker in the family, going to enormous lengths to try and keep everyone calm. They do this in order not to have to suffer the reflected emotional pain. The other direction such children may take is to externalise the reflected pain by rebelling. Usually such children become angrier and angrier until they're placed in some kind of therapy.

There are an enormous number of children with undefined emotional systems that are being medically treated for no reason whatsoever. This is the great danger of generalisations. You cannot treat everyone as though they are the same. Consider for example, a child with an undefined emotional system who is sent to a therapist with a defined emotional system. The chaos begins all over again because the child will never know their true nature when faced with such conditioning.

HEALTH AND THE EMOTIONAL SYSTEM

The emotional system runs the world. There is a great deal of unhealthiness in the way in which the emotional system is currently manifested in the world. The biological associations to the Solar Plexus include the kidneys, the pancreas and the prostate. There is a real danger of problems in these areas if those with an undefined Solar Plexus are constantly identifying with the emotional wave and giving Authority to emotions that don't belong to them. If you have an undefined Solar Plexus, your whole life is about protecting your stomach. The moment that the emotional wave comes into the undefined emotional system and it gets magnified, it can create great physical discomfort. Usually this is often experienced as a queasiness or tightness in the stomach. Over time, this can lead to far more serious problems in this area.

In the same way, the defined Solar Plexus that does not wait out the wave and wait for clarity will make the wrong decisions, which will ultimately lead to illness and disease. Many modern health issues across the planet are a direct result of the collective misunderstanding of the emotional motor. The huge rise in prostrate cancer for example, is a result of the male population being uneducated as to their own emotional nature. If people could learn to wait, who knows how the world might change?

	THE SOLAR PLEXUS CENTRE	
	DEFINED	UNDEFINED
NATURAL STATE WHEN ALONE	An up and down wave of emotions that brings deep clarity after time.	Emotionally still.
HEALTHY STRATEGY OF THE AUTHENTIC SELF 'THE GIFTS'	Experiences a very rich emotional depth in life. The highs and the lows of the wave bring passion, excitement and even beauty in the melancholy. Sexually exciting, attractive and warm. Appreciates the lows as much as the highs. Plays hard to get in decisions and cultivates patience.	Ability to watch and surf the emotional wave, soaking up the highs and the lows without identifying with any of it or allowing emotions to drive it. Never makes an emotional decision but waits to be cool. Doesn't run from confrontation, but accepts emotional conditioning without identifying with it.
UNHEALTHY STRATEGY OF THE NOT SELF 'THE TRAPS'	Hugely impatient, makes spontaneous decisions without waiting for clarity. Tends to identify with a particular phase of the wave, making decisions from that point - e.g. low or high point. Makes up external reasons for feelings, rather than simply accepting the inner chemistry. As a result, tries to escape the low end of the wave, always seeking the highs.	Can feel overwhelmed by the emotional environment and try to avoid confrontation at any cost. Lies to itself and others out of not wanting to rock the boat. Seeks the high end of the wave and tries to resolve or process emotional problems. Allows itself to be driven by emotions of others, or can become so scared of emotions that it runs away from people and relationships altogether.

SUMMARY OF THE SOLAR PLEXUS CENTRE

- The Solar Plexus Centre will eventually be our third awareness, our spirit consciousness.
- In our current evolutionary step, we are learning to deal with the Solar Plexus Centre as a powerful motor.
- Its frequency is the wave and its fears emerge as nervousness.
- The themes of the Solar Plexus Centre are: feelings, emotions, and sensitivity.
- The function of the Solar Plexus Centre is: emotional clarity and emotional well being.
- The defined Solar Plexus Centre is always the Authority: there is No truth in the now. Wait out the wave.
- The undefined Solar Plexus Centre has to avoid all emotional decisions.
- Biologically, it relates to the kidneys, the prostate, the pancreas and the nervous system.
- The Golden Rule of the defined Solar Plexus: there is no truth in the now.

TO FEELINGS, AS FAR AS I'M CONCERNED

'How are you?'

'How are you feeling?'

Dangerous questions, these, asked unwittingly every day. People don't want the real answer. The safest response, the one I usually give, is 'Fine, thank you'. If I'm feeling particularly whimsical I ask, 'How long have you got?' That's guaranteed to make the inquirer back away hurriedly.

Actually, the first response is usually true, if it could be qualified. 'Fine, thank you, as long as I don't look too hard' is more the mark. If you have a defined emotional centre, this is about as close as it gets.

Many years ago I found the following poem by DH Lawrence, and it appealed to me then; it appeals to me even more now:

TO WOMEN, AS FAR AS I'M CONCERNED

The feelings I don't have, I don't have.

The feelings I don't have, I won't say I have.

The feelings you say you have, you don't have.

The feelings you would like us both to have, we neither of us have.

The feelings people ought to have, they never have.

If people say they've got feelings, you may be pretty sure they haven't got them.

So if you want either of us to feel anything at all

You'd better abandon all ideas of feelings all together.

All my life I have been at the mercy of my emotions. I thought everybody felt like I did. I realised that how I felt had a powerful and sometimes devastating effect on those around me. People were 'fine' when I was 'fine' and in a good mood. It gave them a very pleasant ride. If I were not so fine others usually gave me a wide berth – I was too much to cope with. 'Histrionic' and 'sentimental' are two of the kinder epithets that have been used to describe me.

Whenever I needed to share my feelings, I did not want people to fix things, just to listen and try to understand. I just wanted to feel valid. The words a) 'Snap out of it', or b) 'You'll be all right: you always are', although a) possibly well meant, and b) true, are woefully inadequate at the best of times. At the worst of times, they just added fuel to the fire. I might as well have been from another planet as far as others were concerned. I felt people went out of their way not to upset me, and this pussyfoot approach made it worse. I learned that not to let go was best, and became good at pretending. The real thing was too real.

Sometimes the extremes these emotions took me to were quite frightening. The ecstasies could be great, but the agonies were sometimes almost unbearable. I always wanted to be cool, calm and collected, but I could never rely on this, no matter how hard I tried. Anywhere, anytime I could erupt into an emotional outburst, positive or negative, a bit like not even knowing you were near the edge of a cliff until you fell off. You do not have to do this to know it will hurt when you get to the bottom.

I now know that both my parents were undefined emotionally. My very presence obviously sparked things in them I was not aware of at the time. I was taught that you kept your feelings to yourself and did not display them in public. This hurt, too. I can remember at one family funeral that my hand was gripped tightly and 'Don't you dare cry' whispered in my ear. I understand why, now, but did not understand then. Where else did you cry, if not at family funerals?

Over the years I realised that it was not a good idea to rely on the feeling of the moment. Decisions made at either end of the emotional roller coaster were not the wisest, I discovered. Meditation helped the extremes, and led to a greater state of awareness about how emotions worked, and how not to get attached to them, but this was not enough.

My first Human Design analysis was a revelation. There was nothing wrong with me: I did not need to be fixed. The discovery of the chemistry of the wave in a defined emotional centre, that prism of delight and pain, and most of all how it affects both myself and others, was true enlightenment. Reasons were no longer important, just the thing itself. All that need for validation could stop and I could enjoy the roller coaster for the first time.

So, how do I feel now?
FINE!

Ros Taylor
Emotional Manifesting Generator

THE PRICE OF PASSION

I have an undefined emotional centre. Oh … to be filled up in this centre has been my life pursuit. Emotions have intrigued me forever. This pursuit has taken me into so many situations without care, without thought, just the seeking of the passion. The absolute bliss that fills you up and transforms you into another place, a cocoon of pure feeling, no mind, no instinct, everything else dissolves into oblivion. A sense of 'this is what being human is about' … Just to swim in this sea of feeling, simply, feeling an energy so intense, so pure … So clear, there is no confusion, no denying its Presence.

My most favourite thing was being in crowds of people, e.g. at a concert, anything live that got all the emotional people emoting all over the place. You could just be so immersed in the atmosphere, it was amazing I didn't recognise at the time why I loved it so much, not until Human Design. Now I know what the attraction was.

When I lived in the USA, a time in my life when I was exploring the meaning of life, I came across a young Guru from India who became my teacher for a while. What intrigued me and attracted me to this teaching was the way I felt when I was with these people. The bliss you can feel in an open emotional centre in a group of thousands is magical. 'How we delude each other, and ourselves'. The problems came when I didn't feel this bliss. When I was on my own and couldn't find a way to connect with this inner feeling. What was wrong with me? Why could I feel it in the presence of these 'enlightened' people, and yet not have this experience for my very own? This had to be something special. I thought this was the answer to life, this feeling of bliss, what everyone was looking for and should have.

I realise now how my whole life has been conditioned by feelings. Looking for what feels good and trying to fix what feels not so good. This became my authority in everything I did.

So, the price I have paid for this passion is myself. Everything I am has been totally overshadowed by the pursuit and wonderment of this centre. I now realise the enormity of our open centres and why we become such experts in these areas, because that's where we spend our lives.

Linda Lowery
Unemotional Manifesting Generator

4. DIRECTION

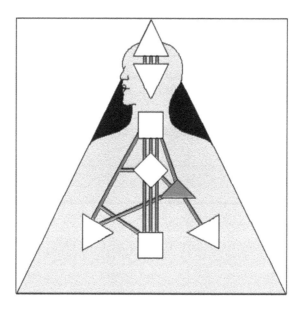

The final three centres, the Heart Centre, the G Centre and the Head Centre may at first glance appear to have little in common with each other. The Heart Centre is one of the four motors, the G Centre stands alone as neither a motor nor an awareness nor a pressure centre, and the Head Centre is a pressure centre like the Root Centre.

However, these three centres do share a commonality, and that commonality is direction. The Heart governs our direction on the material plane, the G governs our direction in relation to all other objects in the Biverse, and the Head governs the direction of our evolving consciousness as a species.

4.1 THE HEART CENTRE: FORM
EGO AND WILLPOWER

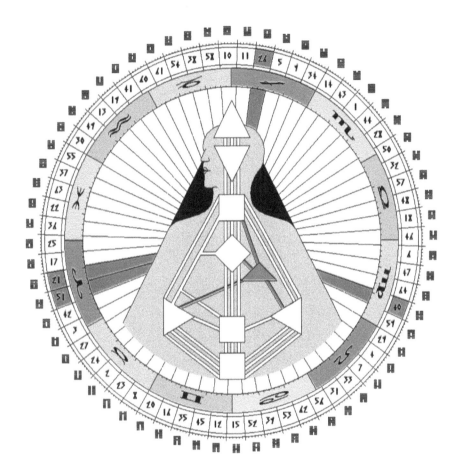

The Heart Centre, also known as the Ego Centre, is an energy system within the body. It is one of the body's four motors. It is the centre of willpower and ego. Although it looks rather small and simple with only four gates, this centre is actually very powerful and very complex.

Thematically, the Heart Centre is all about living on the material plane, and it represents the will to survive on the material plane in established communities. This centre is about making our daily bread, it is about living in harmony with each other, and it is about bonding and bringing children into the world. As a directional centre, it alone is responsible for the creation of all our societies and cultures.

BIOLOGICAL RELATIONSHIP

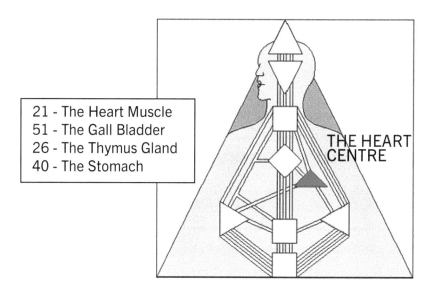

21 - The Heart Muscle
51 - The Gall Bladder
26 - The Thymus Gland
40 - The Stomach

THE HEART CENTRE

In its biological nature, the Heart Centre is very complex. Each of its four gates represents a crucial aspect of our physiology. In the 40th gate, you have the stomach. When the stomach is full, the ego feels good, but when the stomach is empty, the willpower in the 40th gate is driven to go out and find something to eat. In the 26th gate, you have the thymus gland, the gland responsible for the creation of our immune system. When a fetus is in the womb, it is the thymus gland that actually designs the immune system. Thus this channel 26/44 is the only direct connection between the Ego and the immune system in the Spleen.

For the first three years of life, the thymus gland establishes the way in which the immune system will work. The power of the Ego is our main shelter from disease because it is the Ego that releases B-cells that fight disease. Physiologically as well as metaphorically, the Ego is a warrior. The other two gates of the Heart Centre are the 51st gate, which represents the gall bladder, and the 21st gate, which represents the heart muscle itself. Because we find all these organs systems of the body within this centre, it is obvious that it can be the source of many physical problems if a person is unaware of its mechanics in their individual design.

FREE WILL

When we talk about the Heart Centre there is something that is very important to understand. There is a distinction here between will as energy - as we find it here in this centre - and the philosophical concept of free will. Willpower is a powerful energy that arises out of the Heart Centre, but free will is something altogether different. As provocative as it sounds, according to Human Design, free will is nothing more than a myth.

In their great vanity, human beings think that they have a free will. And yet, science has actually shown that everything that we think, say or do is initiated in the deep gray areas of the brain, less than one half-second before we are consciously aware of it in our neo cortex. In other words, if I go to move my hand, the neurons that sent the message to move my hand actually fired before I 'decided' to move it. As any Generator who lives their design immediately experiences, free will is an illusion. It is life that chooses. We as individuals have no choice. We are cells within a huge organism, and the collective 'mind' of the organism chooses through us.

It is only when we identify with our choices that we actually participate in the great illusion of free will. When we awaken through living our own design, we are able to step back from the role we are playing, which is essentially what our design represents. Through our surrender, we see life playing and choosing, and like good passengers, we can sit back and enjoy the ride. Human beings are reactive rather than creative. Free will implies that we control our own process, however we do not. Human beings are here to manifest consciousness in form, but they have no control over any of this. In fact, the very expression 'free will' is a contradiction in itself, because willpower always has to be directed towards a goal. Thus it can never be free. It has to be related to something that you desire.

THE DEFINED HEART CENTRE

Another of the great generalisations we are conditioned to believe in since birth concerns the issue of willpower. Our societies expect that we should all have an endless supply of individual willpower. However, Human Design shows us again that all such things are relative. There are those in the world who have consistent access to willpower. We call them strong-willed. These are usually either people whose Ego is defined and connected to the Throat or whose Ego is defined and connected to the Sacral. Only through definition can the Ego and its willpower emerge consistently.

There are vast numbers of people who are born with undefined Ego Centres, and these people have inconsistent willpower by design. Because it is human nature to survive and succeed, willpower tends to be a value that is exalted, and we are seen as handicapped, lazy or weak when we do not have this wilful capacity. As in the case with all the undefined centres, the strength of this kind of conditioning can break a person's spirit, causing them to suffered terribly within themselves because of what they perceive as failed will.

The defined Heart Centre, as long as it is either connected to the Sacral or Throat, is designed to make promises. It is designed to commit its willpower to goals and targets. If such people do not use the power of their Ego in this way, they will not live their full potential. When a defined Ego makes a promise, you know they have the power to back it up. This doesn't mean they will necessarily back it up and keep their promise, but the point is they have the ability to do so. This is why it is so important for them to make promises that they want to keep; otherwise others will soon lose trust in them.

THE MISUNDERSTOOD POWER OF THE EGO

People with defined Egos should never let anybody repress their sense of 'I'. The ego tends to have a very bad reputation in the world. Society tends to condition us that the ego is arrogant and selfish and should be transcended. For someone with a defined Ego, this is never possible. A defined centre is a fixed theme from life to death. If you have a defined Heart Centre in your design, enjoy the fact that you are an egoist! You have a natural sense of self-value and self-esteem. There is nothing more human than someone with a defined Ego. If they commit their energy in a healthy way, they will give you their absolute loyalty. Defined Egos need to work in life. They have a mechanism inside of them, which always tells them when to work and when to rest.

The ego is a greatly misunderstood power in the world today. Ironically, it is the undefined Egos that have suppressed the defined Egos in the world. Ego is an energy that can appear arrogant, even though that is simply its natural power emerging. Egos are taught from childhood to repress their natural sense of power. These are people who are not easily overruled by others. If they suppress their nature by trying to be 'humble' in order not to upset others, the chances are they will suffer an illness of the stomach or heart.

UNDEFINED HEART CENTRE

The undefined Heart Centre is always looking for willpower. These are people who are conditioned to be go-getters when by design they are not. They wish they had the courage to be willful, and they are determined to prove to themselves and others that they can be. The undefined Ego always thinks it has something to prove. They are always comparing themselves to all the defined Egos and asking themselves questions like 'Why can't I get what they have got? Why can't I be faster or better than them? Ironically, such people have nothing to prove. As we have seen, all human beings want what they are not.

People with undefined Heart Centres have to understand that they cannot rely on their willpower to be consistent. If you have an undefined Ego and you want to conquer the world, you had better make sure that the person beside you has a defined Ego, so that you can take advantage of their conditioning. People with undefined Egos often have a huge problem with self-esteem, undervaluing themselves greatly. However, if they understand their own mechanics, they will see that there is nothing wrong with them, and thus they never need feel a failure in life.

For the undefined Ego, hearing and understanding these dynamics can lead to a real release in the pressure they put themselves under. Undefined Egos are classic overachievers. They try to out-compete everyone else because of the inherent insecurity they feel in not having a defined Ego. Of course, these people don't know that they have an undefined Ego, and their ignorance leads inevitably to disaster, usually based around their health.

The Heart Centre is called the Heart Centre for good reason. It is the heart of what it is to be a human - to work, to make money, to support the family and the community, and to be rewarded for doing so. An undefined Ego has to understand its limits. These are not people who can push their way forwards in life by sheer force of will. If they force themselves in life, it is usually their heart that pays the price. Many undefined Egos end up dying of heart attacks.

THE CONDITIONING OF THE UNDEFINED HEART

Let's imagine a scenario: You have an undefined Ego, you are a smoker and you want to give up smoking. All of a sudden, one day, you see an advertisement for a therapist who specialises in empowering people to give up smoking. You sign up for the programme. The only problem is that, unbeknown to you, the therapist has a defined Ego.

The scenario that follows is one of the classic reasons for what psychology calls 'the transference of Authority'. You, the client surrender your Authority to this therapist with a defined Ego. The reason you surrender is because the conditioning is so strong. Remember that undefined centres reflect and amplify the chemistry around them. So, from the moment you sit down with this therapist, you are being conditioned by their willpower. When you are with them, you feel such a huge empowerment within your body, and you are absolutely convinced that you can and will give up smoking.

You leave that person's office with a great swelling feeling of power within you; as though you could do anything you pleased. Then, an hour or so later, out of the aura of the therapist, you begin to slide back into your old habit, and before you know it, you are having a cigarette again. Naturally, you feel weak, guilty and self-judgemental. However, every time you return to the therapist, you feel the same power welling up within you and because you keep identifying with it, you keep going back in the hope that you can somehow make it last.

Of course, you cannot fix what is not broken in the first place, and so you begin to slide into a pattern of feeling inadequate and disappointed in both yourself and others. Patterns such as the one above are incredibly common at all levels of our society. The undefined Ego is the breeding ground for co-dependent relationships.

Reflection and magnification is a very important reality to grasp. When the therapist said to you that you could do anything you wanted through the power of your will, and you believed him, it wasn't your own willpower that was coursing through your body. It was his willpower, and you were magnifying it through your undefined Ego. It was all conditioned in you, and the moment that you broke the aura, you went back to having an undefined, open Ego system that operates inconsistently.

PROMISES — THE GOLDEN RULE

The Golden Rule of the undefined Ego is very simple: don't make promises. There is nothing more damaging to the health of an undefined Ego than trying to make and keep a promise. The simple reason for this is that the undefined Ego can never know that they have the consistency of will to back up their promise. They may be able to force themselves to keep their promise, but at what cost to their own health?

These people are not designed to be wilful, and if they pretend to be (and many of them do a very convincing imitation), their heart, stomach and immune system may well pay the price. The undefined Ego should simply avoid putting themselves in situations where they have to be willful. Whenever they make a promise they can literally break their heart.

THE GIFTS OF THE UNDEFINED EGO

The reality is that willpower for the undefined Heart Centre is wholly dependent on the people around them. They can actually take advantage of the conditioning of defined Egos around them when they understand their own mechanics. They can be even more competitive than defined Egos, and they can enjoy that competitiveness without identifying with it. Because their Ego is undefined, they can be very sharp judges of other people. They can feel who is capable of what within a community, family, organisation or business. Ultimately their great wisdom is to show others how to value themselves for their own abilities, and how to make the most out of those abilities by gaining maximum reward for the minimum input of energy.

	THE EGO/HEART CENTRE	
	DEFINED	UNDEFINED
NATURAL STATE WHEN ALONE	Has consistent access to will power.	No impulse to be willful.
HEALTHY STRATEGY OF THE AUTHENTIC SELF 'THE GIFTS'	Has a natural sense of self-esteem. Handles the competitive field through exerting its will power or not. Can thrive on the material plane through making deals, bargains or promises to ensure it is valued. Knows that it is here to work, but its true aim is to make enough money as as not to have to work.	Has no need to make promises in life. Has nothing whatsoever to prove to anyone. Enjoys and takes advantage of the conditioning of defined Egos (e.g. competitive field) but can let it go at any time. Loves to spend money.
UNHEALTHY STRATEGY OF THE NOT SELF 'THE TRAPS'	Can engender distrust in others if it shies away from striking a bargain or making a promise. Can become ill if it allows its will power to be controlled or suppressed. However, can lose the trust of the community if it overvalues its importance. Shies away from having to work and loses its true power and self-esteem.	Compares itself unfavourably with defined Egos and tries to overachieve in life by sheer force of will, driven by lack of self-worth. Either believes it is competitive and damages its heart and stomach, or shies from competition for fear of losing. Makes promises it can't keep.

SUMMARY OF THE HEART CENTRE

● The Heart Centre is a powerful motor that drives our willpower.

● It has very important biological attributes: the heart, stomach, gall bladder and thymus gland.

● The theme of the Heart Centre is to survive on the material plane.

● A defined Heart Centre must keep its promises for its own self-esteem.

● The Golden Rule of the undefined Ego is: don't make promises.

4.2 THE G CENTRE: LOVE
LOVE AND DIRECTION

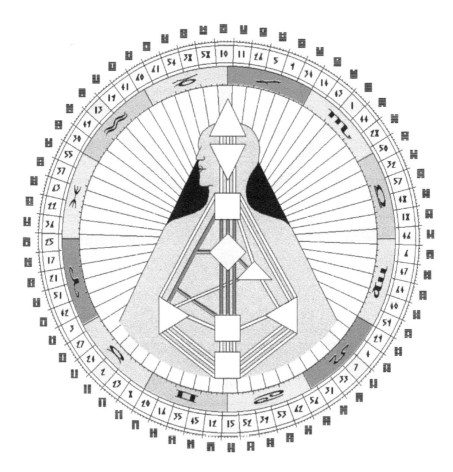

In the geographical centre of the human Bodygraph, is a diamond-shaped centre called the 'G'. Also sometimes known as the Self Centre, no one knows for sure why it is called the 'G'. It is one of the mysteries of the Human Design revelation. What is for sure is that the G Centre governs our direction in life. It acts like an individual global positioning system within us, holding us on our trajectory as we hurtle through space. As such it is one of the most important and extraordinary centres in the Bodygraph.

THE MAGNETIC MONOPOLE

To understand the G Centre requires an understanding of the magnetic monopole, which we have already heard about in Part I of this manual. The magnetic monopole, we may recall, is like a magnet with only one pole, and all that pole does is attract. The monopole is rather like the centre of our galaxy, in that it creates a centre around which all else revolves.

The centre of our galaxy in turn, revolves around another greater centre, hidden from our view. Within this spinning picture, every object has its own monopole, and together, all the monopoles spin in harmony. In other words, what the magnetic monopole does is holds us all together in increasingly wider fractal patterns that are all knitted together. It is somewhat similar to being a cell within a great body. The monopole actually creates the illusion that each cell is separate from each other, even though each cell is a tiny fragment of the greater pattern. In this last respect, the G Centre shows us our individual identity in relation to the whole.

This attractive force that holds everything together in the biverse is the true source of all love. In other words, love is the force that holds the universe together. In Human Design, we distinguish different forms of love. There is this greater love that moves us through life, connecting us to our destiny or geometry. Then there is sexual love, which is rooted in the emotional system, and finally there is love as attraction, which arises when people meet each other in a channel. This is called electro-magnetic love. In the G Centre, the main theme is love of the self. This love pulls everything into its oneness again. As we saw above, the secondary function of the magnetic monopole is to give us our correct trajectory in life as we move through space. Thus, the nature of our identity is about love in movement.

THE HARMONIC STRUCTURE OF THE G CENTRE

The eight hexagrams of the G Centre form two giant crosses in the zodiac. Both of these crosses have names. The first one is called the Cross of the Vessel of Love and it is made up of four gates – the 10,15, 25 and 46.

The second cross is called the Cross of the Sphinx and is made up of another four gates – the 1,2,7 and 13. The names of these crosses show us the two great themes of the G Centre; the Vessel of Love being about love and the Sphinx being about direction.

THE CROSS OF THE VESSEL OF LOVE

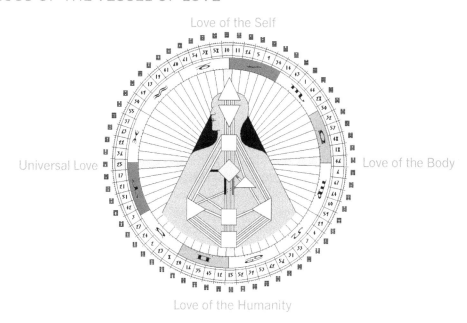

The Cross of the Vessel of Love represents the four archetypes of the love of the self, which we study in depth during the Rave Cartography training.

THE CROSS OF THE SPHINX

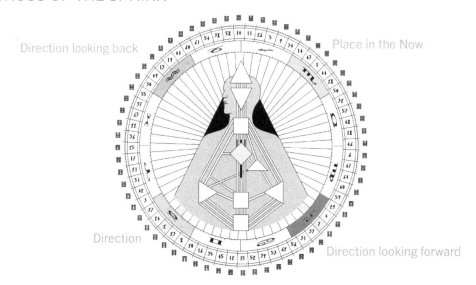

The Cross of the Sphinx represents the four archetypes of direction. Its name is derived from the ancient astrological archetypes of the sphinx: the man (13), the lion (7), the bull (2) and the ancient sign for Scorpio, the eagle (1).

These two crosses are very magical. They are exactly equal in their distance to each other in the wheel. In order to move from one G Centre hexagram to the next it takes exactly 8 steps. This is based on the fact that the Chinese broke up the I-Ching into 8 groups which they called houses, with each house consisting of eight different hexagrams. To understand this graphically, look carefully at the bottom three lines (called a trigram) of each hexagram around the wheel. You will see that each of the eight houses of the wheel is made up of hexagrams whose bottom three lines are identical. In other words, the eight hexagrams of each house share the same foundation.

AS ABOVE SO BELOW

The symmetries of the G Centre are endless. If for instance, you look at the 1st and the 2nd hexagrams, you will see that they are exact mirrors of each other. The first hexagram is all yang lines, while the second hexagram is all yin lines. No matter where you look in the wheel and whichever hexagram you look at, you can see its exact mathematical opposite mirrored in the opposite side. You can see that this wheel is like an ancient mandala for all life, as it graphically represents the duality of life. If you look again at the hexagrams of the Vessel of Love, you will see that they are all cusp hexagrams, meaning that they form the points where two astrological signs meet. For example, you may see that the 25th hexagram is partly in Pisces and partly in Aries. Thus, the four hexagrams of the Cross of Love cover eight zodiacal signs, whereas the Cross of the Sphinx includes the other four remaining zodiacal signs.

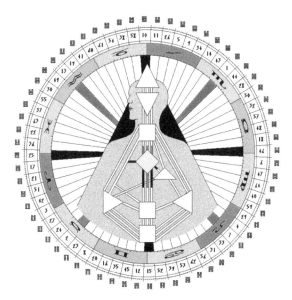

The point of all this geometry is that collectively, the hexagrams of the G Centre represents the lead hexagram of each of the eight houses of the I-Ching as well as being directly connected to all twelve signs of the zodiac. These eight gates of the G Centre represent the macrocosm that becomes the microcosm in us. 'As above, so below'. The G Centre is where everything flows inward to the magnetic monopole, and the monopole is the core of love within each of us.

THE CALENDAR

The sacred geometry of the G Centre is an archetype that man has unconsciously aligned himself with for millennia. The eight hexagrams of the Cross of the Vessel of Love also mark the beginning of the four seasons.

The spring equinox takes place when the sun is in the 25th hexagram on March 21st. The summer solstice always occurs when the sun is in the 15th hexagram on the 21st of June. The autumn equinox is when the sun is the 46th hexagram on September 21st and the winter solstice begins when the sun enters into the 10th hexagram on December 21st. Seeing these patterns rooted in the G Centre actually allows us to use the Wheel as a kind of genetic clock to map the cycles and seasons of our individual lives as well as the movement and direction of the totality.

BIOLOGICAL RELATIONSHIP

Biologically, the G Centre relates to the liver and to the blood. We know that alcohol is destructive for the liver and thus it is also destructive for the self. It can literally destroy a person's identity. It is also of note that once damaged, liver cells cannot be replaced.

There is a great tradition in stating the spiritual nature of the liver, which has its root in ancient Indo-European ideas about the importance of the liver. Many ancient cultures believed that reincarnation took place through the liver. In Human Design terms, this is correct, because the magnetic monopole is directly responsible for our incarnating process. It draws us into the body and it takes us out of the body.

THE DEFINED G CENTRE

People with a defined G Centre have a fixed identity. They also have a fixed potential for love and a fixed direction in life in which they have to trust. For example, if someone has their identity defined through the channel 29/46, known as the Channel of Discovery, they are here to discover what life is, otherwise they cannot live out their true identity and ultimately be fulfilled in life. The defined G Centre always chases after the undefined G Centre because essentially the defined G is eternally looking for itself. In this sense, it is fundamentally narcissistic.

People with defined G's have a fixed way of being. Their character, morality and culture are consistent, and because of this, they are always looking for someone just like them. When the defined G meets the undefined G, what they actually meet is a mirror of themselves, and they say to themselves: 'They are just like me. I feel terrific with them'. The most common relationships are those between a defined G and an undefined G. This is just the basic law of being attracted to what you are not.

RELATIONSHIPS BETWEEN DEFINED G AND UNDEFINED G

Because the defined G Centre is a fixed aspect in someone's design, it is impossible for such people to understand what it is like not to have a fixed sense of self. This difference can lead to misunderstandings between people with defined and undefined G Centres. For example, the defined G Centre assumes that the person they are with (who has an undefined G) is exactly like them, and when the undefined G is in their presence, this is exactly true.

However, the moment the undefined G goes out into the world, their identity changes depending on whom they are around. This often leads to the defined G feeling frustrated with the undefined G because they begin to hear that they are living a double life. Below is an example of this kind of conditioning:

JILL   JACK

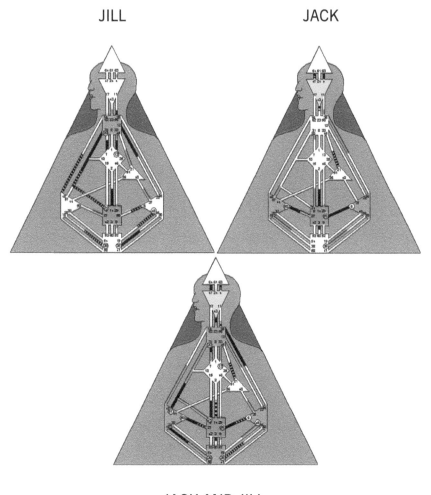

JACK AND JILL

You can see from this relationship that Jill defines Jack's G Centre. It is actually defined through the 13/33, known as the Channel of the Witness, one of the main themes of which is retreat. Thus Jack is quite happy living with Jill in their home. He is actually conditioned by her to stay at home and enjoy the privacy of their life together. However, the moment Jack walks out of the door of the house, he is released from the conditioning field. Then he goes to see his friend Bill, who also has a defined G Centre but who conditions Jack through the 29/46, the Channel of Discovery.

Suddenly Jack takes on a seemingly new identity. He leaves his role of being a witness and becomes a pioneer. He finds himself going out to all kinds of wild parties with his friend Bill. This is how conditioning works. The irony here is that Bill, in his fixedness, cannot understand why Jack lives such a boring home life, and Jill thinks Bill is simply a bad influence of Jack. Both think they know the 'real' Jack. People with defined G Centres really do have a fixed way of being, and as long as they accept that that is how they are, they can always find fulfilment.

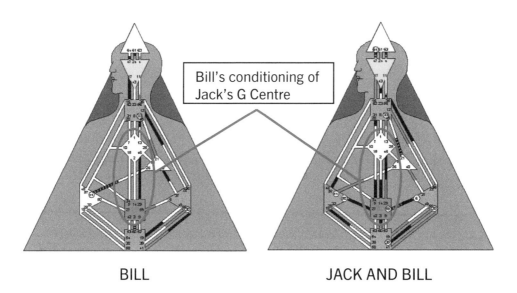

Bill's conditioning of Jack's G Centre

BILL   JACK AND BILL

THE UNDEFINED G CENTRE

From the above example, you can have a fairly good impression of what it might be like to have an undefined G Centre. With his undefined G Centre, Jack has no fixed sense of identity. In other words, he changes, and often quite dramatically, depending on who is connecting up his G Centre and how. The truth is, no one knows the 'real' Jack, and least of all Jack.

People with undefined G Centres have no fixed sense of identity or direction. Such people have to understand that there is nothing wrong with having no fixed identity. For instance, it can be very difficult for them to feel comfortable with a single role in life, but this need not be a handicap. The undefined G Centre is like a chameleon, blending with whomever they are around and fitting in everywhere, but at the same time, nowhere.

WHO AM I? — THE CONDITIONING OF THE IDENTITY

If you have an undefined G Centre, it simply isn't possible for you to know who you are. You are no one and everyone. In a nutshell, you are whomever you are with; since the person standing next to you is conditioning which role you are playing. Therefore the great conditioning for the undefined G Centre is to try and seek who they are. Remember, human beings always want to be what they are not, and the undefined G Centre wants to find a fixed identity in life. They really want to know who they are. Because of generalisations, it is assumed by most people that you are supposed to know who you are and what you want in life, and especially in the New Age. People think there must be something wrong with them if they don't know who they are and what they are supposed to do in life.

For the undefined G Centre, not knowing who you are is not a handicap. It is not the same as not knowing how you operate. As long as you understand your inherent design and its mechanics, you have no need to philosophically guess what your nature is. You are who you are with, and it always changes. So many people with undefined G Centres spend their whole lives trying to get to the bottom of who they are. This is why the understanding of one's design can be such a profound liberation. Having an undefined G Centre means that you can embrace anyone because you mirror who they are. This doesn't mean that you have to like them or dislike them. It simply means that you can identify with them and they immediately feel comfortable with that. The undefined G is rather like being on a divine stage. You get to wear all the costumes and play all the roles, but underneath you will always know that you are acting.

WHERE AM I SUPPOSED TO GO? - THE CONDITIONING OF DIRECTION

With its eightfold sacred geometry, the G Centre acts rather like a compass within us, locating both where we are, and where we need to go next. It is no wonder then, that so many undefined G Centres spend their lives feeling lost, since they do not have an internal compass that tells them where to go and what to do. The undefined G Centre has an inner compass that only spins according to the G Centres of other people. In other words, with an undefined G, your direction in life is entirely influenced by others, whether you like it or not, or whether you know it or not. These people are deeply impressionable to other people who define their G Centre, and it is very easy for them to become immersed in somebody else's identity and life.

PLACE — THE GOLDEN RULE OF THE UNDEFINED G CENTRE

There is a Golden Rule for the undefined G Centre, which is: 'If you are in the wrong place, then you are with the wrong people'. This simple mantra is all about place. As we have seen, the undefined G is conditioned to go in certain directions according to the people they meet in life. In this sense, they are designed to be guided by others, though not in the normal sense of the word. By experiencing different directions coming through different people, the undefined G learns which direction is right. The secret to knowing which direction is right is the physical place you end up in. If your inner compass doesn't feel right in a certain house, restaurant, country or workplace, then the one who took you there was not the right person.

TAKING ADVANTAGE OF CONDITIONING

Undefined G Centres have to see the beauty of their mechanics. Everybody who has a defined G Centre is their servant! All the defined G's show them where everything is, taking them to the important people, places or jobs. This is the great advantage of the undefined G Centre. They never have to worry about where to go, because it is always up to others. That is a wonderful thing to know, and simply knowing the mechanics of this will change their life. Instead of feeling lost, the undefined G can enjoy what is shown to them. They can enjoy the places they are brought to, and they can take advantage of the guidance of others.

If for example, you have an undefined G Centre and you are looking for a new place to live, all you need do is call either your friends or a few agencies and tell them. Then you sit back, wait and experience what others have selected for you. Just by physically going to each place, you will know immediately which one is right for you. This is simply something you feel by being there.

Furthermore, if someone has found the right flat for you, you have to understand that you don't owe them anything. You don't have to become their partner or their friend, and you don't need to hold on to them just because they were of service. You either pay them for their service, or if they happen to be a friend, you simply thank them. This is the way the open G Centre loses its vulnerability. If you ever try to locate your own flat, or try to find your own direction in life, you are always vulnerable. If you have a undefined G Centre, then your gift is ultimately to be able to recognise what is the right direction by experiencing many different directions.

LOVE

The final big theme of the G Centre is love. Whereas the defined G Centre has a fixed experience of love, the undefined G is always uncertain about it. There is nothing more tantalising to an undefined G Centre than a person who brings a sense of love into their life. The undefined G is forever trying to hold on to love in their life. They can be very uncomfortable with the fact that both love and a sense of direction for them comes and goes. It can make them very unhappy and leave them with a sense of feeling lost. They have times in their lives when they know where to go and other times where they don't.

It is so important to understand that this does not mean that they cannot find consistent love in their life. Rather, for the undefined G, love is something that is always a mystery because it always comes from others, and it comes in many guises and roles. They simply have to be very patient and wait to see what kind of love life offers them. The moment they stop trying to chase after love, they allow it to come to them, and when it comes, they always know whether it is right for them or not.

SUMMARY OF THE G CENTRE

As you can see, the undefined G has many traps to avoid and many gifts to offer. These people have to let go of trying to direct their life. They have to surrender to something outside of them, and when they do so, they can really see the eternal dance of life. They can see the vast movement of all the monopoles around them in all beings.

They also have to understand that they are never going to have a fixed identity in their life. That does not matter, nor does it make any difference to them. The most important point about the undefined G Centre is that they are not here to initiate. They are here to be initiated by others. When they are able to accept this about themselves, their true potential emerges. So many of the dilemmas that haunt the human experience are simply the result of ignorance. In not understanding the mechanics, one is so easily propagandised by other people, by books, teachings or philosophies.

The greatest potential of the undefined G is to truly understand the nature of love and the nature of direction, and direction in the larger sense of the word - the direction of humanity - where we are all going together. However, the vast majority of undefined G's lead a life of uncertainty. They lead a life in which they are afraid more than anything of never finding love, and a life in which they are never really certain that they are going in the right direction. Ultimately, there is no better guide in life than an undefined G Centre. By letting go of their need for identity and love, they are able to step into anyone else's shoes and offer truly loving, correct guidance.

	THE G CENTRE	
	DEFINED	UNDEFINED
NATURAL STATE WHEN ALONE	Fixed sense of self.	No fixed sense of identity.
HEALTHY STRATEGY OF THE AUTHENTIC SELF 'THE GIFTS'	Has a reliable sense of self and knows what it is able to give. Has a defined way of offering love and does not need to cling to love coming from another because it always knows it can return to itself. Has an ability to know where and how it wants to make its progress. Potentially has a defined sense of its quest or mission in life.	Deep sensitivity to environment and location. Knows it will never know who it is. Enjoys the mystery of playing many roles that are conditioned by others and surroundings. Allows others to be way-showers without becoming attached to them. Surrenders to not knowing where it is going next. Allows love to come and go without holding on to it.
UNHEALTHY STRATEGY OF THE NOT SELF 'THE TRAPS'	Can get depressed if it represses what it knows deep down about itself, in order to please others. Can behave/feel like an undefined G if it has never got to know itself. Will feel lost and have no sense of its place or direction in life.	Tends to get lost in who or what it has merged with. Tries to find and hold on to love, and to assume a strong identity often drawn from others. Worries about not being in control of its own life, and tries to latch onto things and people that give it a false sense of security and solidity.

- The G Centre has two themes: love and direction

- Its biological attributes are the liver and the blood.

- The hexagrams of the G Centre are all an equal distance from each other (45 degrees).

- The defined G Centre has a fixed identity and thus a fixed way of experiencing their self.

- The undefined G Centre experiences love and direction through the conditioning of defined G Centres.

- The Golden Rule of the undefined G Centre: 'if you are in the wrong place, you are with the wrong people'.

4.3 THE HEAD CENTRE: CONSCIOUSNESS
THE PRESSURE TO THINK

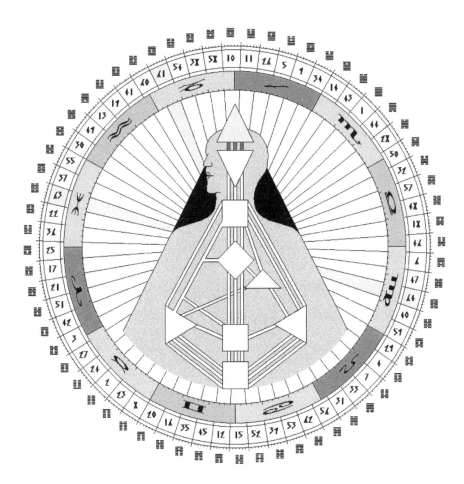

Just as we began our journey through the centres with a pressure centre, we end our journey with a pressure centre. We have travelled from the Root to the Head. Just as the Root Centre represents the pressure of the form to stay alive and evolve, the Head Centre represents the pressure of consciousness to find its way deep into the form.

As we saw at the beginning, we humans are in a pressure sandwich. We have seen how our direction on the material plane is focused through the power of the Ego Centre, and how our direction as an evolving species is focused through the Love within the G Centre. Now we can see how our direction as a consciousness is focused through the mind through the medium of the Head Centre.

The Head Centre is unique within the Bodygraph. Although it is a mirror of the Root Centre, it does not have access to any centre other than the mind, which it duly puts under continual pressure. This is the very pressure of consciousness itself. This continual pressure that the Head Centre exerts of the Ajna Centre ensures that the human mind cannot stop thinking and therefore evolving. It is what we know as inspiration. This pressure of inspiration is often a difficult pressure to deal with. It can bring about a great deal of mental anxiety, because inspiration is always about what has not yet been grasped. This is why there must be doubt and confusion that come with the pressure.

On the other side, there is a genuine sense of wonder and mystery that can follow the inspirational process as it emerges from the Head Centre. The moment that this pressure is present, in other words, when the Head Centre is defined, it creates the pressure on the brain to conceptualise and make sense of the inspiration.

Inspiration is rooted in both our visual and acoustic life. It comes from within us, but only as a result of experience. In other words, you see something or you hear something, it goes through you, and suddenly it comes back to you as a question. Something that you see or hear creates a mental pressure within you that you have to somehow resolve, and this pressure can lead to a deep anxiety.

BIOLOGICAL RELATIONSHIP

The Head Centre is associated with the pineal gland. It is the outlet from the deep, grey areas of the brain into our neo-cortex. It opens up into the Ajna Centre where our pituitary glands are, the master glands, the master endocrine glands for the functioning of our body system.

Biologically, the Head Centre is associated with our pineal gland. It is the outlet from the mysterious deep gray areas of the brain into the neo-cortex. One way to understand the function of the pineal gland is to imagine it as a kind of border guard. It sits in its little box on the border, and it has a flap that it can lift up and down to allow passage in and out of its border. In other words, it filters information between the deep gray areas and the neo-cortex. This is precisely what happens between the Head and Ajna Centres. What people normally assume when they hear the word 'inspiration' is that it is coming from the outside.

However, as we have seen, it actually comes from inside us, since the vast majority of our mental processes actually take place in the dark. We don't know anything about it. More than 90% of our mental process takes place in the deep gray areas of the brain where we have absolutely no access to them. Inspiration comes from within as a result of experience.

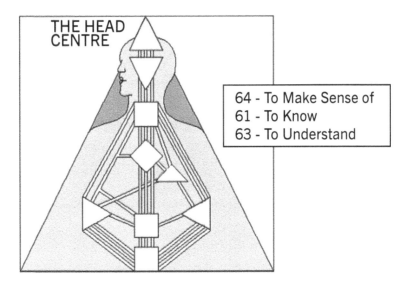

THE HEAD CENTRE

64 - To Make Sense of
61 - To Know
63 - To Understand

There are three basic pressures in the Head Centre.

THE DEFINED HEAD CENTRE

Someone with a defined Head Centre always creates the potential for inspiration in their environment. They actually put everyone else under pressure to think! How they condition others is dependent on the nature of their definition in the Head Centre. They can inspire flashes of inspiration (61/24), they can invoke doubts and/or answers (63/4) or they can create confusion and/or resolution concerning the past. Such people are always fueling a specific conceptualising process, which means that there is a mental pressure in these people to understand, make sense or know exactly what their inspiration is about. The bottom line is that they cannot stop thinking, and they are not designed to!

The final point of importance regarding the Head Centre is that it is not a motor, not does it directly connect to one. In fact, it is more cut off from the four motors than any other centre in the Bodygraph. People with defined Head Centres should always heed this warning: inspiration is not about doing - it is about reviewing.

THE ANXIETY OF THE HEAD CENTRE

The anxiety of the Head Centre is essentially the anxiety that comes with trying to explain a deep concept that you see within your mind. The anxiety is about whether you can communicate your inner concept clearly to someone else.

HEAD TO AJNA

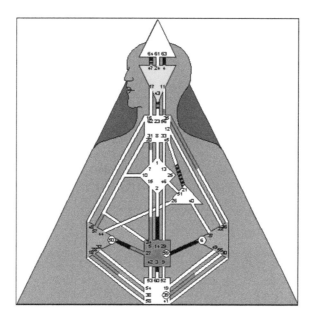

In the example above, you can see a very common configuration in Human Design.

Notice that the Head Centre is defined to the Ajna Centre but there is no connection through to the Throat. In such cases, there is a terrific mental pressure on this person to express their thought process. Every time they are able to express the inner workings of their mind, they will feel a temporary release in the pressure. Ironically however, without the consistent connection to the Throat, these people can never say what they want to say when they want to say it. They are dependent on others to condition the timing and style of their expression.

This is the design of anxiety, and it is also the design of someone who can be enormously inspiring for others. The price you pay for being inspiring to others is this continual pressure to make sense of your own thought process. So often, these people can feel very uncomfortable. They can suffer from headaches or migraines or problems with their eyes. This does not mean to say that they are unhealthy or that they cannot be deeply fulfiled. As ever, it is simply a matter of honouring one's Type and Authority.

This kind of mind, being cut off from the Throat, is known as a projected mind. If you have such a mind in your design, the key for you is to wait for others to invite you to speak. If you have the courage to resist the pressure to speak, your aura will do the talking, and the pressure of your Head Centre will actually force the other to invite you into a conversation.

THE UNDEFINED HEAD CENTRE

JULES VERNE

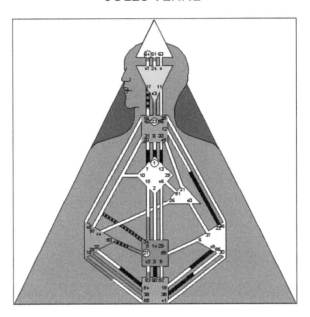

If you have an undefined Head Centre, then the process by which you conceptualise is always conditioned from the outside. Think about that for a moment. It means that other people influence the way you actually think. In other words, you have no fixed style of thinking. You may have a fixed style of expression like the example above (the channel from the mind to the Throat), but you cannot think in a consistently similar pattern.

These people are conditioned in terms of what inspires them. What fuels their conceptualising process is coming from the outside. An undefined Head Centre suffers from a mental pressure, which is simply not theirs but is conditioned and magnified in them whenever they step into the aura of a defined Head Centre.

If you have an undefined Head Centre and you think there is a mental concept that you need to somehow resolve, you are probably being conditioned, either by someone else, or the transit of a planet. All you need to do is relax and allow it to pass. Otherwise, you will end up with your head in a complete spin because you are trying to understand something that is unnecessary to understand. The resulting anxiety can be very uncomfortable for you because you have no fixed way of processing these nagging questions within you.

Conditioning is not the enemy. Ignorance of conditioning is. Any conditioned field can bring positive impact, including the Head Centre. What is essential to grasp is that we cannot afford to give Authority to what we are not. In other words, somebody can pressurise us at the mental level to think about a certain dilemma that has to be resolved. But if it is not our dilemma and it is not our Authority, then it is not our responsibility to carry that burden that we cannot resolve in the first place.

THE HEAD AND ROOT CENTRES

The same conditioned patterns in the Head Centre operate in the same way in the Root Centre. However, when you know what is you and what isn't you, you have a huge advantage in life because you don't have to get lost in the pressure. You can take advantage of it or avoid it altogether. In recognising what you are not, you can totally eliminate its pull over you. The net result is a great potential for wisdom. In the Head Centre, this wisdom is the potential to be able to recognise whose aura really is inspiring, and whose aura simply leaves you feeling confused or pressured.

As human beings, it is a fact that we are under constant stress. We are under stress to stay alive and remain healthy through the Root Centre, and we are under pressure to communicate and inspire each other through the Head Centre. These are the two essential processes that humanity is designed to go through – evolution and involution – to grow and know.

△	THE HEAD CENTRE	
	DEFINED	UNDEFINED
NATURAL STATE WHEN ALONE	Continual pressure to resolve thought process.	Lack of mental pressure.
HEALTHY STRATEGY OF THE AUTHENTIC SELF 'THE GIFTS'	Accepts mental pressure without trying to turn it into action or escape it. Knows confusion, doubt and clarity as natural processes with their own inner timing and resolution. The ability to uplift and empower others with both insights and inspiration.	Knows that questions are never its own questions. Therefore doesn't take on the pressure of other people's need for answers. Always open to new insights and mental sparks coming from who is in its aura, and loves to be 'filled' with inspiration. Enjoys the pressure to know more without becoming identified with it, or overwhelmed by it. Withdraws when confused or doubtful. Can know clearly who is inspiring and who is confusing.
UNHEALTHY STRATEGY OF THE NOT SELF 'THE TRAPS'	Turns mental pressure in on itself, allowing itself to be driven into deep anxiety, self-doubt or depression when it can't resolve the pressure. Attempts to resolve the pressure through outside action, making hasty and inappropriate decisions. Inability to remain patient, resulting in missed opportunities for inspiration.	Can easily become lost or overwhelmed by doubt and confusion which actually belongs to others. Ends up trying to resolve other people's questions. Takes on the worries of others and tries to release mental pressure through action ('I want this resolved now'). Unable to clean the head out and relax in its own space.

SUMMARY OF THE HEAD CENTRE

- The Head Centre is a pressure centre but not a motor.
- The Head Centre's theme is inspiration.
- Its biological attribute is the pineal gland.
- It fuels the mental conceptualising process.
- The defined Head Centre has a fixed inspiration.
- The undefined Head Centre is inspired by who is in their aura.

PART 3: A GUIDE TO TYPE AND STRATEGY

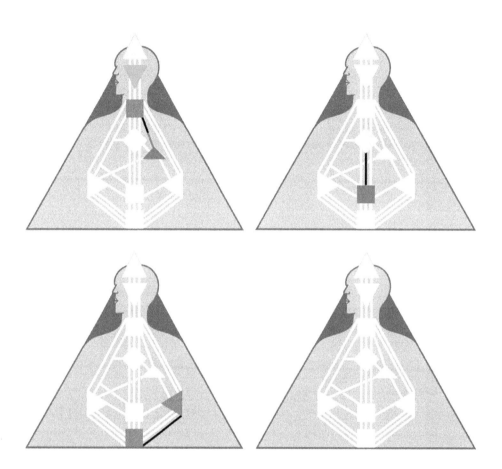

1. INTRODUCTION

This third and final Part of this book is really the most practical and accessible information you will learn. Whether you are using this book to further your own personal interest in Human Design or whether you intend to train to the next level or even the professional level, this information about Type, Strategy and Authority is the essence of Human Design itself. This is the information that changes people's lives. No matter how keen you may be to learn more about the depth and detail of Human Design, it all comes back to Type, Strategy and Authority in the end. If all you can tell someone is how their Type works and what their Authority is, you are giving them the most powerful information they can ever receive from anyone. The simplest truths are always the most profound.

The majority of this section of this book is focused on Type. Strategy is in fact a by-product of Type, since you can only access your Strategy by first knowing your Type. We have also discussed Authority, our own unique decision-making process, throughout this manual. Authority is a deeply complex subject that is fully covered in the professional Analyst programme. However, you can find a brief summary of the main Types of Authority after the following section on Type.

TYPE

According to the current statistics (2002), the human population is made up of an estimated 6 billion people. Despite this incredible diversity, Human Design reveals that we are in fact, not nearly so complex as we like to think. According to detailed and verifiable statistical analysis of thousands of birth charts, it has been shown that there are only four basic Types of human beings. Despite the fact that each Type still has millions of different variations, it is classified by a pattern that is very simple to understand, and each Type has a Strategy that is very easy to follow. The four names given to the Types are: Manifestors, Generators (including Manifesting Generators), Projectors and Reflectors.

Type, a key construct in Human design System theory, was verified in 5 samples of 5000 birth records drawn at random from a general population. Type holds up as a highly significant differentiating variable in all groups far beyond the 99% level of confidence. Furthermore, all groups tested have consistent frequency of occurrence of each Type. For further information about these fascinating discoveries, go to www.ravelifesciences.com.

Type is the most important aspect of Human Design. By only knowing your Type, you can immediately begin the process of finding out your own nature. It is a tool to help you accept yourself and recognise your own values. To live your Type is to release your true being into life. It is nothing less than being yourself. Your Type and its Strategy is rather like the user's manual that goes with your particular genetic vehicle. It allows you to live the life you were born to live.

As you may already have begun to see, Human Design is a vast and complex science with many far-reaching implications. However, the simplicity of this system is revealed in the ease of its practical application to any human being's life.

Essentially, all you need to know in life are two things – your Type and your Authority. Whilst your Authority governs your decision making process, your Type is the mechanical Strategy stamped within your genes. It governs how you enter into any situation in life. Authority comes after that, when you are required to make an actual decision. By only knowing these two things about yourself, your life can be healthy and deeply fulfilling.

AUTHORITY: A SUMMARY

There are in fact, a total of ten different types of Authority within the field of Human Design. Each type of Authority represents a different way of making decisions. However, for the purpose of simplicity, we have only discussed the most common types of Authority in this training. These are summarised briefly below:

1. Emotional Authority – Wait out the emotional wave before making any kind of decision
2. Sacral Authority – Wait to respond, ensuring that you are not being conditioned by someone near you to take a decision
3. Splenic Authority – Follow your spontaneous instinct without hesitation
4. No Authority – Reflectors and mental Projectors – talk your decisions over with as many different people as possible before deciding on a course of action

EXPERIMENTATION IS THE KEY

Many people are deeply sceptical when they first hear about Human Design. To many it looks like another 'new age' self help system or cult. If you know anything about Human Design, you know that it is nothing but practical, and all you have to do is try it. You can study Human Design for the rest of your life and never get to the essence if you don't actually apply it in your own life. It isn't about believing in anything. It is about experimentation. All you need to do is to experiment with the pattern and the Strategy of your Type to see its power in action.

Over ninety percent of the world's population has a design to wait, and over ninety percent of those people have probably never tried waiting. Experimentation relieves you from trusting in something. You get to test it for yourself and then you find out whether it's valid. Most Human Design websites now have a free chart service, which means that anyone can easily find out which Type they are and immediately begin their experiment with their design.

HOW TO CLASSIFY A TYPE

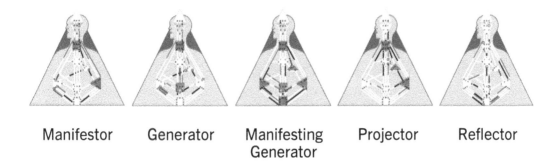

Manifestor   Generator   Manifesting   Projector   Reflector
                                        Generator

Type is derived from definition in the Bodygraph, and in its classification, it is both the Throat Centre and the Sacral Centre that play the key roles. There are only two basic possibilities that determine Type – there are energy Types and there are non-energy Types. In order to be an energy Type, you must have either a defined Sacral Centre and/or a motor centre connected to the Throat. (The 4 motors are: the Sacral (the primary life force energy), the Heart/Ego (the ego, will power), the Root (the adrenal pressure) and the Solar Plexus (the emotional system).

In order to fit into the non-energy category, you cannot have either a motor defined to the Throat or a defined Sacral. Any other configuration in the Bodygraph will confirm that you are a non-energy Type. The two energy Types are the Manifestor and the Generator and the two non-energy Types are the Projector and the Reflector.

Type in Human Design has nothing to do with the many personality types found in popular or esoteric psychology. We are talking about the existence of four distinct genetic Types, which determine our psychology, health, sexuality, relationships and even our dream life. This Type structure establishes the genetic order of the totality.

We will discuss each Type by looking at it through a variety of different lenses: Technical Definition, Role in History, Gift and Handicap, Strategy, Relationship, An individual Example, Metaphor, and Some famous Participants.

2. THE MANIFESTOR

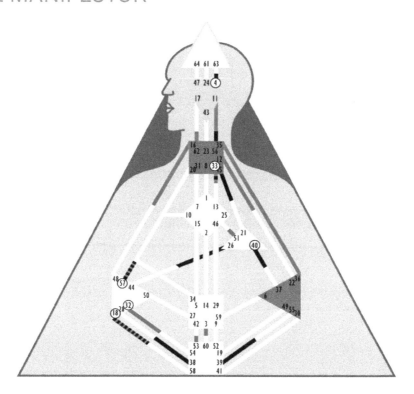

TECHNICAL DEFINITION

To be a Manifestor, you have to have one or more of three motors directly or indirectly connected to the Throat, and the Sacral Centre cannot be defined. In other words, if either the Heart/Ego, Solar Plexus or Root Centres are defined and connected to the Throat Centre, you have a Manifestor. Statistically comprising only 8% of the population, the Manifestor is comparatively rare.

ROLE IN HISTORY

Each of the four Types interlocks with each other, creating a natural genetic hierarchy on our planet. These evolutionary genetic roles are currently undergoing major changes as we transform from being a seven-centred being to a nine-centred being. Historically and mythically speaking, the role of the Manifestor has always been that of the king or high priest. They have ruled throughout history, simply because they are the only pure 'doers' and thus it has been easy for them to gain all the power and Authority. They have established the basic human laws, and all the spiritual and material hierarchies that we see today are a result of their attempt to maintain control in order to avoid being challenged. This is a distinctly patriarchal and male energy, known as the Yang/Yang principle. Because of the current evolutionary changes, the traditional rule of Manifestors is coming to an end. Genetically speaking, the age of the Manifestor came to an end in 1781 around the time the planet Uranus was discovered.

GIFT AND HANDICAP

The one Type that everybody dreams of being is the Manifestor. This is because it is the one Type that is immediately capable of acting on its words. Manifestors are designed to 'do', as opposed to the other three Types, who are all designed to wait. Thus, the Manifestor's gift is just this - to act independently without waiting. Because of this gift, it often seems to Manifestors as though the rest of the world is somehow going in slow motion. The Manifestor can get things done without interacting with other people, and in this respect, Manifestors do not easily fit within society, as they are always perceived as 'uncontrollable'.

It is because Manifestors are designed to operate 'independently' within the hierarchical structure of the four Types, that their very gift often becomes their greatest handicap. Society holds a general concept that all human beings should depend on each other, and society doesn't like exceptions. This is why Manifestors are usually vehemently resisted from the moment they are born. They are regarded as dangerous and unpredictable, which ironically is why everyone idolises them.

MANIFESTORS AS CHILDREN

Let's first talk about how Manifestor children are treated by their parents. The parents of Manifestor children are often stressed, because from a very early age, their children appear to be beyond control. They do not behave like the other children they compare them to, and thus many parents attempt to deal with this problem using hard discipline. Unfortunately, Manifestors do not respond well to enforced controls, since their nature is to be independent. From a very early age, most Manifestors receive the message that they are not permitted to be themselves, and the result is a latent anger that builds inside them as their self-esteem slowly gets eaten away. The irony is that most parents think they are doing the best for their child by disciplining them in this way, and yet for the Manifestor, it feels like being put inside a cage.

Depending on their conditioning, Manifestor children will respond to this kind of enforced control in one of two ways – they either rebel or conform. If they rebel, they will rebel against the whole world, and the chances are that they will end up feeling angry and cut off from other people. They will begin to believe that they need no one and that no one needs them. If they conform, they will deeply repress their rage and live a life based on fear. The greatest fear of the Manifestor is that they will be punished simply for being who they are.

So how should parents react when they discover they have a Manifestor for a child? They need to realise that they have a child that will need different standards from most other children. All children need some discipline, but the parent needs to understand the sensitivity of their child to discipline. Every time they tell their child not to 'do' something, it will feel as thought the world has caved in to that child. Thus, parents need to treat their Manifestor children with respect. They have to teach them to simply ask permission before they do something. That way, they won't be so hurt when they are denied permission to do something.

Furthermore, if the parents do have to deny them permission, they always have to give a sincere and logical reason why they cannot do that thing. Manifestor children need to learn good manners and courteous behaviour more than other children, because this is the way they can protect their children from being hurt and punished later in their lives.

STRATEGY

When we talk about Strategy in Human Design, we are talking about behaving in such a way so as to eliminate resistance and support the process of becoming oneself. Your Strategy is not a philosophy or a gimmick. It is simply the way in which your vehicle is genetically designed to operate. This is why if you don't live your Strategy, you feel unfulfilled and cannot find true peace in life.

The Manifestor's Strategy is different according to their age. As a child, they should be guided to ask permission before they do something. As an adult they have to inform others before they do something. This is their law. This is their way to eliminate resistance in their lives and to protect themselves from being alienated and misunderstood. When they obey this law, they will learn for themselves what a difference it makes to their lives. People stop resisting their actions and support them. This may seem so simple for a Manifestor, but you have to understand how difficult it is for them to tell anyone anything before they do it. It is simply not something that occurs to them, and they often resent having to inform others of their actions. However, if the Manifestor has the courage to experiment with this Strategy, they will find out for themselves what a difference it makes.

Remember, it is never too late to start being who you really are. When you start living your Type, you will see how rewarding that can be. You discover something inside of you that was always hidden due to conditioning. You find that place inside yourself that you can always trust to know what to do about anything in life. Your Strategy is a way to discover your uniqueness so that you no longer have to compare yourself to others. It lets you know that it really is okay to simply be you. The other thing that your Strategy ensures is that you will find your inner essence and learn what the true purpose of your life really is. These things naturally unfold when you begin to follow your Strategy.

THE EMOTIONAL MANIFESTOR

For every Type, there is an emotional version. The emotional Manifestor is different from the non-emotional Manifestor of them informing before they act. Emotional Manifestors have to wait out their wave before they know when, why and whom they should inform about what. The defined Solar Plexus means that they always have to await clarity first, so the emotional Manifestor can't just do, since they cannot know what they are about to do is correct in that moment. It can feel like a real burden for such people to hold back the emotional energy and wait. However, it always pays off in the end.

THE MANIFESTOR'S QUESTION: WILL I BE ALLOWED?

Each Type has a special archetypal question. The Manifestor's question is 'Will I be allowed?' As doers, they don' t need anybody to act and therefore they are deeply reluctant to ask others. They can feel as though they are giving over their power to others when they inform, so they usually don't bother informing and just take what they want when they want it. Their greatest fear is compounded in those words 'Will I be allowed?' Most Manifestors never learn how to ask or how to inform, and thus they do end up being punished, which feeds their distrust of others, and so the circle continues.

THE MANIFESTOR IN RELATIONSHIPS

Because Manifestors are able to do what they want to do when they want to, this is how they tend to behave when it comes to relationships. Especially in men, this can emerge as an attitude of: 'You are mine. I am taking you'. Relationships that begin in this way will end in disaster. Added to this, Manifestors have a latent theme of anger carried from childhood, thus if they do not enter into a relationship correctly, they bring this theme into the relationship. Many problems of violence in relationships stem from Manifestors who did not follow their Strategy to begin with. Manifestors need to be courteous and inform the other person that they want them. This is the hardest thing in the world for Manifestors to do! It usually makes them angry just to think about it - 'Why do I have to tell her? Doesn't she know? Doesn't she see it?'...

All Manifestors have to face their initial fears when they inform someone that they love or want to be with them. They do not know how they will be answered. They simply have to trust in the integrity of their Strategy. If it doesn't work out, it would never have worked out. Let's take an example of how a Manifestor not informing can damage a relationship:

A Manifestor is sitting with his partner and they are watching TV. The Manifestor is a smoker, and he finds he is out of cigarettes, so according to his nature, he simply goes out to get a new pack at the shop down the road. The moment he leaves, his partner begins to worry about where he may have gone. Manifestors are totally unpredictable, and she has no idea where he may have gone. These are the kind of fears that a Manifestor aura can elicit. So the partner begins to get really angry and imagines all kinds of scenarios in which the Manifestor is playing out her fears. All of this is totally unknown to the Manifestor, who comes back from the shop smiling with a pack of cigarettes. Of course, when he returns five minutes later, he faces a storm of anger and protest - 'Where have you been? Why do you always do that? Why didn't you say where you were going?' The Manifestor is absolutely shocked because in his mind all he did was innocently go out for a packet of cigarettes. He has no way of understanding why his partner turns that minor incident into such a drama. Then the fireworks begin and a shouting match ensues, in which all the Manifestor's stored rage from childhood erupts.

Every time a Manifestor encounters this kind of resistance, it brings up all the anger from their childhood. All along, some simple information would have averted the crisis. If the Manifestor had simply informed his partner 'I'm just going out for ten minutes to get some cigarettes', there would be no resistance and no crisis.

EXAMPLES
An Individual Example: Ra Uru Hu

RA URU HU

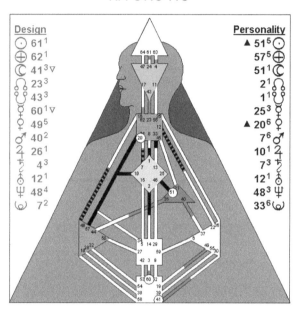

Ra Uru Hu is a Manifestor. He has the Heart Centre connected to the Throat by continuous definition. Thus he manifests out of his Ego and acts out of pure willpower. He is a single definition Manifestor because there is a continuous flow of energy within his design since all the definitions are linked to each other.

For Ra, getting things done was never a problem. He was very well educated and has done many different things in his life: he has worked as an educator in both art and science, as an entrepreneur, a magazine publisher, an advertising executive and media producer, an artist, poet, writer and storyteller, musician, composer and performer. He is a thinker, a traveller and an explorer.

We know that Manifestors have a huge potential through their ability to follow through with their words. However, their potential is usually unlived, because human beings, as we have learned, live out what they are not. Thus, Ra never experienced his strength as a Manifestor, because he lived out what he had undefined, instead of what he had defined. He spent the majority of his life not knowing why he was the way he was.

Before coming into contact with Human Design, Ra described himself as a very arrogant, self-concerned and self-possessed man.

It was very easy for him to be like that because of his Manifestor structure. He never informed anybody of what he wanted to do. He left his family without telling them where he was going. He had the ability to do anything, but he never did what he really wanted to do. Most of what he did was tainted with guilt, blame and shame and the expectation of others.

Being ignorant of the mechanics of his design, Ra lived out the 'not self' of his three undefined motors. The undefined Root Centre conditioned him to constantly seek large audiences in order to get an adrenaline rush. The undefined Sacral Centre led him into myriad diverse partnerships and love affairs, and the undefined Solar Plexus Centre brought him a chaotic emotional life.

CONDITIONED AUTHORITY

When you are looking at the design of a Manifestor who doesn't know their own design, instead of seeing a tremendous strength, you only see the manifestation of their weakness. The main reasons Ra was weak was because he never informed anyone of what he was doing and he constantly gave Authority to his undefined Solar Plexus Centre by making emotional decisions. Having found that emotions led to chaos, Ra also found that letting his mind make the decisions was equally unreliable. He ignored his real Authority, which is his Splenic system, because he could not hear it.

He has a very powerful health system as his Spleen Centre is connected to the Throat and in turn to a motor, the Heart/Ego. According to him, it was this strong Splenic system that actually made it possible for him to survive his mystical experience in 1987. Regardless of this, the Splenic intuition that should have guided his life before his experience was simply overpowered by his mind and emotions. The most common experience he remembers from that time was that after something happened, he would realise, too late, that he had known all along what to do or what not to do. This was clearly the instinctive power of his Spleen Centre trying to talk to him.

As an undefined emotional person, he hated emotional tension and felt very uncomfortable around others who were at the low end of their emotional wave. His experience was always that he was calm and cool when he was away from emotionally tense people, so he tended to keep away from people in general. Unaware of his emotional structure, he drew the conclusion that since he simply wanted to be happy and it was evident that others didn't allow him to be, he would rather be left alone. His only emotional theme is based on acceptance and rejection (the 49th gate), which led him to reject others whenever they made him feel unstable and accept him whenever they made him happy.

STRATEGY AND CORRECT AUTHORITY

Ra never lived the life he was meant to live until he had the experience with the voice. Now however, he fully embodies the power of what it means to be an uncontrollable Manifestor. Before his awakening, he was controlled by guilt and shame and by people's sexuality, adrenaline and emotions. Now he is no longer a victim of his undefined centres. He has recognised that he is a Manifestor who has to make spontaneous decisions out of his intuition.

Because his Spleen is directly connected to the Throat, his intuition emerges in the now, allowing him to always trust his spontaneous decisions. Now he also has learned to follow his Strategy by informing people what he intends to do before he does it, and thus he avoids resistance. After going through his deconditioning, he also now has access to the wisdom of his open centres, and he can share this wisdom with others. Out of his totally undefined Sacral Centre he understands well how the nature of sexuality functions. Out of his undefined emotional centre, he learned about all the different frequencies of the emotional wave and how best to deal with it.

We always need to remember that most Manifestors are uncontrollable and dangerous in an unhealthy way, because they do not follow their Strategy. If you look at their open centres, you can always see where their weak points are. People always live out what they are not. Thus, most Manifestors are deeply unhappy because they suffer from being controlled. However, when you tell a Manifestor how their life is supposed to look, they always know you are right, somewhere deep inside them.

As long as Manifestors tell others what they is going to do before they do it, they can use their power without being constantly threatened. The Manifestor has to be allowed his power in order to be uncontrollable. This is their nature and their purpose. Manifestors are the most metamorphic of all the Types, and Ra Uru Hu is a great example of this. Being an archetype of the first true Aquarian teacher, he transmits the knowledge of Human Design and brings a totally new synthesis into the world that will lay the foundation for a new consciousness. His manifesting qualities have helped him to spread it in America, Europe and Asia despite the initial rejection that he met in the beginning, when he tried to publish this knowledge.

SOME FAMOUS MANIFESTORS

Adolf Hitler, Johannes Kepler, Helmut Kohl, Elisabeth Kübler Ross, Krishnamurti, Hermann Hesse, Jack Nicholson, Bruce Springsteen, Mao Zedong

METAPHOR

During this discussion of Types, we will use the metaphor of a football team to understand the role of each of the Types in relation to each other. In this team, the Manifestors would be the forwards. They are the talent, the ones we all like to glamorise. They are the ones that get things done; they are the goal-scorers. Their style is often wild, unpredictable and full of genius. They have a lot of fans, the audience always either loves them or hates them and the press constantly talks about them. But they pay a price for being in that limelight, and the price is often the sense of isolation that comes from others resisting and resenting their true nature. If they can learn humility at the same time as retaining their wildness, then they can live deeply fulfilling and powerful lives.

3. THE GENERATOR

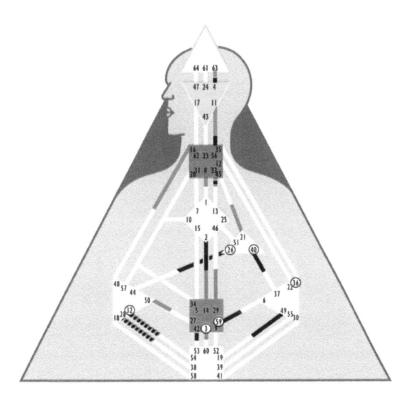

TECHNICAL DEFINITION

It is very easy to spot a Generator in the Bodygraph. You have only to look at the Sacral Centre and see if it is defined. If it is, then you have a Generator. Since Human Design has evolved, we have learned to distinguish between two distinct types of Generator: pure Generators and Manifesting Generators. A pure Generator is someone who has a defined Sacral Centre with either an undefined Throat or a Throat connected to a non-motor. A Manifesting Generator has a defined Sacral and a motor (including the Sacral itself) connected to the Throat.

The ratio in the population is: 37% Generators, 33% Manifesting Generators. Over the past few years, there has been much hot debate within the Human Design community over whether the presence of the Manifesting Generator means that there are in essence five Types rather than four. What is most important in terms of awakening people through their Type is that although there are distinct differences between the two variations, there are four strategies, not five.

ROLE IN HISTORY

Metaphorically speaking, the Generator's role in history has been one of enslavement. Generators have long been controlled and manipulated by the Manifestors, since the Manifestors have always appeared to have the power. Over 70 % of humanity have therefore lived like slaves, being kept ignorant of their true potential and being deeply frustrated from being unable to compete with Manifestors. The new role of Generators however, is something very different. With the natural decline of the Manifestor's power, comes the awakening of the true potential of the Generator, which is to become the builders. As Generators give up initiating and trying to copy Manifestors, their responses to life make them capable of building absolutely anything. The clear commitment of a single awake Generator is an awesome power to contend with. They are after all, the essence of creation and creativity itself.

GIFT AND HANDICAP

Making up over 70% of humanity, the Generator is the most common of all the four Types. We live in a Generator world. Generators have an enormous wealth of energy and power, although they cannot use it directly. As we have seen, the key to the Generator's power is response, and there is nothing more powerful than a Generator who acts out of response. When a Generator waits, they become like a magical black hole that attracts everybody to them. Because the Sacral Centre represents the energy of life itself, this centre exerts a certain pull over everyone within its orbit. When a Generator waits, what happens is that others come over and ask them, because this is precisely what they are designed for. Every Generator has a deep fear that if they do nothing, no one will ask them anything, but every Generator who has the courage to wait soon sees how unfounded this fear is. Generators are something like the priestesses of Delphi, in that you have to come to them and ask, otherwise they give you nothing. This is the perfection of being a Generator.

The great handicap of all Generators is impatience. Most Generators have been brought up to see waiting as a road that leads nowhere, and the result is that they spend their whole lives trying to make things happen for themselves. The irony is that even if they succeed in attaining their dreams, they remain deeply unsatisfied, because they never waited to see what their dreams really were. This is where manifesting propaganda enslaves Generators. Whilst the Manifestor usually knows what they want and actively seeks it, the Generator cannot know what they want until it comes to them and they respond to it. Thus the dreams of a Generator unravel as they go along, but they can never really know what they are until they have attained them.

When you meet a forty or fifty-year-old Generator who has never lived and doesn't know their design, they have no idea who they really are. It is very difficult for them to suddenly change their whole life by waiting to see who they really are. It can be a frightening thing for such people as they are so used to being someone that they are not. They are afraid to be themselves and can be very uncomfortable with the new self that begins to emerge as they respond to life. When you first try to live your design, you have to start at the surface. It takes seven years of hard work to begin the process of being yourself. It is no easy business.

GENERATORS AS CHILDREN

In a certain sense, a Generator cannot know anything unless they are asked. Because most Generators are not correctly understood from an early age, they never develop their natural pattern of response. These are children that need to be asked everything in order that they can feel the quality of their response. Thus, most Generators grow up under the shadow of expectation. They are expected to know what they like and what they want to be in life, and if they do not know, they are expected to go and find out. No Generator can go and find out what they do or do not want in life. They have to wait and see. They do not even know what they want to eat until they respond.

As an example, a Generator that claims to be a vegetarian cannot be living their design correctly, because they do not know how they will respond until the lunch is placed before them. Even though they may have responded to not eating meat for 10 years, there may always come a day when suddenly their response changes, and they eat meat.

The problem, as always, is conditioning, and particularly from the mind. Whether, a Generator has a defined or undefined mind, it will tend to undermine their response by preempting what they think they want. The mind may well say 'mmm, when I get to the restaurant, I'm going to have pasta', and when they get there, they totally deny their spontaneous response from telling them what they really want.

Over 70 % of our planet is frustrated. Over 70% of our planet is made up of Generators. The two themes go together. Most Generators today are in the wrong jobs, living with the wrong people, eating the wrong food and consequently feel a lack of true purpose in life. The main reason for all this frustration is ignorance, and because parents do not understand how to raise children as Generators. The Generator child has to be raised in a way where they feel no pressure whatsoever to know anything until they are asked. For example, you cannot say to a Generator 'Go and clean up your room'. You are not giving them a chance to feel their Sacral respond. Even though they will probably respond 'no' to being asked to clean up their room, you still need to allow them this chance to hear their own response. Then, once you have given them their integrity, you can reason with them that the room has to be tidied!

SACRAL SOUNDS

When Generator children answer with their true voice, they are usually told that this is not polite. The Sacral Centre makes a wide range of grunting, squealing and mewing sounds! Thus these children are forced from an early age to stop making sounds and to articulate in words. This is where the conditioning begins. By being allowed these early response sounds, Generators develop the correct patterns in life, both emotionally and mentally. If they are not encouraged to express themselves through healthy (even if sometimes uncomfortable) sounds, their doorway to the truth closes and they are cut off from developing self-esteem and self-love.

STRATEGY

The Strategy of the Generator is to wait to respond. This Strategy is all rooted in the power of the Sacral Centre. As we have seen in the chapter on the Sacral Centre, it can only express a response through the centre it happens to be connected to. In other words, the Sacral can only respond through one of five centres – the Root, Throat, Spleen, Solar Plexus and G. Every decision that a Generator or Manifesting Generator makes must be rooted in one or more of these five connections.

One of the best ways to understand the expression 'wait to respond' is through the negative variation. In other words, you could also say that the Generator's Strategy is to resist the temptation to initiate. Generators should never take the first step. Action for them always arises out of receptivity. Generators have to trust in the power of waiting and come to grips with being patience.

All the power of the Generator lies in their response. In responding, Generators ensure that it is always they who set the terms, rather than those who ask them. As pure energy Types, Generators also have to see that their Strategy is always at work, 24 hours a day, every day. Their Sacral is the source of life and it will go on responding to life as long as they are alive. In fact, Generators are responding to life all the time. There are so many types of response. You can respond to sounds - rain drops on the windowpane or the wind in the leaves of a tree. You can respond to people in a conversation. You can respond to things you see – a flyer in a shop window or a signpost. Essentially, all life is a response, which is why Generators are the essence of life. The response of a Generator can have the tonal quality of the sacral sounds or it can be simply a silent response, a feeling inside. As long as a Generator doesn't initiate, they are always on track. Generators who experiment with their Strategy almost always get immediate rewards and slowly learn to trust their role in life.

Strategy in Human Design is the key to eliminating resistance. The Generator eliminates resistance through waiting to respond. When Generators follow their Strategy, their tendency to overwork and over commit themselves is one of the first things in their life that comes into harmony and balance. They begin to feel their own life power and learn to share it productively with others on their own terms. If they ignore their Strategy, they tend to get stuck in the wrong careers and the wrong relationships, and instead of seeing their life force generating, they just observe it degenerating into decay.

EMOTIONAL GENERATORS

One of the most powerful and deeply frustrating combinations is a defined Sacral Centre and a defined Solar Plexus Centre. These people have a Strategy to wait to respond which is deepened by having emotional Authority as well. They have to wait to respond and then they have to wait again, to be clear about their response.

If they trust in their design, they will be a deeply surrendered and patient person. If they cannot learn patience, they can be very unhappy, frustrated or angry with their lives.

Emotional Generators cannot respond immediately. They have to play hard to get. When they are asked: 'Do you want this job?' and they hear themselves answer: 'ahuh' they have to add: 'even though it feels perfect right now, I have to sleep on it. Can I let you know next week?' This is their correct behaviour pattern, because they cannot know what to generate unless they have gone through their emotional wave. The Emotional Generator should get used to saying: 'Yes, but...' since the law of the Solar Plexus Centre must always be obeyed – 'there is no truth in the now'.

Emotional Generators have to see that being emotionally defined is not a burden. It is simply not about spontaneous knowledge. It is a way of hearing, seeing and learning that takes place over a movement in time. However, that full movement has much greater depth than the fraction of a second that the Splenic system recognises.

THE GENERATOR'S QUESTION: WILL I BE ASKED?

This question: 'Will I be asked?' is the deepest fear of every Generator. Asking in this sense doesn't have to be vocal. More broadly speaking, it means, 'Will I get the opportunity?' or more succinctly, 'If I don't do anything, will anything ever happen?' For Generators, there is only one way to answer this question, and that is by waiting and trying it out. In the beginning, every Generator has to learn to ride out their frustration. We are dealing here with the Sacral Centre, the centre of life itself, and life has its own timing. If Generators can't wait to be asked, they can never respond, and if they cannot respond, they cannot know what is right for them. Generators get more frustrated because they do not want to wait to respond. They do not think that they will be asked the right questions.

The great irony of being a Generator is that they have the easiest opportunity to become awake of all the four Types. Their path to enlightenment is very simple. All they have to do is respond. Nothing else. If they live that, they will actually see what and who is perfect for them and they will eventually see why the timing moves in the way it does. The Generator is designed to flow with the current of life, taking their cues as they appear. The Strategy is that easy, but the challenge is overcoming the fear of not being asked.

RESEARCH INTO THE FOUR TYPES

Manifesting Generators – You are different!

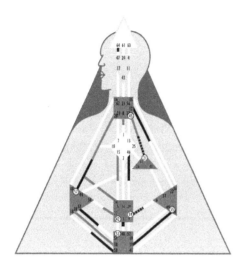 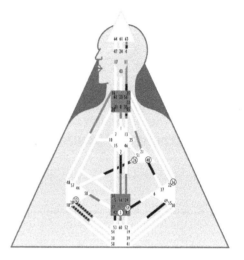

Manifesting Generator   Pure Generator

There has been much talk in recent years within the Human Design community over the differences between pure Generators and Manifesting Generators. Rave Life Sciences (RLS), the US based organisation that oversees all health applications of Human Design has run all kinds of statistical research on the subject of Type, at many different levels. Their findings suggest that there is a far wider chasm between these two types within Types than was previously thought. Indeed, their differences are seen far more clearly when they are asleep!

RLS ran statistical differentiation analyses between all the Types on both waking designs and sleeping designs. When we are asleep, we operate through a different matrix, know as the 'Dreamrave', which shows how we are programmed by the neutrino stream differently when we are asleep. The bottom line is that at this level of awareness, pure Generators and Manifesting Generators are programmed as if they are different Types altogether (for a full description of these findings, please visit the RLS website – ravelifesciences.com). However, on waking, they fall into the same category once again.

What all this research is suggesting is that the two types of Generator are in fact very different at a profound level. Certainly, anyone who has lived with and observed both types of people can experience this difference very clearly. The fact that both the Generators are aligned far more closely when awake shows that they are only similar on the surface. However, when we are looking at Type as a genetic construct, we are only really dealing with the surface of humanity. Type is an extremely broad categorisation of humanity after all. For the purposes of this training, we are only interested in these surface mechanics, rather than the hidden and deeper implications of RLS's findings.

The most important aspect of Type is Strategy, because Strategy has the power to transform a single person's entire life. The conclusion of this discussion is therefore that even though there may be five Types when asleep, there are four when we are awake, because the only thing that is important when we are awake is that we follow one of the four strategies. Manifesting Generators, you are very different from pure Generators, but there is no getting away from the fact that you are designed to follow a Generator Strategy!

OBSERVED DIFFERENCES IN PURE GENERATORS AND MANIFESTING GENERATORS

We know then, that both Generator Types have to wait to respond, since both operate out of the power of the Sacral Centre. However, the greatest difference between the two happens after they respond. Once the pure Generator has responded, they have to go through all the classic sacral stages of development (see the chapter on The Sacral Centre), i.e. they go through the stage of feeling stuck, make a breakthrough, then feel stuck again. This is how manifesting occurs for the pure Generator. However, for Manifesting Generators, it is very different. Once they have responded, they can go right into the action after their response. In other words, they can behave like a Manifestor once they have responded, without the experience of moving through all the different levels of mastery. What often happens to Manifesting Generators in this respect is that they move through their process with much greater speed than pure Generators, and in doing so they usually skip some of the essential steps along the way. It is very common for Manifesting Generators to have to go back to these steps that they have missed earlier on, and as long as they responded correctly in the first place they will not mind having to retrace their steps. The great joke about the two kinds of Generators is that neither is better or quicker than the other. They both arrive at the goal at the same time, but in different ways.

The second difference that has been observed concerns how Manifesting Generators respond. Often the Manifesting Generator will respond by immediately taking action. For example, someone may ask them: 'would you like to go out for dinner?' and their response might be to stand up and start putting on their coat. However, the Manifesting Generator then has to respond to their action to know that it is correct. Thus they may find themselves at the door with coat in hand, only to realise that they would rather stay and eat at home. In other words, they have to respond to their response. This is a subtle but powerful difference between the two types of Generator.

MANIFESTING GENERATORS

The Manifesting Generator is in a sense, a hybrid Type. They are a combination of the two energy Types, the Manifestor and Generator, and they have to balance gifts and challenges from both sides, for example, they have to process both the anger of the Manifestor and the potential frustration of the Generator. They can be the most erratic and impatient of all the Types, but they also have the greatest potential. Below is an extract from the Gene Keys Profiling Pack on Manifesting Generators. We thoroughly recommend these packs for all beginners to Human Design as they illustrate Type, Profile and Authority with great depth and simplicity.

YOUR TYPE AND STRATEGY

You are a Manifesting Generator. You are a pure energy dynamo with the greatest potential of all the Types, even including the pure Generator. Like the pure Generator, your success and fulfilment in life is directly dependent on your ability to be patient. Your Strategy in life is to wait to respond. Patience is likely to be the hardest lesson and the greatest gift in your life, and in this respect you are your own worst enemy.

Within the four Types, you are something of an anomaly. It is as though you are a Manifestor that has somehow been compressed to fit inside a Generator vehicle. This can be a deep dilemma for you since the Manifestor part of you always wants to leap into action while the Generator Strategy always holds you back. You are someone that has to learn things the hard way! Every time you leap into something without waiting to respond you will meet resistance, both from others and from life itself.

As a Manifesting Generator, you are designed to be doing what you love in life. If you are not fulfilled, you will be deeply frustrated and angry. The way for you to find fulfilment is twofold: You must follow your Strategy of waiting to respond, as well as your Authority (outlined separately). Once you have responded to something, you need to double-check that it is something that really feels right for you. Many times, you will begin something only to find a short while later that it doesn't feel right. This is normal and correct for you. If it doesn't feel right, it isn't right.

When you are responding to life correctly you have an advantage over all the other Types. Unlike the pure Generator, you do not have to master things by riding out your frustration. Your Strategy of waiting only governs how you begin new experiences. Once you are in the door, your manifesting power takes over. Having two Types living under the same roof has as many perks as problems. Your highest potential is to counterbalance the raw power and presence of the Manifestor alongside the patience and surrender of the Generator.

PURE GENERATORS

In a certain sense, pure Generators have it easy. They do not have to harness the dramatic power of the Manifesting Generator, and they do not have to deal with such a deep level of impatience and anger that goes with that Type. More than any other Type, the pure Generator is here to attain mastery in life. Once they have learned to relax and respond, pure Generators have to understand their life as a journey through different plateaus. Even though it feels like they keep getting stuck at a certain level, they soon discover that they are never stuck. The moment a Generator is feeling stuck it is an indication that they are about to make an evolutionary leap in their process of mastery.

Ironically, it is at this very point that most Generators give up. So long as the pure Generator begins their process correctly (relationship, career, etc), they will always find the staying power to move through the different levels to mastery. Ultimately, this staying power is their own sense of fulfilment in whatever they are doing.

GENERATORS AND MANIFESTING GENERATORS IN RELATIONSHIPS

Despite what our conditioning may like us to believe, Generators are not here to initiate their relationships. Generators can never walk up to someone and tell them that they want to be with them. Unlike Manifestors, Generators always need someone else or something outside them to initiate their response. When it comes to relationships, Generators have to learn to play with their own Strategy. People new to Human Design often ask the question: 'What happens when two Generators are in a relationship together? If neither of them can initiate the other, what on earth do they do?'

USING YOUR STRATEGY

To answer the above question, you have to understand the difference between 'playing' and 'not initiating'. If you are a Generator, it doesn't mean that you can't walk up to someone and say good morning. Obviously, that would be somewhat extreme and impractical. Being a Generator means that you have to learn to 'flirt' with your own energy field. As a Generator, you cannot embark on a preconceived conversation with someone, but you can begin a conversation and then wait to see which way your response moves. No one knows which way the conversation will go until it goes there, if indeed it goes anywhere!

This is how two Generators use their own Strategy within a relationship. One of them has to assume the role of the initiator, even though they are not designed that way. It is rather like playing with a ball. Someone has to throw it first, and then they can get a response going. An example of this might be one Generator turning to another and saying: 'would you like to go out tonight and have Chinese food?' to which the second one can respond and know what is right for them.

However, the Generator that first asks the question has no idea of whether they themselves would like to have Chinese food, since the idea did not come as a response. Thus the second Generator has to fire the same question back to the first one, so that they can also feel their own response. The final result may be that they both decide to stay and eat at home! Although, this may seem a banal example, it is actually a very dynamic and powerful way for Generators to manage their relationships.

Generators have to be very awake to the sounds that they make. If one of their friends happens to ask them one day: 'Are you happy in this relationship?' and they hear themselves groaning in response, it actually tells them very clearly what they really feel. Many Generators actually end up in relationships that are detrimental for them and cause them deep frustration. The cause is usually because they decide that they like someone through their mind rather than having the patience to wait and see who life brings to their door.

EMOTIONAL GENERATORS IN RELATIONSHIPS

Because the emotional Generator has a Strategy of playing hard to get, they are designed to actually torment their potential admirers! The Strategy of the Generator is to wait to respond, and the Authority of the emotional system is to wait to be clear, therefore these are people who cannot afford to make commitments right away.

The emotional Generator has to keep meeting people a number of times in order to take them in through their changing emotional wave. That is the only way they can truly get to know anyone. The conditioning of the emotional system is extremely powerful. Since the Solar Plexus Centre is the hub of pain and pleasure, it is where our passions are stirred. When we meet someone and fall in love (or lust) with them, there is such an overpowering urge to act on our passions, and yet for the emotional Generator, this is extremely dangerous. If the emotional Generator is able to truly play hard to get, they will discover which passions are fleeting and which are consistent. Only then can they find the right relationships with the right people.

Entering into a relationship correctly can be a very magical thing, because it no longer matters how long that relationship lasts. If it begins at the right time and in the right way, then it will end in the right way, if indeed, it does end. Such relationships can end naturally and beautifully, with no blame or guilt. Going out of a relationship correctly is just as important as being in a relationship.

What usually happens to human beings is that they meet through their 'Not-Selves', meaning that they are not chemically correct for each other and do not know how to be together. Thus the tension steadily builds up until the relationship falls apart, and unfortunately it takes them a seven-year cycle to release the pain of their relationship from their physical bodies.

If you did not enter into your relationship properly and you don't go out properly, you carry a wound inside of you, and that wound conditions you negatively in every other relationship you meet. Every time you meet someone in this life, your only imperative is to be yourself. If you are not being your true self, then you never meet the experiences that truly belong to you, and you never realise the intense pleasure that comes when you are being yourself.

EXAMPLES
An Individual Example: The Dalai Lama

THE DALAI LAMA

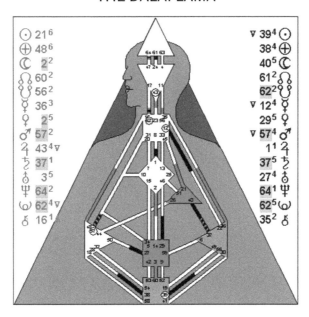

When we look at the above chart, we can see a defined Sacral Centre connected to the Root Centre. We also notice that the Throat is undefined. Because he also has another separate definition between the Solar Plexus and the Ego Centres, we know that this is a split definition Generator.

We have chosen this chart as an example in order to give Generators a glimpse of how the power of their aura can work, as well as what the mastery of patience can look like. The Dalai Lama is the perfect example of Sacral receptivity.

When we take a look at the above definitions, we can see both the Channel of Mutation, the 3/60, and the Channel of Community, the 37/40. When we keynote his energy using these two terms we can see him as someone who mutates communities when he responds. His truth speaks through his desire to act in the Root Centre. However, because his emotions are split off from his Sacral Centre, he has to wait to be clear before his response can be verified.

Whenever you see the Sacral Centre defined, you also need to see which channel defines it. In the Dalai Lama's case, his Sacral is defined through the channel 3/60 – the Channel of Mutation. This means that whenever he is responding, his Sacral is actually measuring every response through its potential to be mutative. In other words, when he feels an inner 'Yes', the intelligence of the Sacral is saying that this decision can have a deep impact in the world.

When his Sacral says 'No', there can be no mutative capacity. However, as we have seen, the Dalai Lama has a defined emotional centre which is split off from his Sacral. This means that he cannot be sure of his response in the now. Only through time can he measure whether something will be mutative or not. This is the design of someone who can only have a real impact on the world through listening to the changing qualities of his feelings over time. He has to wait to respond, and then he has to wait again, to be clear. One can see that the Dalai Lama is indeed a mutative force in his effort to support international understanding. He also mutated the Buddhist tradition by changing some of the strict rituals and opening up the way for female followers of Buddha. Thus he has greatly improved the position of women in Tibetan Buddhism.

The Dalai Lama is a title, representing the highest authority of Tibetan Buddhism. His real name is Tenzin Gyatso, and he was officially chosen to be the XIV incarnation of the Dalai Lama when he was four years old. The final proof that he was indeed the real Dalai Lama was the result of a test given him by a delegation formed to find him. They gave him two drums, two rosaries and two walking sticks to choose from, and in each instance he immediately chose the ones that previously belonged to the XIII. Dalai Lama. It was these Sacral responses made during his childhood that mutated his life.

Everything in the Dalai Lama's life is about the pressure to act in order to create positive change. The 2 other activated gates in his Sacral Centre are the 29 and the 27, which are about commitment (29) and caring (27). He says about himself that sympathy has always been a trait of his character. As a small child he always felt sympathy for suffering animals and when he saw children fighting with each other, he would always interfere and help the weaker child. You can see from his design that what is defined is truly what makes him who he is.

Now let us turn to the undefined centres. Having an undefined G Centre, the Dalai Lama takes his direction from the cues of his environment and from responding to the needs of others. His open G Centre also means that his identity can harmonise with anyone in any situation, making him an excellent diplomat. The Dalai Lama also has an undefined Ajna Centre, which is a sign of natural intelligence and mental agility. Studying has always been one of his major occupations. When he was six years old he began to study the classical disciplines such as drama, art, music, astrology, poetry and writing. Later on in life, he also added healing, Sanskrit, dialectics and metaphysics to his list of studies. He was also trained in memory techniques very early in life and spent much time researching the teachings of the different Dalai Lamas. Then, when he was eleven years old, he met the Austrian writer Heinrich Harrer, and had his first opportunity to open himself to the West.

Under Harrer's instruction, the Dalai Lama learned English and science, the latter allowing him to develop his technical and mechanical skills and he soon found a passion for repairing the old cars that had belonged to his predecessor. The Dalai Lama's undefined Spleen Centre tells us several things about him. Firstly, that he doesn't always feel good in his body and secondly that he is very sensitive to the suffering of others.

Thirdly, he is conditioned by certain fears, namely the fear of failure in the 32nd gate and the fear of authority in the 18th gate. These two fears are patterns that he will have to learn from throughout his whole life, and as he does so, his immune system will actually become stronger.

At the age of three, he had to leave his parents and live in a monastery. Naturally, he was full of fear and felt terribly homesick because he had no idea what it meant to be a Dalai Lama. Then, at the age of sixteen, in the face of the Chinese threatening his country, he had to take up his office and was given the full responsibility of leading his country. This challenge brought up his deep fears of failure because he knew so little about what was going on in the world at that time, and had no experience with politics. However, he faced his fear and went to see Mao Zedong in 1954, because he had thought of a peaceful solution. In meeting Mao Zedong, he realised that his country and his culture were in danger.

In 1959, the Chinese occupied Tibet and the Dalai Lama had to flee to India. In the following years, his task was to coordinate the stream of refugees and to find them a new home. Even now, when people set all their trust in him to help them and expect him to improve their situation, he suffers from the fear of failure, because he is knows that what he can offer is so limited.

Out of his receptivity and his Buddhist culture, the Dalai Lama learned early in life not to initiate speech but to wait to respond. Thus during his childhood, he had access to the gifts of his undefined Throat, which is to learn about communication. In the long years of living in exile, he has had the opportunity to travel a great deal and thus has met many famous personalities and known religious teachers, all of whom he has enjoyed talking to and getting to know their cultures. He points out that communication is the human way and the best means of building bridges between different cultures, and this is what he has devoted his own life to.

He is generally recognised for his openness, his communicative skills and his great respect towards people of different faiths. This is reflected in his open Spleen, Throat and Ajna/Mind. In fact, he is a classic example of an open Throat because he articulates the concerns of others; he speaks for the Tibetans by informing the world about Tibet's destiny.

The Dalai Lama also has a defined Solar Plexus Centre connected to his Ego - the centre of will. As a wilful child he used to become very angry if he could not get what he wanted. He says about himself as a child that his actions were always driven by his emotions, until he learned composure through meditation. He now knows how to be an observer of emotions as they move through him and no longer needs to identify with them. This is the highest potential of any Solar Plexus Centre, whether defined or not - to not get caught up in the emotional drama of life.

The Dalai Lama's unique gift is to remain a man at peace despite being the leader of a suppressed nation who has to live in exile.

For him, accepting disastrous events does not mean instant discouragement and depression. He tries to overcome problems and tragedy while remaining calm and stable. As a pure Generator, the Dalai Lama is an example of a man who has learned to follow his Strategy and live by his Authority in life.

SOME FAMOUS GENERATORS

Pure Generators: Albert Einstein, Carl Gustav Jung, Mozart, Madame Curie, Luciano Pavarotti, Dustin Hoffman, Greta Garbo, Madonna, Elvis Presley, Walt Disney

Manifesting Generators: Mother Teresa, Vincent van Gogh, Friedrich Nietzsche, Alois Alzheimer, Marie Antoinette, Mata Hari, Arnold Schwarzenegger, Bruce Lee, Charlie Chaplin

METAPHOR

In our metaphorical football team, the Generators are the defenders. They are the backbone of humanity. They have to wait until the ball comes to them, and if they can accept this limitation, then they can truly excel at whatever they do. The Manifesting Generators are also, like pure Generators, natural defenders. They have to let the ball play into their hands while resisting the temptation to rush to the place of action. If they manage to wait, then when the ball does find them they can move with great speed to the forefront of the game and score goals alongside the forwards (Manifestors). The glory is all theirs if they manage to wait.

4. THE PROJECTOR

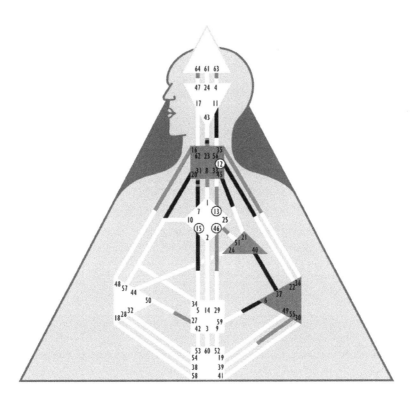

TECHNICAL DEFINITION

A Projector is someone with no motor connected to the Throat Centre and no defined Sacral Centre in their design. Projectors can be so complex that as many as eight of the possible nine centres are defined without the potential of generating or manifesting. Because there is no means of either manifesting or generating energy, the Projector is the first of the two non-energy Types. 21% of the world's population are Projectors.

ROLE IN HISTORY

Historically, the Projector has had the least opportunity to fulfil its potential, because the rulership has always been in the hands of the energy Types. Basically, Projectors have never been recognised for their potential. The natural place for the Projector is at the top of the hierarchy of the four Types, since they are designed to guide the energy Types, and in particular Generators. As the Generators begin to regain their natural power as creative builders, it is the Projectors who will emerge as the administrators and leaders of the new order.

GIFT AND HANDICAP

The first thing to recognise about the two non-energy Types, the Projector and the Reflector, is that their greatest gift is to be able to guide and understand the energy Types. Their true role is to manage the energy Types. Projectors have a talent of recognising the capabilities of the energy Types and of guiding these people in the most efficient use of their energy. This is their gift. Their handicap is that they do not have consistent access to energy within themselves, but have to rely on others recognising their gifts. In other words, they are the only Type that depends solely on others in order to fulfil their purpose in life. Although they are at the top of the hierarchy, they are not given the power. Ironically, the power is given to the Generators, who do not really know how to use it without the help of Projectors. Thus, these two Types are designed to be deeply interdependent.

Being a non-energy Type does not mean that you do not have any energy. In fact, the opposite can appear to be true. Because Projectors do not have consistent access to generative or manifesting power, they are designed to use the energy of others. This can either make them invaluable to others if they know their design, or a drain on other's resources if they do not know their design. One of the great themes of the Projector is exhaustion. If they try to behave as an energy Type, they soon become exhausted.

Projectors are great organisers and networkers, and they have the gift of bringing people together in the right combinations in order to achieve specific tasks. They are the natural middlemen between the two energy Types, and it is ultimately down to them to know how to maintain harmony in the world.

RECOGNITION

There is really only one thing that a Projector ever wants in life; they want to be recognised for who they are, so that they can put their gifts into action. The great secret for Projectors is people. They have to have the right people in their life, and for a Projector, the right person is only someone who recognises you. Anyone that does not recognise you is a drain on your resources. It is a fact that Projectors actually get more recognition than any other Type, because it is in their design to be seen. However, other people often only see what they want to see in Projectors, rather than seeing who they actually are. This gives rise to great resentment in Projectors, which is one of their themes in life. The Projector who does not insist on working with people who recognise them will end up feeling bitter inside.

Because Projectors are rarely seen for who they are, they are often confused themselves about what it means to be recognised. In the example above, you can see that this Projector has two definitions, one in the mind and one between the Root and Solar Plexus Centre. This is therefore someone who has to be recognised either for their inspirational mind and/or their depth of feelings about things. If someone comes up to this Projector and says: 'You have a very nice voice', even though that may sound nice, it is not true recognition for them since they do not have a defined Throat Centre.

Likewise, if someone says to them: 'You are so courageous', they do not feel deeply recognised since courage is an energy particular to the Heart Centre, which is also undefined. These kinds of recognition can so easily land the Projector in trouble because they like hearing that kind of thing! However, relationships founded on the wrong recognition can never work out well for them. When the Projector above hears someone say to them: 'I always feel so inspired when I am with you', every cell in their body literally lights up, because that person has truly recognised them.

EXHAUSTION

As we heard earlier, Projectors often suffer from fatigue and exhaustion. Many Projectors actually end up in life with debilitating diseases and a shorter lifespan than normal. The single cause of all these is misplaced commitment. Projectors have a genetic need to be seen, and if they cannot wait for recognition to find them, they spend their life trying to attain recognition and make all manner of compromises in the process. With their undefined Sacral, it is very easy for Projectors to take on the burdens and commitments of others. In fact, every Projector needs to understand that every person in their life who does not recognise their needs and respect their design is a physical burden on their energy system and health. For Projectors, there can be no compromises. If they are not recognised, there is no relationship possible with that particular person, and it is never a personal thing when they are not recognised, it is simply that there is no match between their chemistry with someone.

When you have a Projector chart in front of you, you have to realise that you are dealing with someone who feels they have never lived to their full potential and they probably feel resentful of that fact. They have probably never waited to see who recognises them because they didn't know that they could simply trust in waiting. Most people are terrified of waiting. When you are looking at a Projector's design with them, all you need do is describe the channels that are defined in their design and they will feel recognised. That feeling of recognition is the key to their passage through life. If they do not feel it, they simply have to move on. As a Projector, if you do not wait to be recognised for who you are, the energy you take in from those around you will make you physically sick. It will put you into the wrong environment and you will continue to attract auras that are unhealthy for you. As a Projector, you are not someone who is supposed to take on the burden of doing all the work of others. Your true role is to guide the energy Types and let them do all the things that you are not equipped to handle.

PROJECTORS AS CHILDREN

Every child is conditioned by its parents to be a 'doer'. When a Projector child comes into the world, all it wants is to be seen. There are many different types of Projectors and each one has to be seen for their respective gifts. The mental Projector needs to be intellectually recognised when they are young and nurtured in that direction. The emotional Projector needs to be recognised for their depth of feeling and given time and space to process life through the emotional wave. The Splenic Projector needs to be encouraged to trust in their instincts from the very beginning of their life.

These are just three examples of the hundreds of possibilities of how Projector children need to be raised according to their design. Parents who fail to recognise their children deny them the possibility to early realisation of their full potential. They do that in ignorance of the mechanics, because parents want their children to grow and to be happy. They think they can make them happy and successful in trying to show them how to be a Manifestor, and in making them independent and showing them how to find what they want without relying on others.

Projector children are actually very easy to nurture as long as you know their design. If you give them the right recognition, they can really excel.

STRATEGY

In Human Design, there is a clear distinction between those who have a design 'To do' and those who have a design 'To wait'. Like the Generator, the Projector has a design to wait, but unlike the Generator, they are not simply waiting to respond. The Projector has to wait for a specific invitation rather than a broad set of energetic responses. Whereas the Generator responds all the time, the Projector only receives invitations once in a while, making their 'style' of waiting very different, and in many ways, much harder. Projectors are waiting for investors to recognise their special skills, and the invitations that are correct for them have to be perfectly tailored to fit their design.

The Strategy of a Projector is not a moment-by-moment Strategy like the Strategy of the energy Types. It is only a Strategy that needs to be applied for major decisions in life. The formal invitations they are waiting for in life are basically only about four things: the invitation to love, the invitation to career, the invitation to bond with others and the invitation to a place to live. For the rest of their lives, the Projector simply has to follow their Authority, whatever that happens to be.

What most Projectors discover when they hear about their Type, is that they immediately resonate to the keyword 'invitation'. They also get to see that instead of waiting to be invited in life, it is usually they that do all the inviting. In their restlessness and deep insecurity, Projectors tend to treat others the way they themselves should be treated. However, this is not how their mechanics work. The Projector has to understand that if they relax and stay silent, their aura does the talking and soon brings out the invitation of others. When the Projector learns to trust in the silent magic of their chemistry, many opportunities begin to come their way.

The mantra for the Projector is to wait for the formal invitation that is just right for them. That is how their Strategy eliminates resistance in life, and this is how their life loses its sourness and finally becomes sweet. Everything else will unfold for them, if they just trust in the mechanical structure of their chemistry.

THE PROJECTOR'S QUESTION: CAN I BE NOTICED?

The golden question for every Projector is 'can I be noticed?' Projectors need more than any other Type to understand the power of their aura. The Projector's aura is very specific. It is a bio-energetic field that can be felt across a room, and it is coded to a certain very distinct frequency. Anyone who is not attuned to that specific frequency will never really notice the Projector, and anyone who is attuned to their frequency cannot help but pick them out across a crowded room. The Projector's aura is magical. Not only does it ensure that they will get exactly the right recognition and draw it towards them, but also it serves to protect them. Anyone who is not naturally drawn into the Projector's aura is not going to be healthy for them. All the Projector really has to do is sit back and wait to see who comes forward and who does not.

THE EMOTIONAL PROJECTOR

We know that every Type has an emotional version, and this emotional definition redefines the Strategy. We know that a defined Solar Plexus is always the Authority in a chart, and for the Projector this means that they cannot accept an invitation right away, because there is no truth in the now for them. They have to sleep on it and then they have to be re-invited. Obviously, this Strategy is very testing, since it often seems as though they are throwing away a perfect opportunity. However, they soon learn that what appears to be a great invitation when they are up in their wave can turn into a horrible commitment when they are down in their wave. Thus an emotional Projector has to test each invitation for authenticity by pushing it away or delaying it. If the invitation is perfect, then their aura will naturally coerce the other person to renew their invitation.

We are all conditioned to be polite and answer spontaneously whenever someone invites us for a job or an event. However, an emotional person can never be spontaneous. Take the example of an emotional Projector child with the channel 40/37 (Channel of Community). This child has to be invited to the potential of their definition without the pressure of accepting the first time. They have to be invited into groups without any pressure (e.g. which playground they want to be in) to stay with that group. Such a child has to be allowed time to consider things and always needs to be re-invited. Only if this child is in the right community will they grow and develop correctly. If they are put under pressure to accept the invitation, the chances are they will end up in the wrong community and will be deeply unhappy.

THE PROJECTOR IN RELATIONSHIP

As we have seen, the Projector has to receive a formal invitation to love and to bond with others. This is the only way that they can correctly enter into a relationship. So, for example, if a woman happens to be interested in a male Projector, contrary to popular culture, she will have to do the inviting. She may like to invite him home for dinner for example. If two Projectors are interested in each other, they will have to go through an extended courtship in which they both invite each other. This is the only situation in which a Projector can invite another person. The fact of the matter is that there must always be a formal invitation where Projectors are concerned.

Projectors are here to be able to manage energy. They are masters of reading energy through their undefined Sacral Centre. For the Projector, what is important is the quality of the energy that is offered to them. If you invite them to McDonalds, they will have a different impression of the kind of energy they have available to manage than if you invite them to a fancy restaurant. Each Projector needs an invitation that matches their frequency. Most important of all is the nature of the invitation. If you don't invite them at all, but instead you tell them that you want to be with them, then that relationship will be full of bitterness.

Non-energy Types always get more recognition than energy Types; they get more opportunities to find partners than the energy Types. Energy Types have a built in limitation in terms of how they meet others, but Projectors are designed to be noticed. Their biggest downfall in relationships is their inherent 'need' for energy. If they do not enter into a relationship in exactly the right way, then they will always fall in with the wrong person, and in doing so they will usually become the 'needy' partner in the relationship. Projectors have to be very clear that just receiving an invitation from a nice looking person does not mean that that is the right kind of relationship for them! It simply means that the basis of finding out if there can be a match is established.

Projectors have a unique role in the world because they represent the only part of the population that transcend class and status, in the sense that they can be born poor and end up being very rich. They can be the kind of people that are born without culture and end up being deeply cultured. In other words, they are designed to move through the strata of the social structures of our society. The Projector is there to do well with their mate.

This is why they have to be very clear that they are being recognised by an energy that it makes sense for them to manage, because it is out of managing that energy that they are going to have their future. They have to make sure that there is a place for them to go in that recognition. They need the energy, either of an energy Type or another Projector or Reflector that defines the Sacral.

EXAMPLES
An Individual Example: Pablo Picasso

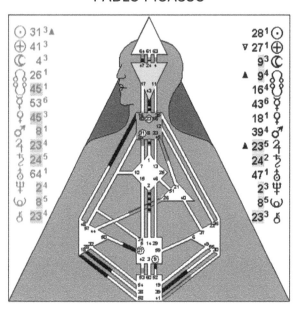

Above we can see the design of Pablo Picasso, arguably the most famous painter of the 20th century. Picasso is a Projector because he has no Sacral Centre and no defined motors to the Throat Centre.

As a Projector, we know he needs to be recognised for what is defined in his design rather than what is not. Looking at his definition, we can see that he has two defined channels; he has the Channel of Abstraction (64/47), which is essentially about making sense out of a flood of images rooted in past experience, and has the Channel of Structuring (43/23), which is about expressing his unique insights. When we put these two channels together, you have the design of a man who is here to express his past in a totally unique, individual way. It is clear that Picasso did indeed get worldwide recognition for these very qualities.

The reason why we have chosen Picasso as an example for the Projector is because we intend to show you how important early recognition is in a Projector's life. When a Projector is recognised early in their childhood, it allows them to build the correct energy in order to be successful with their specific qualities.

Before he could even talk, Picasso made himself understood through painting what he wanted to eat, and his first word was 'piz' which means 'lapiz', the Spanish word for pencil.

In Picasso's case, his father, José Ruiz Blasco who was a painter, recognised him early. He became his first teacher and supported his talent in exactly the right way from the beginning. He taught him to draw hands and feet and to improve his sense for detail.

When Picasso was 11, his father then sent him to an art school where he received an academic education. The recognition culminated when his father gave up his own career as a painter in order to support his son, whom he considered to be a genius. In a symbolic act of recognition, he gave Picasso his own brushes and colours. As a young man of only fourteen, Picasso was deeply impacted at being valued in this way, since he was to be very bad at school due to his dyslexic problems.

There is another important fact by which we can assess the amount of recognition. As he grew up, Picasso's fame and recognition spread. During the Second World War, he was in fact the only artist who was allowed to move relatively freely in Paris when the Nazis occupied France. They left Picasso alone, because they were afraid of the world press taking a stand against them.

Now let's have a look at what is undefined in Picasso's design. We can see immediately that none of the four motors are defined. This is the kind of Projector that needs to work with other people in order to take advantage of their energy. Indeed, since he was five years old, Picasso found that he needed an 'audience' for painting. This audience consisted of his cousins, who wanted him to paint animals for them.

It is fascinating to see how dependent Picasso really was on other people in order to unlock his potential. He was an extremely productive artist, painting as many as 50.000 pieces of art and amassing a fortune of as much as 260 million dollars. None of this would have been possible without all these different people who moved in and out of his aura, each one contributing to his genius in their own unique way. In fact, in the famous Picasso biographies by Arianna Stassinopoulos Huffington, there are so many people mentioned - painters, poets, art dealers, philosophers, friends, and relatives - that it even gets confusing.

It is clear from his life that Picasso hated to be alone, and he surrounded himself by others nearly all the time. He would probably have found it very difficult to get things done without the presence of others. Remember, Projectors actually need the physical presence of other people in order to benefit from the aura of their energy. All Projectors have to understand how they are conditioned by this need to be around others. If they understand it clearly, they do not become a victim of their need but are able to use it objectively and then enjoy being alone as a balance.

All Projectors need to be able to get away from all the people around them in order to purify their open centres and in particular, the open Sacral. We know that as a child, Picasso was desperately afraid of being alone, insisting that his father had to accompany him to school and give him a pledge that he would always come back and collect him again.

He also has an undefined Sacral Centre. This is a man who was famous for having endless love affairs and a lifelong ambiguity about the role of women in his life. On one hand, women were the core of his life, but at the same time he was deeply disgusted by the demons that overwhelmed him. It seems that contempt was his only way of dealing with this fear of female power, and this is clearly reflected in many of his paintings of deformed women. His confusion about women and sex are rooted in his being an unwitting victim of conditioning in his undefined Sacral Centre. So often, simple understanding of mechanics frees us from this kind of confusion.

An undefined Sacral Centre is a sign of someone with a deep fascination, whether hidden or obvious, for sexuality. Picasso was driven to discover the mystery of sexuality, and he was excited to experiment sexually with what was not permitted. For instance, he had a love affair with a minor - Marie Thérèse - which would have been severely punished by imprisonment at that time. He wanted to break down sexual barriers and taboos to find out the connection between sexuality and transcendence.

He was deeply attracted by women, but at the same time, he realised to his great frustration that he could not control them. Being a classic macho, this was a dilemma that he really suffered from. There was only one woman in Picasso's life – Francoise Gilot – who actually left him. Filled with bitterness at not being recognised, he systematically tried to destroy her life, making her career options impossible just to take his revenge on her. His famous statement about women is a testament to the potential bitterness that a Projector can feel: 'It is easier for me to carry a woman to her grave than to see her happy with somebody else.'

We have also learned that fertility is also conditioned in people with undefined Sacral Centres. Picasso had four children from three different women, but he was not the caring father, taking little notice of his children and spending very little time with them. These children just happened to him, and he was too self-concerned and obsessed with painting and living out his definitions.

The open G Centre shows us that Picasso has no fixed identity as a painter. Indeed, he was a versatile creative force: he painted on canvas and walls; he made sculptures, ceramics, etchings, lithographs, linocuts, drawings, and sketches. He worked for the 'Ballets Russes' as a stage designer. He also wrote poems and stage-plays. Together with George Braque he developed a new style called analytical cubism. His only gate in the G Centre is the 2nd gate, which is the gate of direction, which was obviously what he gave to the art world.

The undefined Spleen tells us that Picasso needed others in his aura in order to feel good, which is another reason why it was uncomfortable for him to stay alone in his house. More than that, Picasso suffered from the fear of death, being his sun theme in the 28th gate. When he was thirteen years old, his sister Conchita died of diphtheria, which was a traumatic experience for him. He prayed to god that god should save her life and that he would sacrifice his painting. When she died, Picasso drew the conclusion that destiny was against him and god was nothing but evil. For Picasso being busy was the only way in his life to suppress his fear of death.

A small incident of his biography is very revealing in the context of his conditioned fear of death. In his late eighties, one of his old friends, Pallarés, came to visit him. Picasso insisted that he did not spend the night there. Because Pallarés was older than him, he was afraid that Pallarés could die in his house and infect him with death. His undefined Spleen ensured that he had a continual theme in his life of having to deal with fear.

Being so open in his design, Picasso was an emotionally disturbed man. His undefined Solar Plexus Centre caused him much turbulence and misunderstanding. He was famous for his rage and his outbursts as he identified with and mirrored the emotional wave of others in his aura. This gave rise to his eccentric and sometimes very cruel nature, but most of all, he lived out the conditioned emotional wave in his pictures. With all his open centres, Picasso was a seismograph for all the conflicts, the rebellion and the pain of his time. Remember that his definitions were about bringing out unique pictures. Through his art, he expressed the gloomy and crushing vision of his century, giving painting the same vision of decay that Kafka and Beckett contributed to literature.

SOME FAMOUS PROJECTORS

Nelson Mandela, J.F. Kennedy, Queen Elisabeth II, Fidel Castro, Josef Stalin, Karl Marx, Baghwan Shree Rajneesh, Mick Jagger, Barbara Streisand, Marilyn Monroe, Woody Allen, Steven Spielberg, Princess Diana, Thomas Gottschalk, Berthold Brecht

METAPHOR

In our metaphorical football team, Projectors are the midfielders. They move between the forwards and the defenders (Manifestors and Generators). They set up the ball for the forwards, and feed it back to the defenders. Their skill is to direct the entire game by coordinating with the other players as and when they are needed, seeing where the energy can be efficiently used in order to create a goal. In fact, they are the most recognised of all, since it is really the Projectors who keep the wheels of the world turning.

THE TRICKY BUSINESS OF PROJECTORS

There is an unusual phenomenon that takes place when one becomes a Human Design analyst. That is, whenever one gives readings to the public, they always come in patterns. Every analyst I have spoken to has had this same experience. This week I have had Projectors. Out of 12 readings I've seen 9 Projectors. That's 9 people desperate to be recognised for who they are, and most not knowing who they are. You can imagine what kind of a week it's been!

However, all these Projectors have got me thinking. From my sixth line view of being on the roof, I have spent much time observing Projectors, and my final conclusion is that they are a tricky business.

In the hierarchy of our genetics, the Projectors are designed to be at the top. They are the natural guides for humanity and in particular for Generators and Manifesting Generators. The gods however, have a funny sense of humour, because in placing the Projectors at the top of the global hierarchy, they also made sure that they couldn't abuse their power. They put them at the top, but they gave them no power of their own. What the gods did is give them the power to guide others. There is no way that any Projector is ever going to be able to fulfil their destiny unless they are recognised.

Let us consider then, the marketing strategy of the Projector. What can they do to enhance their chances of being recognised? Most Projectors know that if they try and draw attention to themselves actively, it usually ends in disaster. They have a design to wait after all. Sitting at the top of the hierarchy, every Projector carries a certain sense of genetic arrogance. I am not talking about the arrogance that comes from the ego. This is a cellular arrogance carried in their aura, almost undetectable. What it says is: 'I have exactly the thing that you need, but I'm not going to give it to you. You are going to have to come and find me and ask me for it, and even then I might not consider you to be worthy of my guidance.'

That is what every Projector is really saying at the level of their chemistry. It's powerful stuff. If they have the courage to trust in this hidden power, all they have to do is wait for the right person to come along. In the meantime, what they can do is carry a role that matches their strategy. In other words, they assume a role that lets others know what their particular gifts are, and that they are open to invitations. Then they sit back and wait. They also need to charge a high price for their gifts because this really matches their strategy. Strangely enough, this does the opposite of putting people off. So few Projectors claim what is theirs by right. They have to insist on recognition, from their friends, their clients, even their family. If they are not being recognised, then they are being drained and they should pull their energies away from that alliance.

People are always asking me what the real difference is between the Generator Strategy of waiting to respond and the Projector Strategy of waiting to be invited. The difference is vast. The Sacral Centre simply responds to life all the time, depending on which centre or centres it's connected to. This is an ongoing process for the Generator. For the Projector, invitations are rarer and very specific.

The Revelation

Remember that the Projector Strategy is only for the most important things in life, such as job, relationship, environment etc. The rest of the time, Projectors simply live according to their authority (whatever that may be) while they are waiting for the big invitations. Sometimes Projectors have to wait for years just for one invitation, but when it comes, the rest of their life is riding just behind it. I have seen this happen. One big invitation is the introduction to a whole career.

So the tricky business of Projectors is about waiting for the big invitations. It takes a lot more courage than simply responding to life. I have one Projector friend who was given her Human Design reading 3 years ago and is still waiting for the big invitation. Obviously, her life has been going on as usual, but all the time she is waiting for her real recognition. But she is no longer willing to compromise. The magic of Human Design is that even if you don't get the invitation right away, your waiting still transforms the cells of your body. My Projector friend has become more and more assured of her strategy as she becomes less and less in need of recognition. She has seen her strategy work in so many small ways that she knows that the big invitation is only a matter of time.

The deconditioning of Projectors is the trickiest business of all. Many of them do not last the course. What waiting does for the Projector is show them how desperate they are for recognition. It shows them how in the past they have been willing to compromise their lives even to get the wrong recognition. So many Projectors are recognised for the wrong things, and even though others may think they are great, they simply don't feel fulfilled inside. For Projectors the greatest irony of all is that it is only when they let go of caring whether they are seen, that they finally are seen. This is what waiting does for them. It shows them how to let go and trust in their design. It teaches them to hold out for the perfect invitation instead of just muddling through their life with only half-recognitions. Projectors have to find the courage to claim what is rightfully theirs; the best, most luxurious and most expensive seat in the house.

Richard Rudd

5. THE REFLECTOR

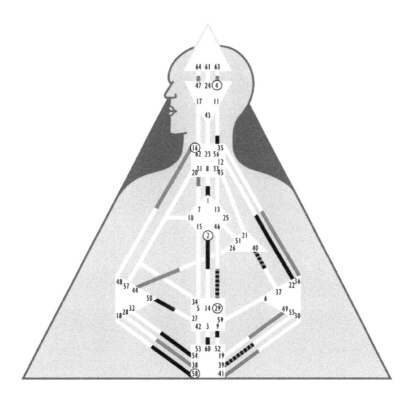

TECHNICAL DEFINITION

Technically a Reflector is very easy to determine because they have no definition. In other words, all the centres remain white. However, having said this, they do have a lot of activations acting as potentials, sticking out of the single centres.

The Reflector is an extraordinary being, making up less than 1% of the population of our planet. Even so, we are still talking about billions of people, given the population size of humanity. The most important thing to understand about the Reflector is that the way in which they process experience is different than any of the other Types.

THE GENETIC HIERARCHY

In the image above, you can see the three other Types that we have looked at arranged in a triangular structure, with the Reflector in the middle. In terms of the genetic hierarchy, the Reflector has a unique view and role. The Manifestor, Generator and Projector are all solar Types, which means that they operate in a generalised imprinting program rooted in the neutrino stream coming from the sun. The Reflector is the only Type that can be described as 'lunar' since it operates in an imprinting program that is reflected through the movement of the moon as it passes through the solar neutrino stream.

ROLE IN HISTORY

In history, the Reflectors, like Projectors have been generally ignored, since the energy Types have ruled throughout our history. The future lies in a new direction however, with the unfolding of the natural genetic hierarchy. The Reflector's place in this new order will be as an embodiment of the ultimate form of social and global justice, since their potential is to reflect everything around them with perfect equanimity.

GIFT AND HANDICAP

Because Reflectors have no fixed definition in their design, there can be a quick assumption that they are somehow more vulnerable than the other three Types. This is not strictly true. We have already seen that the undefined centres are not necessarily a handicap if they are operating correctly. In fact, we have shown throughout this manual that it is the undefined centres that can be the deepest windows on wisdom.

It is true that Reflectors are indeed vulnerable, but if they know their design clearly, they are absolutely protected from identifying with anything at all. Because the Reflector's chemistry magnifies everything and everyone, they have the potential to see everything that is really happening in a way that no one else can. They are a key to a global consciousness, because they participate through their openness in filtering the general consciousness field.

The role of the Reflector is to be one with the totality. They are extremely important to us because their unique perspective is much closer to our future emerging consciousness than for example, the perspective of a Manifestor, which is deeply selfish in comparison. Their greatest ability is to read others. Added to this, Reflectors have a deep kinship to the moon, and thus they have an opportunity for a mystical life that most of us cannot know. They can know a deep connection to a celestial body in an ongoing and profound way. In a certain sense, Reflectors represent the moon on earth.

The greatest handicap of a Reflector is their greatest gift; their openness and vulnerability. If they do not know how they function, and if they identify with what they are mirroring, they will easily get lost and confused. Because of their impressionability, they can become very dependent on those around them and therefore they have to be very careful about who they allow into the inner circle of their lives. Reflectors come into the world full of wonder, but so often, having me the not-self of the world, they suffer from a deep disappointment.

REFLECTORS AS CHILDREN

Reflector children obviously need a deep understanding from their parents and peers. From early on in their life, they need to be given a great deal of personal space so that they can learn to discriminate between all the different auras that move in and out of their chemistry. Contrary to what many people think, Reflectors do not need any more attention than other children. Indeed, it is children such as Manifestors that will need a greater care. Reflector children do not need to be protected from other people or children. They need to be right in the heart of the community or school so that they can learn from all those who are around them.

The Reflector child has to learn that the world is made up of all kinds of forces and people. They have to learn that there is no good and no bad in the world, but only different perspectives and energies. Thus their early upbringing needs to provide a haven where they always know they can go to shake off the conditioning that they are constantly taking in.

This is a habit that needs to be encouraged in their lives; that they regularly withdraw to their own space or take a walk or play for a while on their own. The parent of a Reflector child has a special responsibility. They need to ensure that their child grows in a balanced way without identifying with all the natural tension of life. The parent also needs to understand their child's monthly lunar cycle in order to help them find their deepest stability in life.

STRATEGY

Since Reflectors have no fixed definition in their design, it appears at first as though they have nothing fixed in life that they can rely upon. However, there is an element in their lives that they can rely upon, and this factor is the moon. Since the moon moves around the entire Human Design Wheel once in every month, it also opens up a regular pattern of energy in our chemistry each month. Moving very quickly in comparison to the other planets, the moon activates every single gate in the wheel during each monthly cycle. This sets a deeply stable pattern of conditioning at the core of their lives, so long as they are aware of it.

This is where Reflectors can find stability. In other words, for them, they have regular cycles each month where they can live out all the other 3 energy types. For example, they may have 3 days in every month when they are a Manifestor, then 4 when they are a Generator, etc. It is important for Reflectors to know about these rhythms within themselves in order that they take advantage of them fully. Ideally, Reflectors need to learn to work with a Human Design ephemeris because this gives them the ability to chart the movement of the moon in detail.

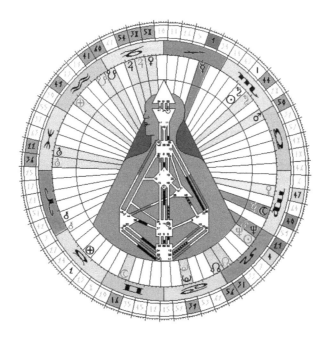

Being a Reflector means that the way in which you process information can only take place after each lunar cycle. Thus, when Reflectors have to make a major decision in their lives, they always have to wait out the lunar cycle. In other words, if for example, they have to decide on a new job, they have to be given one month to make up their minds. During that month, they also need to talk about their prospective job with as wide a variety of people as possible. Feedback from the aura of others is an essential part of their process.

The reason that Reflectors need to talk things over with others is not because they are seeking advice from people, but rather that they simply need to collect their thoughts during the cycle. Each conversation on the same theme can bring a different perspective of what is really going on inside of them, because each time it is reflected back through their chemistry through a different person's aura. At the end of the cycle, they are in a position to know exactly whether they can accept or reject the job. Although it may appear to be an unusual way of making decisions, this is the Reflector's Strategy.

THE REFLECTOR QUESTION: CAN I BE MYSELF?

The big question for a Reflector is always: 'Can I be myself?' It is so important to tell Reflectors: 'Yes, you can. There is a 'You' to discover.' This can be very relieving for them to hear because it takes away their greatest pain, which is that they feel as though they are invisible. However, the only way that Reflectors can truly be themselves is over their monthly lunar cycle. They have to understand that they are a moving, rippling rhythm that repeats and repeats endlessly until the day they die.

The Reflector goes through their lunar rhythm 14 times a year. That pattern is who they are. Reflectors are one of the few types of design that have no inner Authority. This means that there is nothing inside of a Reflector to say to them that yes and no is correct. In their process they must accept the Authority that comes to them from being with others. The people who the Reflector shares their life with define who they are, thus they have to chose very carefully who they live and work with. At the deepest level, this is exactly what the Reflector is here for: to be open to the outer Authority of the world around them, and to take it in and to filter it. But they don't filter the world as blind conditioning. They do have an inherent structure, but it is a moving lunar structure that is at the heart of their nature.

A REFLECTOR IN RELATIONSHIP

As we have just seen, the Reflector has no definition and no inner Authority. Therefore, they have no direct mechanical way to either affect or understand the nature of any relationship that they are about to meet. The Reflector does have certain repeating themes, which exist in their gate activations, but as a Type they are completely open. There is something rather unusual to understand about Reflectors in relationships: which is that they are always at the mercy of the person who wants to have a relationship with them. A relationship with a Reflector is a deeply narcissistic relationship, because the people that meet the Reflector get themselves back completely. In other words, if you fall in love with a Reflector, you have really fallen in love with yourself! This is what Reflectors do. They always mirror the other person.

In life, people who do not like themselves often fall in love with themselves through somebody else, and often through Reflectors. This can be a discovery process for people to find themselves, but for the Reflector a relationship is only of value when it is fertile and productive. For example, if the Reflector or their partner gets pregnant, then the Reflector really feels like they are in a relationship for the first time. Reflectors who have children almost always feel good about their relationship. Naturally, this does not necessarily mean that their relationships work.

Reflectors can have a very hard time because they are not here to be secure in their decision-making process. They can become dependent on those who do have the Authority to make their decisions for them. For the Reflector, there are no rules in relationships. There is only the Authority of waiting out their lunar cycle to be clear before they enter into a relationship. This is the only way for them to know whether someone is right for them. Each Reflector holds a deep hope within themselves that the rest of humanity will figure out who they are, so that they don't have to be messed up reflecting everyone's pain, and instead they can reflect their truth.

EXAMPLES

An Individual Example: Richard Burton

RICHARD BURTON

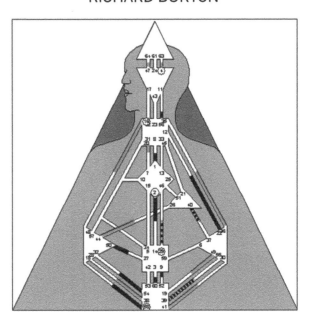

Richard Burton is our famous example of a Reflector. A man of extraordinary talent and depth, Burton is totally undefined in all of the nine centres. As we know, this is either a recipe for being totally distracted and confused, or the potential for a great natural wisdom.

Being a Reflector, we know that Burton had no reliable mechanism inside to tell him what to say yes or no to, and thus his life was all about finding the right people around him in whose Authority he could trust. Because he had the gift of being open to anyone, he was also open to those that were not good for him, and it was perhaps this that led to both his fame and his downfall.

The son of a coal-miner and born in the industrial heart of Wales, Richard Burton was the twelfth of thirteen children. He grew up in the aura of many brothers and sisters, which as a Reflector would give him a deep sense of stability, had it not been for his father, who was an irreverent man and an alcoholic. As a Reflector, his childhood required that he had space and understanding from his siblings and his parents, neither of which were particularly true. The result was that Burton couldn't wait to escape the cramped poverty of his early life. It was clear to him that he was very different from all those around him and his only escape was learning and books, of which he read one a day.

Once he was at school, Burton's intelligence was immediately recognised by his teacher, Phillip Burton, whose surname he later adopted. Finding an ally who was healthy for him, the young Burton excelled at school and was awarded a rare scholarship to Oxford University, enabling him to finally escape the difficult aura of his childhood and pursue his dream of becoming an actor.

With all his undefined centres and particularly his open G Centre, Burton made the consummate actor, being able to adopt any role that suited him with ease. He also became well known for the power and resonance of his voice, reflecting the potential gifts of having an undefined Throat Centre. Throughout his acting career, he played an enormous array of roles, saying in his own words: 'I've played the lot; a homosexual, a sadistic gangster, kings, princes, a saint, the lot.'

Richard Burton was famous for his sexual exploits and constant womanising. His undefined Sacral led him to experiment with many women and even try homosexuality at one point in his life. His fame really exploded when he played alongside Liz Taylor in the epic 'Anthony and Cleopatra', although it was not so much the film that shot him to fame so much as the scandal of his love affair with Liz Taylor. Thus began the relationship for which he became famous and his subsequent 'fall from grace'. His relationship with Liz Taylor was explosive, passionate and erratic, leading to two divorces and a growing addiction for alcohol and women.

Burton's life was characterised by his deep-seated confusion about what made him happy and who he really was. As a Reflector, it is clear that he tried to find stability in the auras of other people, and in many cases, those who were clearly not healthy for him. He was in many ways the archetype of a deeply disappointed man, and caused a huge scandal in Britain when he refused to play a role of Winston Churchill for the BBC, labelling him as 'inhumane'.

Burton's disappointment seemed to be for the whole of humanity rather than anything personal, and those who knew him closely speak of him as a man 'too sensitive for his own good'. It seems that he was at his happiest when he was acting either on stage or for film, since these were the times when his depth of genius came through the clearest. Liz Taylor once said of him, that when she first faced him across the stage, she was genuinely terrified on account of him losing who he was and totally forgetting himself in the part he was playing. She said that there was no way she could possibly compete on stage with 'a man who was not there'.

A REFLECTOR MONTHLY STORYLINE

Below is an example of a typical lunar monthly chart given to a Reflector. This chart was done for the month of December, but on learning to use an ephemeris, it is very easy to apply the same pattern for every month for the rest of one's life.

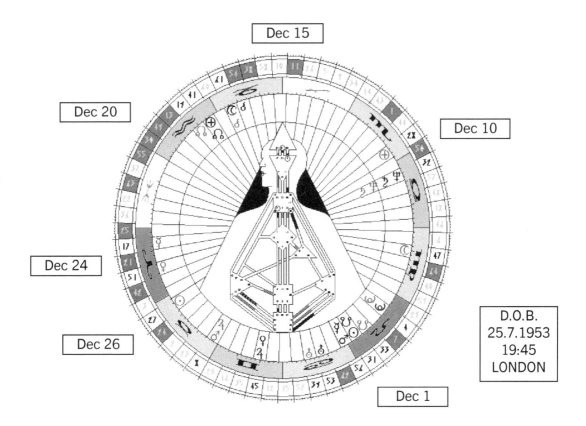

CYCLE OF DEFINITIONS

50	Generator	Lunar Birthday:	Cycle Begins Sacral	(1 day)
1	Projector	Creative Burst	G Centre	(3 days)
11	Projector	Ideas/Caution	Ajna	(1 1/2 days)
38	Projector	Struggle	Spleen	(1/2 day)
54	Projector	Transformation	Spleen	(2 1/2 days)
13	Projector	Retreat	G Centre	(1/2 day)
49	Projector	Material needs	Emotional	(1/2 day)
30	Projector	Desire/Fantasy/Expectation	Emotional	(1/2 day)
55	Projector	Low Spirit/High Spirit	Emotional	(1 day)
63	Projector	Doubt	Ajna	(1 1/2 days)
25	Projector	Initiation	Ego	(1 day)
21	Manifestor	The Peak	Ego	(1 day)
42	Generator	Closing of Cycle	Sacral	(1 1/2 days)
24	Projector	Inspiration	Head	(5 1/2 days)
62	Projector	Organisation/Service	Ajna	(2 days)
7	Projector	Leadership	G Centre	(2 days)
64	Projector	Taking Stock	Head	(3 days)

Your monthly cycle is clearly divided into 2 phases - an introverted 'study' phase and an extroverted 'communication' phase. In saying that, it doesn't mean you can't communicate in the first phase or that you can't study in the second. These are simply general patterns in your particular cycle.

The cycle begins each month with the moon in the 50. This activates your unconscious sun in the 27th gate, which is about looking after yourself. It is also when you have generative energy, so it's a major point in your month. It's like a mini birthday in each month when it comes round, so it begins your monthly process of figuring out what you are going to care about that month and what is of value to you within the community (50). It's about providing for yourself, NOT others. It's interesting that you will have to keep coming back to this every month. It says that you can only help others when you put yourself first. It sets the tone of each lunar cycle with 'OK, what do I want for ME this month?'

You then have about 16 days as a Projector, which is basically about your study period.

Here's the storyline: Once the tone of the month is set by the 50, you have a creative burst when the moon goes into the 1. This yang energy gets the ball rolling. Again, this is creativity that is inward facing rather than outward. The fact that there is no further lunar definition for the next 3 days means that this creative energy lasts for that long as a theme.

Next the moon defines the Channel of Curiosity by going into the 11th gate of ideas. Out of the creative energy flow new ideas. Be careful not to get overexcited at this point. The ideas are not grounded. They are the beginning of a process. This activates your personality mercury in the line of caution. Be careful what you communicate. This phase lasts until the next definition about 1 and a half days later.

Now the moon goes into the 38 and activates your design earth in the 28, (now you have several days with a defined Spleen because the moon follows by going into the 54). This is when the ideas have to be grounded. You have to struggle at this point, and if there is a point in the month when you may get ill, it is here. This is when you have to take the thing that you are studying and ground it in the material realm (Channel of Transformation 32/54). You have to transform your mental ideas into something lasting and practical.

Then the moon goes into the 13 and takes you deeper into retreat. This is a natural time for you to be alone and reflect on the struggle you've just gone through. You will also need this little pause in order to deal with the next 2 days, which mark your emotional cycle. You will have 3 definitions, all in different streams: the 49, when you have to figure out your material needs, the 30 when you are moved by desires, fantasies and dreams and the 55 when the emotions may or may not begin to clear so that you can make sense of what is happening to you. These 2 days are always going to be foggy for you because you cannot yet see clearly what process you are in. You are still in the introverted half of the month. This is not a good time to make any decisions because you may feel nervous. On the other hand this can be a very rich time as well. The 55 is the gate of spirit, so it can give you a real sense of depth.

The emotional period is immediately followed by doubt. You doubt whether what you are feeling is really the truth. The doubt really tells you to wait until things are clearer. Also, this activates both your Pluto's, which means this is a real key moment in your cycle. This is when you have to come up with an excuse to go back indoors.

Next you have your only 2 days of ego definition. The 25 is a real test for you every month. This is the Channel of Initiation. All the inward energy of the month is about to turn into outward energy so there is great pressure in this particular moment in your cycle. The test is to hold out from releasing the energy and the ideas unless they are called out or invited. All your Projector days say just this, in fact. Don't do anything unless someone calls on you first. If you can hold out for this one day, then you will always get your reward when the moon goes into the 21 because then is the natural time for manifestation. It is the peak of your month. This is a day you always need to know. Put it in your diary because you will see that all the energy of your cycle is moving towards it. It is the natural time for you to reach others with all that you have worked on inwardly in the month.

After the manifesting peak, you get a little rest. For the next 11 days or so, the energy is going outwards and it is the natural time for you to be invited out and recognised. If you wait, you should see this. The 21 is followed by the 42, which is the gate that ends your lunar cycle. It is the gate of completion. It gives you this power to follow through with your process until the end of the month.

Then the 24 comes and brings out your natural brilliance in the 61 line 2. This is a time of inspiration for you and for how you impact others. It is the best time to communicate your inspiration (again it needs to be invited).

The next 4 days of your cycle are essentially your most transpersonal time of the month. You finish with 2 logical definitions, which point you towards the future. For the first 2 days, you have the 17/62, which is the design of an organisational being. So you get everything together at this time. You sort out what the month has brought you and you get ready for the next beginning. It is also when you can best communicate with others. It is when your 'Bodhisattva' line gets defined, so it is a natural time of service in the world. This is the time at the end of your month energetically, so if you have been waiting out an important decision (your Strategy) for the month, it is here, with the moon in the 62, that you get all the details (gate of detail) so that the decision can be made.

The penultimate 2 days are marked by the 7/31, the design of Leadership. Your organisational capacity opens up your greatest opportunity to influence and guide others.

Finally, and rather neatly, your month finishes with the 64/47, activating your design moon in the 47.1 - the line of 'Taking Stock'. This is all about you finding inspiration from your own past. In other words, it is your time to sit back and take stock of your month and all that it has brought you. This is a quiet time that is really all about you clearing out your aura and turning inwards once again. The fact that your lunar cycle ends with your design moon in this gate and line is a wonderful piece of Reflector choreography! Then you are back to the same theme of personal needs with which you began the cycle. This is where you say: 'OK, this bodhisattva stuff is fine, now I've got to have time to myself again to clear out all these auras I have been taking in'.

So you can see how your energy diary should be laid out. It begins with generative power in the 50 and peaks with manifesting power in the 21. Before the 21 is about YOU, after the 21 is about OTHERS. In the middle you have to deal with a lot of mundane struggle and emotion. After the 42nd gate closes the cycle, it's basically a cruise back down the other side of the mountain (the only potential difficulty here could be the moon in the 24 since those next 5 and a half days can be irritating if no one shows up to listen to your inspiration!) However, if you wait, it will naturally be the time when you are around others.

Now, you have the pattern, you can watch for it. You may not see it all immediately, but given a year or so, you should be clearly able to fall into the rhythm of it. It can provide you with an incredible stability in life. This is where you learn that a Reflector honouring their cycle is in fact the most stable human being of all the 4 Types, despite having no definition.

SOME FAMOUS REFLECTORS

Michael Jackson, Rosalyn Carter (wife of Jimmy Carter), Eduard Mörike (a German poet), Thorwald Detlefsen (a German psychologist and author of esoteric literature)

METAPHOR

In our football team, the Reflector is the goalkeeper. They are a rare breed, being perhaps the most crucial single member of the team, even though they themselves do not move around the field like the other players. They operate according to different laws, for example they are able to use their hands whereas the other players cannot. They are perhaps the most limited and at the same time the most unlimited people among us, and their perspective is truly unique.

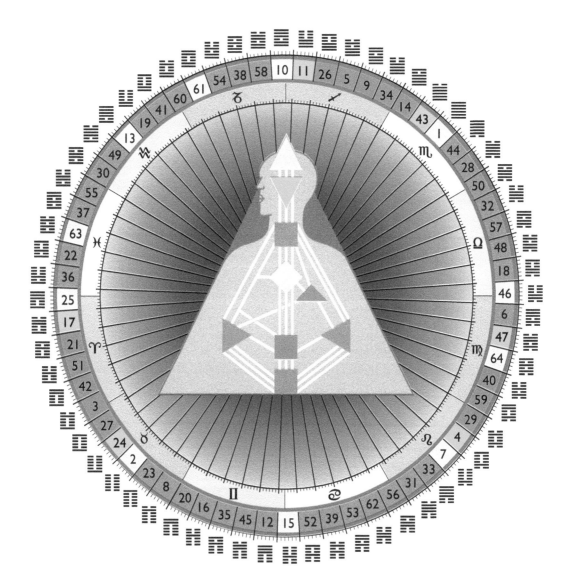

6. FINAL COMMENT

Type and Strategy really is the simplest panacea for transforming a person's life.

Manifestors lose their anger if they inform.

Generators get rid of their frustration if they don't initiate but learn to respond.

Projectors can no longer be resentful if they wait for the invitation.

Reflectors are no longer disappointed if they manage to wait out their 28-day moon cycle.

I hope that this book has encouraged you to explore your Strategy. Human Design is a logical system and I am grateful for any student who is not willing to believe what I say. This is why I invite you to find out its validity for yourself so that you can truly gain confidence in being who you are.

Every journey begins with the first step...

Good luck and enjoy the experiment.

Richard Rudd

Other books by Richard Rudd

THE GENE KEYS
Embracing your higher purpose

Richard Rudd

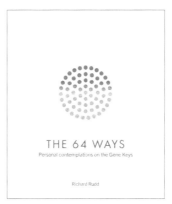

THE 64 WAYS
Personal contemplations on the Gene Keys

Richard Rudd

THE GENE KEYS
GOLDEN PATH

GENIUS
A Guide to your Activation Sequence

Richard Rudd

THE GENE KEYS
GOLDEN PATH

LOVE
A Guide to your Venus Sequence

Richard Rudd

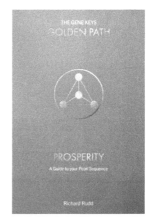

THE GENE KEYS
GOLDEN PATH

PROSPERITY
A Guide to your Pearl Sequence

Richard Rudd

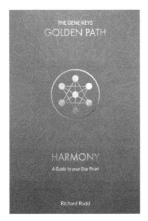

THE GENE KEYS
GOLDEN PATH

HARMONY
A Guide to your Star Pearl

Richard Rudd

DARE TO BE DIVINE
A journey into the miraculous

Richard Rudd

**THE SEVEN
SACRED SEALS**
Portals to Grace

Richard Rudd

genekeys.com/books

Other books by Richard Rudd

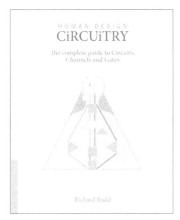

genekeys.com/books

Milton Keynes UK
Ingram Content Group UK Ltd.
UKHW051605290224
438698UK00005B/23

9 781999 671075